Rhetoric, Prudence,
and Skepticism in
the Renaissance

Rhetoric, Prudence, and Skepticism in the Renaissance

VICTORIA KAHN

Cornell University Press

ITHACA AND LONDON

Cornell University Press gratefully acknowledges a
grant from the Andrew W. Mellon Foundation
that aided in bringing this book to publication.

First published 1985 by Cornell University Press.
Published in the United Kingdom by Cornell University Press Ltd., London.

International Standard Book Number 0-8014-1736-8
Library of Congress Catalog Card Number 84-21362
Printed in the United States of America
Librarians: Library of Congress cataloging information appears on the last page of the book.

The paper in this book is acid-free and meets the guidelines for
permanence and durability of the Committee on Production Guidelines
for Book Longevity of the Council on Library Resources.

For my parents

Contents

Es könnte wahrscheinlich auch anders sein.
—Robert Musil

Preface

> For suppose it be granted (that which I suppose with great reason may be denied) that the philosopher, in respect of his methodical proceeding, doth teach more perfectly than the poet, yet do I think that no man is so much *philophilosophos* as to compare the philosopher in moving with the poet. And that moving is of a higher degree than teaching, it may by this appear, that it is well nigh the cause and effect of teaching. For who will be taught, if he be not moved with desire to be taught? and what so much good doth that teaching bring forth (I speak still of moral doctrine) as that it moveth one to do that which it doth teach? For, as Aristotle saith, it is not *gnosis* but *praxis* must be the fruit. And how *praxis* cannot be, without being moved to practise, it is no hard matter to consider.
> —Sidney, *An Apology for Poetry*

This passage from Sidney's *Apology* articulates two of the most fundamental assumptions of Renaissance humanist thought:[1] the belief in the importance of the active life and the conviction that we are best persuaded to ethical praxis by the rhetorical practice of literature. By its reference to Aristotle's *Nicomachean Ethics*, the passage also serves to introduce the subject of this book: the practices of rhetoric which evolved out of the renewed interest in the Aristotelian ethic of prudence and its alliance with the newly recovered classical doctrines of rhetoric in the Renaissance.

Such an alliance should not surprise us, for rhetoric and prudence alike are concerned with the contingent realm of human affairs. As Aristotle tells us in the *Ethics*, prudence (*phronesis*) is that faculty of judgment which provides an internal rule of decorum or authoritative standard of interpretation, one that is not logical but pragmatic, and that enables us to act appropriately within a social and political context. Like rhetoric, prudence involves deliberation

9

(NE 6.1357a); and like rhetoric, it aims at "the kind of truth that is practical and [that] is concerned with action" (NE 6.1139a 26). In the Aristotelian rhetorical tradition, rhetoric and prudence thus both involve an act of interpretation which is itself the precondition of action. It is probably because of this ideal capacity of rhetoric and prudence to mediate between theory and practice, interpretation and action, that the Renaissance humanists began to conceive of literature as a particularly persuasive form of prudence. For, as the quotation from Sidney suggests, rhetoric and prudence are not only analogous for the humanists, they are also inseparable. Beginning with Petrarch, the humanists argue again and again that it is better to do the good than to know the truth, and that we are more effectively moved to right action by the examples of poetry and history than by the precepts of philosophy.[2] As a result, poetry itself comes to be seen as part of practical philosophy, and eloquence is conceived of not only as the cause and effect of prudence, but as a form of prudence itself.[3]

The premise of this book is that the humanists' assumptions about the practice of literature have not been taken seriously enough. While much has been written about the importance of the newly recovered classical rhetorical texts and the renewed interest in Aristotle's *Ethics* for the humanist conception of the *vita activa*, scholars focusing on these issues have tended to ignore the rhetorical practice of the humanist works themselves. Conversely, critics who have focused on the rhetorical practices of humanist and humanist-influenced works have tended to ignore the humanists' arguments for the analogy between practical reason and the practice of rhetoric. Yet it is this practice that affords both intellectual historians and literary critics the best evidence of what the humanists meant when they argued for the inseparability of prudence and eloquence, or of the activity of interpretation, which is practical reason, and the interpretive practices of reading and writing.[4]

Accordingly, precisely because the book is concerned to provide the intellectual history of the alliance of rhetoric and prudence during the Renaissance, the burden of my argument falls on the close textual analysis of a representative selection of humanist and humanist-influenced texts. For while it is certainly an important first step to consider the humanists' thematic statements and those of their classical predecessors about the relation of prudence to persuasion, to read these texts simply thematically is to reduce them to the status of those philosophic precepts the rhetorical inadequacy of which the humanists so consistently deplored. We must remember that the humanists "embed language in action and make activity the object of discursive inquiry," that they conceive of figurative language and the rhetorical organization of their texts as not merely "a cognitive strategy, but an argumentative tactic."[5] For this reason, if we are to take the humanists' claims for eloquence seriously, we must compare their explicit statements about praxis with the rhetorical practice of humanist argument.

In the following pages I will argue that the central assumption of the humanist rhetorical tradition is that reading is a form of prudence or of deliberative rhetoric and that a text is valuable insofar as it engages the reader in an activity of discrimination and thereby educates the faculty of practical reason or prudential judgment which is essential to the active life. In so doing I hope to make a contribution to a "historical poetics," that is, to the recovery of the various conventions of writing and interpretation within a given period and the description of the literary competence necessary for the reader of works of this period.[6] By focusing on the humanists' arguments for the alliance between rhetoric and prudence, I hope to clarify not only the humanists' assumptions about the nature of reading and interpreting texts, but also the extent to which humanist moral philosophy can be understood only through a rhetorical analysis of humanist texts. Rhetoric is not an ornament to such philosophy; it is constitutive of it, with the result that intellectual historians of this aspect of Renaissance thought cannot avoid becoming literary critics. As rhetoric and ethics were ideally inseparable for the humanists, so a contribution to the history of Renaissance moral thought is inseparable from a contribution to a "historical poetics."

VICTORIA KAHN

Ithaca, New York

Acknowledgments

Chapters 4 and 5 of this book grew out of a dissertation in comparative literature at Yale University, written under the direction and with the support of Thomas M. Greene. During this time a Fulbright fellowship and a Whiting fellowship allowed me to do the original research for these chapters in Paris. I thank the individuals who recommended me for these fellowships, as well as two of the dissertation's original readers, Margaret Ferguson and the late Paul de Man, for their thoughtful reader's reports.

Since then, time and the good fortune I have had in friends and teachers have taught me the difference between prudent and expedient revision. I am particularly grateful to Charles Trinkaus for his encouragement and intellectual generosity over the past four years. A three-year Mellon fellowship at Johns Hopkins University enabled me to do the work on the Quattrocento humanists. I am indebted to Nancy Struever for sharing her unpublished work with me and for reading an earlier draft of the manuscript. Her epigrammatic comments and, more important, her example have taught me much of what I know about how to approach intellectual history. Thanks are due as well to Joseph Marino for introducing me to the computer. Also at Johns Hopkins, Steven Lally read Chapter 2 with care and discussed it with me over many lunches. Charles Trinkaus and Thomas Greene have read more versions of the manuscript than I think any of us cares to remember.

Earlier drafts of several chapters have already appeared in print. Chapter 3 draws on "The Rhetoric of Faith and the Use of Usage in Lorenzo Valla's *De libero arbitrio*," *The Journal of Medieval and Renais-*

sance Studies 13:1 (Spring 1983): 91–109, copyright © 1983 by Duke University Press; as well as on "Giovanni Pontano's Rhetoric of Prudence," *Philosophy and Rhetoric* 16 (1982): 16–34. Chapters 4 and 5 are revised and expanded versions of "*Stultitia* and *Diatribe:* Erasmus' Praise of Prudence," *German Quarterly* 55 (May 1982): 349–69, and"The Sense of Taste in Montaigne's *Essais*," *MLN* 95 (1980): 1269–91, respectively. I am grateful to the journal editors for their kind permission to use this material.

Life in Baltimore would not have been possible without the conversation, wit, moral support, and intellectual example of two friends, Neil Saccamano and Nancy Troy. Neil Saccamano read most of the manuscript over four years. I learned a great deal from our discussions, as well as from his own work on Spenser and Shakespeare. Brian Vickers first suggested that I work on Hobbes. I am grateful also for his invitation to give a paper on Salutati at the *Vita Activa–Vita Contemplativa* conference in Zurich in June 1981. Eugene Garver shared his published and unpublished essays on Aristotle, rhetoric, and Machiavelli. My editor, Bernhard Kendler, and the anonymous readers for Cornell University Press made helpful suggestions regarding revision, and a year at the Society for the Humanities at Cornell gave me the necessary time. Thanks are due in particular to Timothy Murray for recommending me to the Society. At Bennington College, Dennis Aebersold spent many hours teaching me the intricacies of word processing and suffered my questions in phone calls, notes, and computer mail for over a year. Without his help and hospitality, final revision of the manuscript would have taken much longer than it did.

Every book has a secret history that is not easily discerned in the final draft. My real literary education began in the courses of the late James Zito at Sarah Lawrence College. I want to thank Andrea Simon, with whom I first began to discuss the issues raised in these classes and to think about skepticism. The epigraph to the book acknowledges this friendship and intellectual debt. I also want to thank my sister Madeleine for rescuing the original notes for chapters 4 and 5 from a locked and abandoned apartment in Paris. My greatest debt, however, is to my parents, who taught me to love learning and to appreciate a good joke.

V.K.

Abbreviations and
Note on Translation

Apology   Sir Philip Sidney, *An Apology for Poetry*, ed. Geoffrey Shepherd (Manchester, England, 1973).

De doctrina   Saint Augustine, *De doctrina christiana*, trans. D. W. Robertson (New York, 1962).

Ep.   Coluccio Salutati, *Epistolario di Coluccio Salutati*, ed. Francesco Novati, Fonti per la storia d'Italia, 4 vols. (Rome, 1891–1911). Volume is indicated first, followed by page number.

EW   Thomas Hobbes, *The English Works of Thomas Hobbes*, ed. Sir Thomas Molesworth, 11 vols. (London, 1839–45).

L   Thomas Hobbes, *Leviathan*, ed. C. B. Macpherson (Harmondsworth, Middlesex, England, 1975). Chapter is indicated first, followed by page number.

LB   Erasmus, *De libero arbitrio*, in Desiderius Erasmus, *Opera omnia*, ed. J. Leclerc (Leiden, 1703–6; Hildesheim, 1962). Vol. 9 except where otherwise indicated.

LE   Martin Luther and Erasmus, *Luther and Erasmus: Free Will and Salvation*, ed. E. Gordon Rupp, A. N. Marlow, Philip S. Watson, and B. Drewery, Library of Christian Classics, vol. 18 (Philadelphia, 1969).

NE   Aristotle, *Nicomachean Ethics*, trans. Martin Ostwald (Indianapolis, New York, 1962).

OO   Lorenzo Valla, *Opera omnia*, ed. Eugenio Garin, 2 vols. (Basel, 1540; Turin, 1962).

PLQ   *Prosatori latini del Quattrocento*, ed. Eugenio Garin (Milan, Naples, 1952; Turin, 1976).

Rhet.   Aristotle, *Rhetorica*, trans. W. Rhys Roberts, vol. 11 of *The Works of Aristotle*, ed. W. D. Ross (5th ed.; Oxford, 1971).

WA   Martin Luther, *De servo arbitrio*, in *D. Martin Luthers Werke*, kritische Gesamtausgabe (Weimar, 1928). Vol. 18 except where otherwise indicated.

15

The following abbreviations have been used to refer to works of Cicero:

Acad.   *Academica*
Ad Her.   *Ad Herennium*
De fin.   *De finibus*
De inv.   *De inventione*
De nat. deorum   *De natura deorum*
De off.   *De officiis*
De orat.   *De oratore*
Part. or.   *Partitiones oratoriae*
Tusc.   *Tusculanae disputationes*

All foreign-language quotations are translated into English, though in most cases reference to the original text is provided. Unless otherwise indicated, translations are my own. *U* and *V* have been regularized in Latin and English quotations. Greek words have been transliterated.

Rhetoric, Prudence,
and Skepticism in
the Renaissance

1 Introduction

Rhetoric is the faculty of observing in any given case the available means of persuasion.
—Aristotle, *Rhetoric*

Historical knowledge of the humanist emphasis on the activity of reading and judging suggests an analogy with modern critical interest in "reader response"—if by this we understand the assumption that the meaning of a work of art does not exist as a timeless object, but is produced in the reader's interaction with the text, that is, in the act of reading. It also makes clear that reader-response criticism could only be seen as new and fashionable when the assumptions of the humanist rhetorical tradition had been forgotten. As Rosemond Tuve's work has shown, Renaissance rhetoric is by definition concerned with the effect of the text on the reader, and in particular with educating or influencing the reader's judgment. Once we accept this centrality of the reader in humanist rhetoric, we see that the humanists' assumptions about the practice of reading necessarily implicate twentieth-century readers as well. A remark by Hans Robert Jauss is to the point here: "The historical context in which a literary work appears is not a factical, independent series of events that exists apart from an observer. [A text] becomes a literary event only for its reader."[1] The question, as Jauss is well aware, is, Which reader? But this ambiguity, far from being a problem, makes Jauss's remark instead doubly significant for an investigation into Renaissance humanist assumptions about reading and interpretation. In the first case it means acknowledging that the twentieth-century reader approaches an earlier—in our case Renaissance—text with a certain competence and with certain inevitable prejudices. But it also means that the reader must aim at familiarity with "the system of expectations that arises for each work in the historical moment of its appearance" (22). I shall be less concerned to describe the responses of actual readers than to analyze the humanists' rhetorical practices and those of their followers in terms of the humanists' statements about the prudential and deliberative nature of such practice. The issue I am concerned with is precisely the one Jauss describes in a general way when he says that a text becomes a literary event only for its reader. My aim is to specify what this assertion means to the Renaissance humanist.

I suggest that once we see the connection between deliberative rhetoric and an active conception of reading, we will also be able to see how the transformation of this deliberative rhetoric in later humanist-influenced works signifies a questioning of the early humanists' conception of this activity. In early humanism, dialogue and other instances of deliberative rhetoric are encomia of the will: the very fact of written debate is taken to be evidence of the reader's ability to respond, and thus of the existence of free will and the genuine possibility of rhetorical persuasion. In later humanist-influenced works, dialogue turns in on itself and the encomium of the will becomes paradoxical. In the earlier period, the poet's nonassertion, in Sidney's terms, is no hindrance to his ability to educate the reader's prudential judgment—the judgment that will then guide his actions in society. Contradiction—in the form of contradictory opinion—is seen to be capable of resulting in a probable truth, and is thus ultimately subordinate to consensus in interpretation. The activity of the Academic skeptic, who can argue on both sides of any philosophical question (*in utramque partem*), is considered to be analogous to that of the orator and the prudent man: all three are concerned with efficacious action and, accordingly, for all three the criterion of truth is not theoretical reason but probability or "practical certainty."[2] Later, however, in the Northern Renaissance, there is a growing skepticism about the availability of a criterion of practical judgment. The easy alliance of rhetoric and Academic skepticism begins to be undermined by the arguments of Pyrrhonism. The exchange of contradictory opinion is no longer subordinate to a belief in practical certainty; contradiction becomes paradoxical and resistant to a prudent interpretation or practical resolution. Skepticism, in short, is no longer compatible with rhetorical persuasion; instead, it takes the possibility of persuasion itself as its object.

The analogy between rhetoric and prudence—the fact that both involve deliberation about action—is thus a particularly useful point of departure for exploring the relationship of theory to praxis in humanist and humanist-influenced texts. It is historically justified by the humanists' self-conscious concern with this analogy, and heuristically valuable insofar as it forces us to pay close attention to the different rhetorical practices that dramatize an author's interpretation of this analogy. It also allows us to see the particular relevance of the early humanists' debates on the nature of prudence and the existence of free will to a study of the assumptions informing the activities of reading and interpreting in the Renaissance. For the humanists, the prudence that is the intellectual virtue of right judgment about our actions applies to the author's and reader's acts of interpretation as well. Indeed, some humanists go further and suggest that insofar as deliberation, judgment, and writing involve the will, they can themselves be construed as actions. In either case, fifteenth- and sixteenth-century debates about the nature and possibility of prudence and free will are also concerned with the nature and possibility of correct interpretation. Conversely, statements about interpretation can also be read as statements about the possibility of prudence. More important, whether or not a given text makes explicit statements about the act of interpretation, it exemplifies and dramatizes issues of interpretation in its relation to and readings of other texts.

Precisely for these reasons focusing on the alliance of rhetoric and prudence also alerts us to the various ways of understanding the self-reflexive rhetorical practice of the literary text, and in so doing tells us something about the different ways in which literature itself can be conceived. Modern students of literature are familiar with the argument that the text refers to itself as act, rather than directing the reader to an act outside of the text. The early humanists' way of understanding the self-referentiality of the text, however, was to argue that literature is not only the activity in which the self-reflexive nature of the linguistic act is most in evidence, but also the place where that self-reflexivity—conceived in prudential terms—may be seen to have practical and political significance.[3] Within the humanist tradition, it is only those texts of the later Renaissance, in which the analogy between rhetoric and prudence is subject to doubt, that the self-reference of the text tends to be understood in terms closer to the modern conception of "literariness": in the act of referring to themselves as linguistic and political acts, these texts also force us to question the possibility of such reference and such action. For many of these later authors the rhetorical dimension of the text can no longer be contained by practical concerns; rather, it is conceived of as threatening, aberrant, resistant to the author's intention to persuade to right action. The rhetorical strategies that we associate with humanist texts appear in these later works as well, but for different, often ambivalent and ironic reasons. The authors are frequently concerned to engage the reader only then to preclude discussion or deliberation in the humanist sense of the word—whether out of fear of the practical religious or political consequences (Erasmus, Hobbes) or out of a general skepticism about the possibility of such humanistic discussion (Montaigne). The responses to the "crise pyrrhonienne"[4] of humanism are thus various and ambivalent: while an author may accept the arguments of Pyrrhonism and develop a textual rhetoric that looks forward to a modern formalistic concept of literature, the author who, like the humanist, desires to educate and persuade his reader must devise a substitute for humanist rhetoric. Montaigne's skeptical acceptance of the waywardness of language and Hobbes's attempt to control this waywardness represent only the two extremes of a wide spectrum of possible "motives of eloquence" in the later Renaissance.

Of course, humanist rhetoric, with its insistence on argument *in utramque partem*, forces us to problematize this historical scheme even as we propose it. In showing that the same arguments can be used on both sides of a question, and that the same text can be interpreted in different ways, these authors also address themselves to the contrary interpretations that their own texts are capable of eliciting. They call our attention to the fact that within the realm of rhetoric (that is, of language) every figure is "potentially reversible":[5] each can be read as serious or ironic, as simply contradictory or profoundly paradoxical, as undecidable or the occasion for a decision. The humanist emphasis on the act of reading can itself be interpreted *in utramque partem* as conducive to action or as a substitute for action, and in fact has been so interpreted both by twentieth-century critics and by the later humanists of the Northern Renaissance. Fredric Jameson's remark on "the fundamental equivocality of the symbolic" is to the point. The symbolic is "at one and the same time the accomplishment of an act and the latter's substitute, a way of acting on the world and of compensating for the impossibility of such action all at once. . . . Much depends, indeed, on whether you think of art as a symbolic *act* or as an act which is merely *symbolic*."[6] My contention is that the early humanists intended writing to be understood as an act and reading, if not as an act, at least as conducive to action, whereas later critics of the humanist tradition (e.g., Luther in the debate with Erasmus on free will) stressed the *merely* symbolic and therefore illusory nature of such action.

The problem of the reversibility of the symbol as discussed by Jameson raises the issue of the relation of humanist rhetoric to contemporary literary and cultural criticism. I am certainly not the first to suggest that many of the recent developments in criticism involve a return to the Aristotelian and Ciceronian tradition of rhetoric which, since the eighteenth century at least, has been in eclipse. As Franco Moretti has noted, Aristotle's subordination of rhetoric to ethical and political studies prefigures "those researches of the last few decades aimed at demonstrating that rhetorical conventions exist in order to satisfy specifically *social* requirements."[7] What these investigations share is not simply a renewed concern with the social and political context of the literary work, but an awareness of the rhetorical dimension of, and thus the constitutive role of convention in, all forms of discourse. From the perspective of such theory, in other words, all forms of discourse are equally subject to rhetorical analysis. This does not mean that literature is, as has sometimes been argued, the privileged instance of language, that form of language in which "language" is most "itself," but rather that the concept of literature is itself historically and ideologically variable. Accordingly, in the new rhetorically oriented criticism, Aristotle's definition of rhetoric as "the faculty of observing in any given case the available means of persuasion" (*Rhet.* 1355b 25) must itself be historicized. The study of rhetoric becomes the study of the different conventions of interpretation, the different forms of consensus, that are available at a particular historical moment.[8]

This kind of criticism, as Terry Eagleton and others have remarked, is not formalist or aesthetic in our modern understanding of those terms. Neither, I will argue, was the discourse of Renaissance humanism. This should be apparent not least of all in my selection of texts. Quattrocento dialogues, treatises on free will, paradoxical encomia, and essays are all generic possibilities within the comprehensive theory of discourse offered by the humanist rhetorical tradition. Familiarity with this tradition can thus also help us understand why the eighteenth-century development of a formalist aesthetics (which so much contemporary criticism has been concerned to attack) coincided with the redefinition of politics in terms of science rather than prudence. When mathematical certainty is taken as the standard of reason in politics as well as science, then the aesthetic realm of prudential deliberation, and with this the work of art itself, must be redefined in terms of mere subjective experience.

The contemporary attack on formalist aesthetics provides one context for the chapters that follow, but for our purposes the most relevant context for the renewed interest in rhetoric is the debate between pragmatism and deconstruction, that is, between a conception of rhetoric that has affinities with humanism and one that specifically takes the ideology of humanism as its target. Since I shall often refer to the early humanists' pragmatic conception of rhetoric, it will be useful at this point to clarify the ways in which the humanists anticipate contemporary notions of pragmatism. Such a discussion will also help us to see the relation of the rhetorical analyses in the following chapters to the contemporary practice of deconstruction.[9]

The pragmatist, as Richard Rorty has written, is not concerned with finding the one true description of the way things are, but with "a description of the descriptions" that the human race has come up with so far.[10] Thus, as I have already suggested, a pragmatic history of rhetoric will be concerned with the different ways in which literature and rhetoric have historically been conceived. This in turn should alert us to the fact that the meaning of pragmatism is itself historically variable. For example, while the modern pragmatist, according to Rorty, gives up the notion of an ultimate reality to which the truth would correspond (150), the Christian humanist only gives up the notion of correspondence, not that of ultimate reality. As we will see, the Quattrocento humanists' pragmatic conception of truth was constrained by, not simply compatible with but founded on, a belief in a divinely given standard of practical reason.

In one sense, to say that the humanists subscribed to a pragmatic and rhetorical conception of the truth is not to defend the humanists against the common charge that they were uninteresting philosophers, but to admit it. Rorty's comment on the twentieth-century pragmatist theory of truth is apropos: "This theory says that truth is not the sort of thing one should expect to have a philosophically interesting theory about" (xiii). What this means for our purposes is that the pragmatism of humanist rhetoric rejects the validity of universal truth claims and insists instead on the principle of decorum. Truth is not correspondence to a theoretical standard; rather, truth itself changes according to the situations in which one finds oneself. Or, in the words of William James, the true is "whatever proves itself to be good in the way of belief" (xxv; cf. 162). Here the traditional philosophic distinction between the true and the good dissolves: both turn out to be normative notions.[11]

Rorty's three-part definition can serve us further as a grid for charting the humanist notion of pragmatism. First of all, according to Rorty, pragmatism is an antiessentialism, as the quote from James suggests. The pragmatist tells us that "it is in the vocabulary of practice rather than of theory, of action rather than contemplation, in which one can say something useful about truth" (162). That is, in examining statements about the way the world is, the pragmatist does not ask, "Do they get it right?," but "what would it be like to believe that? What would happen if I did?" (163). Second, for pragmatism there is "no epistemological difference between truth about what ought to be and truth about what is, nor any metaphysical difference between facts and values, nor any methodological difference between morality and science. . . . For the pragmatist, the pattern of all inquiry—scientific as well as moral—is deliberation concerning the relative attractions of various concrete alternatives [i.e., *phronesis* rather than *theoria*]" (163–164). In the Renaissance humanist tradition, there is a wide spectrum of interpretations with respect to these first two descriptions of pragmatism. Hobbes's conflation of fact and value, for example, will turn out to be the ironic equivalent of the early Quattrocento humanists' normative notion of truth. But whereas Hobbes uses science as the paradigm for morality, Salutati does distinguish between the two on methodological grounds. In Rorty's terms, then, the pragmatism of the early humanists would be a limited pragmatism. This is clear when we turn to the third characterization of pragmatism as "the doctrine that there are no constraints on inquiry save conversational ones—no wholesale constraints derived from the nature of the objects, or of the mind, or of language, but only those retail constraints provided by the remarks of our fellow-inquirers" (165). Such a characterization is inapplicable to the early Italian humanists, for whom the possibility of consensus is informed by a divinely given natural reason. This standard of reason ideally provides an internal constraint on discourse, as well as a defense against the charge that pragmatism is another form of relativism or irrationalism.

Contrary to Rorty's claims, however, contemporary pragmatism does not anticipate the insights of deconstruction. Whether one conceives of deconstruction as a critique of metaphysics or, as in the practice of some American critics, a specific form of rhetorical analysis, in either case it is incompatible with pragmatism, and thus with the skepticism to which pragmatism may be allied. For, even when the deconstructive critic is concerned to demonstrate the way in which the rhetorical and pragmatic dimension of the text undermines or interferes with the cognitive dimension, this interference can itself never be transcended. There is no practical resolution of the skeptical dilemma, precisely because deconstruction questions the epistemological basis of such a resolution, that is, the skeptic's appeal to common sense or consensus. In doing so, deconstruction is guided by what Rodolphe Gasché has called a "cognitive rhetorics."[12]

In a certain sense, the deconstructive description of the pragmatic skepticism of the humanists is one that the humanists themselves would accept: humanism is defined by its resistance to the epistemological implications of its own rhetoric, by its concern with the "consequences of pragmatism" rather than with the epistemological implications of such pragmatism. In the following pages I will be more concerned with defining the humanists' attempt to construct such a pragmatic rhetoric than with deconstructing such an attempt. For if deconstruction is a critique of metaphysics, of philosophical language in general, it is necessarily a very different task from the reconstruction of the conventions of writing and interpretation in a given historical period. In fact, familiarity with the humanists' conception of rhetoric allows us to see the extent to which the deconstructive view of rhetoric is determined by theoretical and epistemological rather than by pragmatic concerns.[13] Thus, to the extent that Erasmus, Luther, Montaigne, and Hobbes focus on the epistemological paradoxes of humanist rhetoric—on the way in which, for example, the rhetoric of humanist texts undermines their own claims to persuasion—they would seem to provide a deconstructive reading of earlier humanist texts. But in each case a new practical transcendence of the epistemological dilemma—whether through negative theology, faith, Pyrrhonist skepticism, or political science—is offered in place of the humanist one. The success of these efforts could itself be subjected to a deconstructive analysis; but that would be the subject of another book. Finally, it is important to add that the "history" of humanist rhetoric that I have been sketching is not something that impinges on humanism from the outside. I suggest rather that it be construed as a kind of allegory of the tensions constitutive of humanism from the very beginning.

In order to narrate that history, Salutati, Pontano, and Valla have been chosen as representative of the Quattrocento humanists' attitudes toward rhetoric. For all their differences, the Quattrocento humanists share a number of important ideological assumptions, assumptions that are reflected in similar rhetorical practices: they are united by their faith in the compatibility of Christianity, prudential rhetoric, and Academic skepticism, and they believe that the Academic skeptic's way of arguing *in utramque partem* can be used to support their ethic of decorum. Contradiction for these authors is not a logical scandal, but a sign of rhetorical possibility. Skepticism is conceived of not as a threatening relativism, but as an occasion for action. The realization that the same arguments can be used pro and contra, that the same text can be read in different ways, is liberating rather than demoralizing, and the potential reversibility of every figure is seen as the condition of the possibility of change in general. The conviction that it is impossible to have theoretical knowledge of God gives way to a *belief* in free will and to a corresponding concern with practical certainty—the only kind of certainty available to us as human beings. This practical certainty is in turn seen to be manifest in the *consensus omnium* of linguistic usage, rhetorical convention, and social custom. Philology and rhetoric (as the theory and practice of linguistic consensus) and politics (as the theory and practice of social consensus) are then judged to be analogous and inseparable.

Erasmus, Montaigne, and Hobbes, on the other hand, have been chosen for their pivotal, Janus-like position in the development of humanist attitudes toward rhetoric: at the same time that their texts reveal an awareness of the ideal alliance of rhetoric and prudence, their rhetorical strategies prove to be symptomatic of an increasing anxiety or skepticism about the power of rhetoric to persuade to right action. For these authors the Academic skeptic's process of argumentation is no longer simply an ally of decorum: instead, it threatens to undermine the possibility of consensus altogether. This threat is apparent as well in the new uses to which the arguments of Pyrrhonist skepticism are put. The Pyrrhonist arguments borrowed from Sextus Empiricus were often used in Renaissance apologies for the faith to combat the dogmatism of atheist rationalists, since both skepticism and faith were alike in criticizing the authority of theoretical reason. The aim of such arguments was not a radical epistemological critique of the possibility of judgment or of knowledge, but rather the chastising of the rational nonbeliever. Yet these arguments could also be used to suspend the possibility of knowledge, as they were by Montaigne, for whom both the practical criterion of decorum and the theological criterion of faith (and the two are finally inseparable) were subject to doubt. In different ways and to different degrees, Erasmus and Hobbes share Montaigne's doubts about the humanist rhetorical tradition. Accordingly, these later authors are frequently less concerned with persuading us to action than with persuading us to consider the nature of persuasion itself. By emphasizing the problematic nature of interpretation, they force us to reflect on the relationship between interpretive and ethical practice, the practice of reading and practical reason. Thus, while they instruct us in the complexities of the humanist rhetorical and pragmatic conception of literature, they also allow us to perceive the shifting status of prudential rhetoric in the Renaissance and its eventual decline. By the time we reach Hobbes, rhetoric is no longer "regina rerum . . . et perfecta sapientia" (queen of all things and perfect wisdom),[14] but an outcast from the commonwealth.

The following chapter briefly sketches the early humanists' assumptions about the practical and prudential nature of reading, then turns to the skeptical questioning of these assumptions by later figures of the Northern Renaissance. Subsequent chapters present close readings of a number of texts that exemplify some of the different ways in which the analogy of rhetoric and prudence is understood or undermined in the Renaissance. I intend the book to be conceived of in part as a contribution to the intellectual history of Renaissance rhetoric. The later chapters, however, should also be seen as proposing a spectrum of possible interpretations of the humanist rhetorical tradition as it was articulated in the Quattrocento. While this spectrum is clearly not exhaustive, it does represent some of the most important responses to the humanists' rhetorical practices. The positions represented by the authors I discuss are exemplary, and are intended to have an heuristic value for further research in this area.

2 Humanist Rhetoric

Dicere enim bene nemo potest nisi qui prudenter intellegit; qua re qui eloquentiae verae dat operam, dat prudentiae. [For no one can be a good speaker who is not a prudent thinker. Thus whoever devotes himself to true eloquence devotes himself to prudence.]
—Cicero, *Brutus*

Quattrocento humanism was a civic humanism, which means that rhetoric was in the service of the active life.[1] While a thorough examination of the social and political factors contributing to the Quattrocento humanists' interest in prudence and the active life is beyond the scope of this book, it is clear that this interest was determined neither by purely political nor by purely literary factors, but by a combination of the two. Political conditions in the republics and courts of Italy created the need for the humanists' rhetorical activity, at the same time that the humanists' literary interest in antiquity led them to recover classical arguments for the superiority of prudence to theoretical reason within the realm of action.[2] During the fifteenth century, Aristotle's *Rhetoric* and *Nicomachean Ethics* were newly translated from the Greek, not only into Latin but also into the vernaculars.[3] It was at this time as well that the sovereign Ciceronian texts of the Middle Ages, the *De inventione* and the pseudo-Ciceronian *Ad Herennium*, were dethroned: in 1416 Poggio Bracciolini discovered the complete Quintilian, and in 1421, Gherardo Landriani, Bishop of Lodi, discovered the complete texts of Cicero's *De oratore* and *Orator*. But what is decisive about these translations and recoveries is the opportune moment at which they occurred: the moment when they could be read with a new openness and receptivity to the rhetorical ideal they presented. For the humanists, who were professional men of letters,[4] might not have been interested in the classical defense of prudence if it had not been for the further argument—hinted at by Aristotle and developed by Cicero—that the activity of the prudent man is analogous to that of the orator.

While Aristotle limits the province of the orator in the *Rhetoric*, he draws several analogies between rhetoric and prudence in the *Nicomachean Ethics*—not so much in terms of the domain of competence, when this is interpreted as an intellectual discipline or subject matter, as in terms of *the form or the activity* of judgment that both involve. In this respect, while Aristotle's orator may seem to have little in common with the Ciceronian ideal of the good man speaking persuasively, Aristotle's man of practical reason or prudence is very similar. That Cicero himself recognized this to be the case is clear from his many references to Peripatetic ethics.[5] It is because of the implicit, and at times explicit, connection between rhetoric and prudence in the *Ethics* that the Quattrocento humanists, in turn, drew heavily on this text in their defense of their own rhetorical activity. For this reason, a brief sketch of the Aristotelian notion of prudence is in order. The crucial difference to keep in mind in the following summary is that while Aristotle analyzes the formal similarities in the activities of the orator and the prudent man, Cicero insists that the prudent man be eloquent.[6]

Rhetoric, Prudence, and Skepticism in Antiquity

Aristotle recognized both in the *Rhetoric* and in the *Nicomachean Ethics* that rhetorical decorum and prudence share a faculty of judgment that is not logical or theoretical, but practical; that does not subordinate an object to a general rule or concept, but responds to the particular per se (*NE* 6.1141b 14–22; 1142a 25). This is because both rhetoric and prudence are concerned with "problems about which different points of view . . . [can] be maintained, questions open to debate because they . . . [can] be judged only in terms of probable truth and . . . [are] not susceptible to scientific demonstrations of irrefutable validity."[7] Thus, Aristotle writes in the *Rhetoric*: "The duty of rhetoric is to deal with such matters as we deliberate upon without arts or systems to guide us. . . . There are few facts of the 'necessary' type that can form the basis of rhetorical syllogisms. Most of the things about which we make decisions, and into which we therefore inquire, present us with alternative possibilities. For it is about our actions that we deliberate and inquire, and all our actions have a contingent character; hardly any of them are determined by necessity" (1357a).[8] One crucial implication of Aristotle's observation that we debate about things that present us with alternative possibilities is that the arguments with which we debate themselves suggest alternative possibilities—that is, not only can we argue pro and contra a given position, but the same arguments can be marshaled on either side of the question.

The consideration of which figures or forms of argument are appropriate to the end of the persuasion (leaving aside for a moment the question of the ethical status of that end) is analogous to the choice of means by the prudent man. In neither case are general rules simply applied to particular instances. Rather, it is the nature of the rule to be modified in the application (NE 1140a 25–1140b 25). Hence one critic of Aristotle refers to prudence as the knowledge of the rule about choice.[9] The relevant distinction here is between the determinant (logical and necessary) judgment of the theoretical sciences, for which objective or mathematical certainty is the criterion of truth, and the reflective judgment of practical wisdom, which is concerned with action. Thus, A. E. Taylor writes, "Aristotle calls the method of practical wisdom the practical syllogism or syllogism of action, since its peculiarity is that what issues from the putting together of the premises is not an assertion but the performance of an act."[10] Practical wisdom, Aristotle tells us in the Ethics, is much closer to the technical skills required by the applied arts (technai), not only because both are concerned with "things which admit of being other than they are" (1140a ff.), but also because, as Gadamer writes: "Both are knowledge of a dynamic kind [vorgängiges Wissen], and must determine and guide an action. Consequently, they must contain within themselves the rule for the application of this knowledge to the concrete task at hand."[11]

Both Cicero and Aristotle realized that the rule of decorum is only formal if it is not referred to some ethical standard (De off. 1.27.94; NE 1142b 30–35)—hence Aristotle's insistence that deliberation seeks to determine the means, not the ends of action (NE 1144a 7; Rhet. 1362a 18)—and for both such a standard of reflective judgment did indeed exist, whether it was interpreted as an inborn disposition (Aristotle) or innate ideas (Cicero). For both, in other words, the possibility of prudence was grounded in man's natural being (NE 1103a 25, 1140b).

Aristotle argued that man has an innate disposition to moral virtue which must be cultivated by prudence (*NE* 1144b 15), while prudence is itself a potentiality whose realization depends on practice and on moral virtue (1144a 30). Thus, while human beings have an intellectual intuition of the absolute standard of conduct which is the good life, the prudent man incarnates the "standard and measure" (1113a 30) by making the "actual and normative"[12] coincide in every particular act of judgment. His deliberation or interpretation of what is required is intrinsically authoritative, because informed by an intuition of the good. But this rule of behavior is not something that can be conceptualized. It is a combination of intuition or innate predisposition and practice. Thus, Aristotle writes in the *Ethics*, "It is this kind of deliberation which is good deliberation, a correctness that attains what is good" (1142b 20).

It was in terms of such an intuitive standard of judgment that Aristotle first provided a theoretical justification of the dialectical syllogism.[13] He explains in the *Topics* that the dialectical syllogism differs from the apodeictic syllogism in dealing with the realm of contingency rather than that of necessity. It takes the probable as its point of departure, and thus achieves a lesser degree of certainty in its conclusions. The probable is defined in terms of common opinion: opinions "which are accepted by every one or by the majority or by the philosophers" (100b 20). The degree of truth that Aristotle then claims for the conclusion of the dialectical syllogism thus depends on the assumption that common opinion or consensus corresponds in some degree to the truth (*NE* 1140b 20–25). Yet for Aristotle, as for the Sophists, this argument by consensus or probability is not merely a debased form of the apodeictic syllogism.[14] Rather, it is governed by completely different—practical—considerations, and derives its authority from the conviction that, in some practical sense (*NE* 1139a 27), "what all believe to be true is actually true" (*NE* 1173a).

Thus, whereas Plato condemned the realm of opinion as deceptive and illusory, Aristotle granted it a positive status in its own right, and this is important because the contingent realm of opinion is the realm in which persuasion and action can take place. Furthermore, in this realm practical reason takes precedence over the precepts of theoretical speculation, for there can be no science of particulars (see *NE* 1104a 5–10, 1141b 15ff). On the basis of these two assertions, one could then argue—as many of the humanists later did—that the literature that is appropriate to this realm should not

be identified with the sta'
but rather with the dv

While Aristotle d
logism to literatu'
dialectic and r
Both are in
speculati'
as their p
rather than
tle discusses t.
he begins with th.

sciousness in an innat
mediate inner certain
ing all previous tend
seeds of morality w
allowed to develo
virtutum; quae si a
[The seeds of v
allowed to ripe
life].[17]

> We may approach th.
> persons to whom we attr.
> about what is good and adv.
> of a man of practical wisdon.
> good and advantageous in a part.
> thing contributes to the good life in t
> *we speak* of men having attained prac.
> spect . . . when they calculate well with
> end, one that cannot be attained by an appli
> *that*, in general, a man of practical wisdom is h.
> deliberate. [1140a 25–30, my emphasis]

It was no
of pruden
vided the
regardin
orator.
tilian
neces
ness
pr
h
a

It was this belief in a practical standard of judgm.
common linguistic usage that legitimated the orator's ap.
mon sense, his arguments by consensus, opinion, and
place. Accordingly, the rhetorical syllogism was not a false
ceitful form of argument, but one grounded in the com.
imperfection of human nature: imperfection because human affaï.
do not lend themselves to logical formalization; common because,
although based on the probable, such an argument can claim universal appeal by virtue of a shared human nature.[16]

Whereas Aristotle writes of the standard of judgment that guides
the prudent man, and by extension the orator, in terms of potentiality, Cicero gives this standard a content as well. In an article on
the concept of the *consensus omnium*, Klaus Oehler remarks on this
difference:

> Aristotle and Plato already speak of a natural disposition of man to
> morality, . . . [but] it was Cicero who first grounded moral con-

33

knowledge, which gives the individual an im-
y of his ethical conduct [*Wertverhalten*]. Surpass-
encies in this direction, he teaches that the innate
ll in themselves lead us to a happy life, if they are
unhindered: *Sunt enim ingeniis nostris semina innata*
olescere liceret, ipsa nos ad beatam vitam natura perduceret
rtue are inborn in our dispositions and, if they were
n, nature's own hand would lead us on to happiness of

doubt in part because of this more substantial definition
e in terms of "innate seeds of virtue" that Cicero pro-
Renaissance with the classical statement of confidence
g the standard of judgment that informs the activity of the
n *De oratore* (1.18.83, 3.16.60–61, 3.31.122), as later in Quin-
pr. 9ff., 2.16.11, 2.17.43), we read that the good orator is
sarily a good man, and in *De officiis* we learn that moral good-
and decorum, *honestas* and *utilitas*, cannot conflict: "For what is
per is morally right, and what is morally right is proper [*quod*
nestum est, decet]. The nature of this difference between morality
nd propriety [*decori*] can be more easily felt than expressed. For
whatever propriety may be, it is manifest only when there is preexisting moral rectitude" (1.27.94; see also 2.3.9–10, 3.3.11).

This conviction in turn justifies the centrality of the rhetorical and
ethical concept of decorum in Cicero's works. In a famous passage
in the *Orator*, Cicero writes:

> For after all the foundation of eloquence, as of everything else, is
> wisdom [*sapientia*]. In an oration, as in life, nothing is harder to deter-
> mine than what is appropriate [*quid deceat*]. The Greeks called it *prépon*:
> let us call it decorum or "propriety." . . . From ignorance of this mis-
> takes are made not only in life but very frequently in writing, both in
> poetry and in prose. Moreover the orator must have an eye to pro-
> priety, not only in thought but in language. For the same style and the
> same thoughts must not be used in portraying every condition in life,
> or every rank, position or age, and in fact a similar distinction must be
> made in respect of place, time and audience. The universal rule, in
> oratory as in life, is to consider propriety. This depends on the subject
> matter under discussion, and on the character of both the speaker and
> the audience. The philosophers are accustomed to consider this exten-
> sive subject under the head of duties [*officiis*]. . . . the literary critics
> consider it in connexion with poetry; orators in dealing with every kind
> of speech, and in every part thereof.[18]

34

When we turn to *De officiis* we find that Cicero defines decorum in the political realm as prudence. And while he first opposes prudence to theoretical wisdom as Aristotle does, he goes beyond Aristotle when he argues for the superiority of prudence on the grounds that it is concerned with action rather than contemplation. Human society is Cicero's primary concern, and prudence is more appropriate to this society than contemplation is:

> And then, the foremost of all virtues is wisdom [*sapientia*]—what the Greeks call *sophia*; for by prudence, which they call *phronesis*, we understand something else, namely, the practical knowledge of things to be sought for and of things to be avoided. . . . And service [which is a function of prudence] is better than mere theoretical knowledge, for the study and knowledge of the universe would somehow be lame and defective, were no practical results to follow. Such results, moreover, are best seen in the safeguarding of human interests. It is essential, then, to human society; and it should, therefore, be ranked above theoretical knowledge. [1.43.153][19]

In Cicero's view, then, even more than in Aristotle's, the faculty of prudence is inseparable from the ideal practice of the orator. Both the orator and the prudent man are concerned with the domain of probability, and both know that they can only be effective in this domain by acting according to the rhetorical standard of decorum. Just as the orator is guided by decorum in adapting his speech to the exigencies of the moment, so the prudent man enacts decorum in the moral sphere by responding to the particular and contingent in human affairs (*Orator* 71). Furthermore, the prudent man and the orator are not only analogous for Cicero; they are ideally the same, since the good man to be effective must be persuasive, and the orator who is not good is not worthy of the name.[20] Cicero's point is not simply that the orator has the rhetorical skills of persuasion that will enable the prudent man to achieve a particular end, but that the latter is prudent precisely by being an orator. The important consequence of Cicero's argument is that rhetoric—properly speaking—is morally justified.

Cicero's further contribution to the ideology of humanist rhetoric was to argue for the similarities between the orator and the Academic skeptic (an analogy that was already implicit in Aristotle's conception of rhetoric as the art of finding the best available arguments within the realm of the probable).[21] Since man, according to the skeptic, can know nothing absolutely, he is always concerned with the realm of the contingent and the probable, that is, the realm of rhetoric. Furthermore, while the skeptic is traditionally less concerned than the orator with persuasion to action within this realm, he shares with the orator a refusal of dogmatism and an ability "to speak persuasively on any side of any philosophical question."[22] Finally, the Academic skeptic believes that within the contingent realm of human life the genuine exchange of ideas and opposing arguments in rhetorical debate will elicit the practical truth we know as consensus. This is a conception of truth that involves reference not to some absolute ethical norm but rather to a standard of decorum, likelihood, or probability; it thus allows for, indeed depends upon, action but does not thereby abandon the claims of an ethical conception of judgment. In short, what the Academic skeptic has to offer the Ciceronian civic orator is an important argument for the possibility of prudence: that is, the combined acknowledgment of the contingent realm of action and the assurance of a practical ethical criterion within this realm.

Thus, while Aristotle draws an analogy between the orator and the prudent man, it was Cicero's presentation of the orator that was particularly attractive to many Renaissance humanists. As we have seen, this was not simply because Cicero's texts were written in a Latin which the humanists regarded as the model of eloquence.[23] Nor was it only because as professional men of letters they had a vested interest in Cicero's emphasis on the propaedeutic role of a literary education in the training of the orator. While both of these factors contributed to Cicero's influence, the humanists were primarily drawn to the Ciceronian orator as an ideal representative of humanist culture. For Cicero does not restrict the orator's domain of competence in the way that Aristotle does, with the result that the orator is not simply a technician, as Aristotle's orator must have seemed to many humanists, but rather the embodiment of true learning.[24]

Quattrocento Rhetoric

Leonardo Bruni's remarks in his *Isagogicon moralis disciplinae* (Introduction to moral education, 1421–24) are typical of the Quattrocento humanist attitude toward prudence and the active life. While acknowledging the superiority of theoretical wisdom or contemplation, he argues for the greater utility of prudence in the contingent realm of human affairs. In so doing, he illustrates the tendency of many Quattrocento humanists to turn to classical texts for a theoretical defense of the ethic of prudence that was already theirs in practice:

> For in truth, although there are many virtues, as I have said, some are more suited to the life of retirement and contemplation, others to the life of business and civic affairs. For wisdom and knowledge nourish the contemplative life, while prudence governs every action. Each, to be sure, has its proper merits and excellences. The contemplative life is clearly more divine and rarer, but the active life is superior in public service.[25]

In articulating and defending the ideals of civic humanism in the *Isagogicon* and in *De studiis et litteris* (On studies and letters, 1422–29), Bruni appeals both to Aristotle's analysis of prudence and to Cicero's rhetorical treatises. In fact, he conflates them in a way that Cicero would have approved of and that was characteristic of many Quattrocento humanist texts, for he argues that the study of secular literature has the power to make us both prudent and eloquent. The study of history, Bruni tells us in *De studiis* (13), educates the faculty of prudence and provides us with a copia of examples which we can then employ in our own writing. Similarly, the study of orators teaches us how to be both politically effective speakers and eloquent writers, just as reading poetry informs us about "vita moribusque" as well as about its own persuasive way of teaching.

It is now generally accepted that the Quattrocento humanists were decisively influenced both by Aristotle's *Ethics* and by Cicero's rhetorical works. But it is important to recognize that the influence of these works was itself determined by the humanist conflation of rhetoric and poetics. Whereas in the works of these classical authors literature was seen as separate from or a propaedeutic to the acquisition of rhetorical skills, in the Renaissance the two were often combined and literature was conceived of in Horatian and rhetorical terms as having its own persuasive and formative powers. If we interpret this conflation in simple didactic terms as the subordination of the text to some transcendental meaning, then this attitude was certainly already present in the Middle Ages. For Bruni and his contemporaries, however, there was an increasing emphasis not only on the power of literature to present a transcendental Idea but

37

to persuade to right action. This emphasis in turn helps explain the humanists' practical conception of the acts of reading and writing.[26]

Intellectual historians tend to agree about the conflation of rhetoric and poetics in the Renaissance, but are divided as to its causes and its significance. Some have argued that the rhetorical definition of literature was influenced by the early Italian humanists' experience of the political force of their own literary activity, as when Giangaleazzo Visconti is reported to have said that he feared Salutati's letters more than a thousand horsemen ("non tam sibi mille Florentinorum equites quam Colucii scripta nocere").[27] Others have suggested to the contrary that this conflation was owing in part to a more developed sense of the limited possibilities for genuine political action, with the resulting defensive argument that instead of being preparatory to the action of persuasion in the forum or the law court, literature was itself seen as an act of persuasion.[28] What is clear in either case is that the arguments that Cicero and Aristotle had intended to apply to speeches in the forum, law court, or public ceremony were applied by the humanists to written texts. Accordingly, Renaissance rhetoric can be seen as a truncated version of its classical ancestor, since as the legal and political dimension of rhetoric falls away, only epideictic—the rhetoric of praise and blame— remains.

Those scholars who stress the limited possibilities for genuine political action in the Renaissance tend to view this shrinking of rhetoric to epideictic as an anticipation of a properly aesthetic conception of literature. What I want to suggest with specific reference to humanist works is that if the conflation of rhetoric and poetics diminishes the sphere of rhetoric as it was classically conceived, it enlarges the sphere of literature, since the written text now takes on the functions of deliberative and judicial rhetoric.[29] One generic consequence of this prudential and rhetorical conception of the literary text was, as I have already suggested, the prominence of the dialogue among Quattrocento humanist works. Whereas the classical orator was trained to argue *in utramque partem*, that is, on both sides of a question, in any particular case he argued on one side or the other. But when the Renaissance humanist adopted the Aristotelian and Ciceronian rhetorical skills, he was not constrained by the same immediate concerns as is the orator in the forum or the law court. As a result he could actually present both cases and, in so doing, persuade the reader not to any specific action, but to the exercising of the prudential judgment that is required for all actions.

Aristotle reminds us of the practical dimension of epideictic in the *Rhetoric* when he remarks that demonstrative or epideictic rhetoric is inseparable from deliberative rhetoric insofar as praising is tantamount to urging a course of action (1367b 35–1368a 7). But the distinction between deliberative and demonstrative rhetoric breaks down in the works of the Quattrocento humanists not only because epideictic can be viewed as urging a course of action, but also because the deliberation involved in reading is itself understood as a form of the deliberation that leads to action. The Renaissance humanists thus go beyond their classical mentors in conceiving of literature not only as the cause and effect of prudence and right action (i.e., the writer is presumed to be prudent and to inspire prudence in others), but as a form of prudence itself. Rhetoric here is not primarily conceived of in terms of style or ornament, but in terms of its capacity to exemplify and encourage the activity of practical reasoning.

The Quattrocento humanists thus shared two related assumptions that influenced their conception of the act of reading. First, the prudence or practical reason that is deliberation about action in a social and political context is also at work in the artist's production of a work of art. Prudence is, in this sense, the precondition of artistic decorum, just as it is of ethical decorum. As a result, the work of art is seen less as an object than as reflecting a certain process or activity of judgment. Second, and consequently, the reader's knowledge of the literary text (or any other work of art) can only be practical,[30] since the interpretive practice of reading requires the same acts of discrimination, the same judgments of decorum, as does the author's practice of writing. Thus, the practice of interpretation, like the practice of writing, exemplifies for the humanist the inseparability of moral philosophy and rhetoric.

In the Trecento Coluccio Salutati, chancellor of Florence from 1375 to 1406, is particularly eloquent on this point. In his early letter in praise of Petrarch, he argues that moral philosophy is inseparable from rhetoric (*Ep.* 1.179–80) not only because both are concerned with the practical realm of human affairs, but because it is in language that this moral dimension is most fully realized: language raises man above the animals and enables him to create a consensus and community, and language allows for the persuasion of the will to action. Accordingly, the poet and the orator do not perform a merely aesthetic function; rather, the aesthetic dimension is the precondition of the political. This does not only imply that the meaning of the text is inextricable from the aesthetic expression, which is then both pleasing and useful in terms of conveying meaning, or that the intended function of the text is to persuade to right action. It means something particular about the way in which the text persuades to action: unlike the reading of an abstract argument, reading poetry or history involves an "applicatio mentis" (*Ep.* 2.295), a pleasurable activity, exercise, or praxis, which educates us in the very act of reading at the same time that it moves us to the application of prudence in human affairs.[31]

The Quattrocento humanists were decisively influenced by Salutati's arguments. Like Salutati, Giovanni Pontano claimed that literary or rhetorical decorum can educate the reader in the virtue of prudence, both because it can provide thematic examples of prudent actions in the past and because the skills of judgment and discrimination involved in the composition and interpretation of a literary work are similar to those involved in practical reasoning about our actions. Thus, in the *De principe*, Pontano insists on the contribution of the activity of reading to the rhetorical force of virtuous examples (*PLQ*, 1034, 1052), and in his dialogue *Actius* he argues that the portrayal of counsel and debate in historical works will serve to elucidate the truth, while reported speeches will not only provide moral precepts but also make the reader more diligent in examining and reflecting on other passages.[32] Contrary to the notion that epideictic as the rhetoric of aesthetic display is the form of rhetoric most suited to writing (because the written text allows for the appreciation of aesthetic effects),[33] Pontano suggests that writing transforms the auditor's aesthetic appreciation of epideictic into the reader's active participation in a process of deliberation, deliberation that is itself analogous and conducive to action. According to this argument, the reader's process of discrimination in reading must be seen as the imitation not of the text as a product, but of the text as a process.

In the sixteenth century, this educative view of the process of reading is epitomized by Erasmus's famous remark in the *Ratio: lectio transit in mores* (reading passes over into morals [usage, practice, custom]).[34] Yet, while Aristotelian prudential deliberation results immediately in action (*NE* 1095a 5: "The end of this kind of study is not knowledge but action"), in Erasmus's dictum political action is mediated by the exercise of judgment in the act of reading. Praxis in the sense of political action can be the fruit of reading because the practice of interpretation educates our ability to deliberate about such action.

Philip Sidney articulates a similar view in the *Apology* when he writes that the poet "so far substantially . . . worketh, not only to make a Cyrus, which had been but a particular excellency as Nature might have done, but to bestow a Cyrus upon the world to make many Cyruses, if they will learn aright why and how that maker made him" (101). To learn aright "why and how" Xenophon made Cyrus is to imitate the poet's own imitative process, not merely the image of Cyrus. To learn why and how Sidney made the *Apology* is to imitate the activity of judgment, the decisions of decorum, that are manifest in the rhetorical structure of that work.[35]

Even Hobbes, who wants to exclude rhetoric from the commonwealth, constructs the *Leviathan* to enable the reader to understand the logical *process* by which the right commonwealth is produced, for it is only in imitating and comprehending this process that the reader who is sovereign will be able to put Hobbes's logic into practice, and the reader who is subject will accept the necessity of the finished product.[36] Accordingly, the "Introduction" to the *Leviathan* concludes by emphasizing this prudential and reflective moment of deliberation: "When I shall have set down my own reading orderly, and perspicuously, the pains left another, will be onely to consider, if he also find not the same in himself. For this kind of Doctrine, admitteth no other Demonstration" (83).

As I argue in chapter 6, Hobbes dismissed prudential rhetoric on technical rather than moral grounds. But his technical critique is simply the other side of the ethical objections to prudence. If we return for a moment to Pontano, we can anticipate some of the reasons for these objections, and at the same time further clarify the Quattrocento humanist position. For, unlike most of his contemporaries, Pontano explicitly calls attention to the ambivalence with which rhetoric and prudence have traditionally been regarded, and in so doing, obliges himself to offer a defense of their ambiguous status.

As Pontano is well aware, ambivalence about rhetoric or prudence arises when their dual allegiance to the morally right and the expedient is recognized, and when the amoral character of the technical skills involved is judged to be immoral. Just as the orator has the dual purpose of speaking well and persuading his audience, so the prudent man is bound by considerations of both moral correctness and efficacious action, and in each case it is not clear that what is conducive to success need be in conformity with the good. For just as the technical skills of the orator can be seen as capable of serving immoral as well as moral ends, so prudence, which is, strictly speaking, an intellectual rather than a moral virtue, looks as though it might involve the clever manipulation of circumstances without direct regard for morality.

There have traditionally been at least three ways of dealing with the ambivalent moral status of rhetoric. One can (1) condemn it as an immoral pseudoscience (Plato in the *Gorgias*); (2) subordinate rhetoric as a skill to moral judgment, and thereby identify rhetoric with the moral use of rhetoric (Cato, Cicero, and Quintilian: the good orator is necessarily a good man); or (3) acknowledge that there are no built-in constraints and that rhetoric can be used to persuade to evil as well as to good (the Sophists, Aristotle). Similarly, with regard to prudence, one can identify it with theoretical wisdom, in which case it is governed by an absolute notion of the truth (the Platonic ideas); with practical wisdom as the knowledge of good and evil, what to seek and what to avoid (the Stoics, on occasion Cicero); or with a faculty of practical reason which has no precepts but is governed in every particular case by considerations of decorum—of the best means to achieve the end at hand (Cicero, Aristotle).

Depending on how one feels about the claims of social and political action, a rhetoric or prudence that is not subordinate to the fixed moral precepts characteristic of theoretical reason will be more or less attractive. If this realm of action is in all cases to be subordinate to the standards of theoretical reason, then conformity to that standard rather than practical effectiveness will be the primary concern, and prudence in the sense we have been exploring falls away. Accordingly, if one has to choose between speaking well and speaking persuasively, between acting correctly or acting effectively, one will always choose the former. But, Pontano argues, there is another way of looking at things, another system of values that is not concerned with correspondence to some fixed theoretical truth or ethics, but with the creation and maintenance of a social and political community, and thus with compromise and consensus. The agent within this community does not seek preestablished first principles, but rather a practical truth:

> We are speaking about truth here, not that truth which is sought by scientists or mathematicians, which has to do with the certainty of syllogisms in disputations about nature and the disciplines, sciences and faculties of man, but about that truth which shows there is nothing fictitious, deceitful or counterfeit in conversation or speech or customs. . . . Those who have followed this [truth], and hold to it in speaking, business, and domestic habits, are called truthful, and that virtue [is called] truth.[37]

The measure of the extent to which Pontano views this truth as practical appears in the discussion of the positive use of fiction in the *De sermone:* doctors, rulers, priests may all tell untruths without being charged with lying, since their intention is not to deceive their interlocutors but to help them. In this turn to fiction, they are guided by the social and pragmatic judgment of prudence: "omnino prudentiam est hominum munus atque officium" (the entire duty of man is prudence, 58). Poets are thus also exempt from the charge of lying (61–63) since they invent their fables not out of vanity, "but in order that, by this art, men should be deterred from vice . . . or incited to virtue" (62). Finally, ironic dissimulation of the sort Socrates engaged in is not immoral because it is not self-interested. Socrates denied his own learning "not in order to deny what was clear to all [quod in luce expositum est] but to incite others to *humanitas* and modesty" (197). This emphasis on the realm of praxis leads Pontano to justify irony, along with other rhetorical figures, in persuasive rather than cognitive terms: in the case of Socrates, irony is employed to persuade the auditor to the morally good rather than to indicate his own knowledge by a figure of inversion.

Pontano's defense of his practical conception of the truth makes explicit a final assumption that the Quattrocento humanists shared with the Ciceronian orator: the belief that the impossibility of *gnosis*, or cognitive knowledge of the truth, was not a hindrance to ethical praxis. The difference between the two periods is that in the Quattrocento the Ciceronian analogy between the orator and the skeptic is further reinforced by the generally accepted view of the compatibility of skepticism and faith, on the grounds that both involve a critique of the authority of theoretical reason.[38] Salutati is particularly forceful on this point. While in his letters he subscribes to the classical dictum that one must have knowledge in order to be eloquent (*Ep.* 3.602), he adds the at once serious and ironic qualification that the knowledge that is necessary is the knowledge that one knows nothing (*Ep.* 3.602–603); but this recognition is liberating rather than constraining, for it shifts the emphasis from the realm of necessity, that is, from the cognition of logical truth, to that of probability, or of action within a social and political context. Here the criterion of theoretical certainty gives way to that of moral efficacy and rhetoric assumes the divinely authorized function of moving the will.[39]

The early humanist conception of rhetoric thus involves a precarious synthesis of aesthetic, political, and religious factors. Aesthetic decorum is seen to be inseparable from political effectiveness, and in both cases the possibility of such decorum is seen to be not only compatible with cognitive skepticism but contingent upon it. But this skepticism about the power of human reason is itself just the opposite side of faith in divine will. The view that the impossibility of theoretical knowledge leaves room for action and practical certainty then explains the benign role of both skeptical and hypothetical arguments in early humanist texts. As a Christian, the Quattrocento humanist believed that skeptical arguments could be used to destroy the claims of theoretical reason and thus make room for faith. Like the Sophist, the humanist believed that hypothetical argumentation could have beneficial practical consequences. Thus, Lorenzo Valla adopts a Pyrrhonist mode of arguing in his dialogue on free will in order to suggest that we cannot *know* whether or not we have free will but that we can *assume* we practice it. And Erasmus argues explicitly in his *Diatribe* that it is good to assume that we have free will since this hypothesis will have beneficial effects. The humanist's practical transcendence of the epistemological impasse of skepticism can then be seen to be opposed to one traditional analogy between skepticism and aesthetics, according to which the skeptic's detachment is the equivalent of the autonomy of art, or the disinterestedness of the aesthetic experience.[40]

At this point it may be helpful to distinguish the humanist conception of the morally educative activity of reading from the aesthetic conception of reading.[41] In the former, humanist conception, reading is seen to involve a series of discriminations that are analogous to the kinds of discriminations we make in acting in the social and political spheres. This activity of judgment is an interested one. Furthermore, it is not something that supervenes upon the experience of pleasure but is intrinsically bound up with it.[42] While the humanists argue that the activity of judgment is constitutive of the reader's or viewer's response to a work of art, the Kantian, on the other hand, claims that our primary aesthetic response is one of pleasure, which is noncognitive. Only upon reflection do we subject the source of this pleasure to a properly aesthetic judgment.

Despite these differences, however, the practical and aesthetic conceptions of reading are alike in significant ways. While the Kantian aesthetic judgment is noncognitive, and is explicitly opposed to the interested judgments of prudential reasoning, it shares with the prudential judgment of decorum both an authoritative moment of self-reflection and an implicit claim for the moral value of this experience.[43] Just as the judgment of decorum involves reflection on the needs of the judging subject, as well as reference to an internal though not merely subjective standard of decorum, so the aesthetic judgment requires reflection on the subject's experience as grounded in the shared, and thus not merely subjective, human capacity for judgment.[44] Both the practical and aesthetic models of reading, in other words, reject the Pyrrhonist threat to the possibility of cognitive and moral claims; both presuppose the integrity and authority of the judging subject, as well as a relatively unproblematic conception of judgment. The practical and the aesthetic can thus be seen to represent two models of literary judgment, two attitudes toward the text, which are not so far apart as has often been assumed. For if the former places more emphasis on the direct tie between literary and ethical praxis, the latter is far from denying that we are interested in having disinterested aesthetic experiences.[45]

It is important for a number of reasons to establish these differences and similarities between the aesthetic and practical conceptions of reading. In the first case, such clarification guards us against the anachronistic reading of Renaissance texts in purely aesthetic terms.[46] In the second case, it guards us from assuming that the questioning of the humanists' practical conception of reading by many later Renaissance authors necessarily led them to an aesthetic conception of literature (this is one way the conflation of rhetoric and poetics has been interpreted): if the criterion of judgment or of common sense that informs practical reason is open to doubt, the possibility of aesthetic judgment may be threatened as well. The practical and aesthetic conceptions of judgment can then serve as heuristic paradigms, models of reading, which can help us clarify *per contrariam* the rhetorical practices of a number of later Renaissance authors who are skeptical both of the possibility of persuasion to action and of (in Kenneth Burke's definition of the properly aesthetic effect of the text) the action of "pure persuasion."[47]

Skepticism about Rhetoric and Prudence: the Northern Renaissance

To the extent that the humanists embraced the proximate and pragmatic truths of Academic skepticism and of the classical rhetorical tradition, they would seem to be immune to any sort of skeptical crisis. But even before we begin to consider historical causes, this alliance between the humanists' prudential rhetoric and Academic skepticism suggests an internal reason for the vulnerability of the humanist conception of rhetoric to the corrosive arguments of Pyrrhonist skepticism. The problem is that once the moment of practical and rhetorical judgment has been admitted, it threatens to undermine the possibility of fixed ends or of an accessible truth. The legitimacy of the prudential judgment's claim to be something more than mere subjective preference depends on an available standard of judgment, but this standard is ultimately an article of faith that by definition cannot justify itself before the court of skepticism.[48]

Given the vulnerability of the traditional alliance of rhetoric and Academic skepticism, how did it happen that skepticism was all at once perceived as a threat? Why, that is, should it be felt to be necessary, at a particular historical moment, to justify the claims of practical reason? It is here that it is important to make a distinction between the earlier and the later Renaissance, and between Academic skepticism and Pyrrhonism. In the early Italian Renaissance the humanists did not distinguish between these two schools of skepticism, and were not for the most part interested in Cicero's most extended treatment of Academic skepticism, the *Academica*. Charles Schmitt conjectures that this lack of interest was due to Cicero's disconcerting attack in this dialogue on the more traditional schools of philosophy (Stoic, Epicurean, Platonic, Aristotelian).[49] I suggest, in addition, that the early humanists didn't need Cicero's *Academica* because the skeptical arguments presented there were available in Cicero's rhetorical works, or, to put it another way, that the early humanists were less interested in the epistemological questions raised by skepticism than in what the skeptical tradition had to offer the orator.

While the arguments of Academic skepticism were readily available in Cicero's rhetorical works, it was really only with the publication of the Latin translation of Sextus's *Outlines of Pyrrhonism* in 1562 by Henri Estienne, and of *Against the Mathematicians* by Gentian Hervet in 1569, that the more radical arguments of Pyrrhonism became generally accessible.[50] Richard Popkin and Charles Schmitt both place primary responsibility for the revived interest in Pyrrhonist skepticism on the recovery and publication of these texts, and Popkin in particular remarks that publication coincided with the intellectual crisis of the Reformation.[51] Again, I would add that since the first Greek manuscripts of Sextus had already been brought to Italy in the early fifteenth century, this fact of translation and publication suggests that the questioning of received standards of judgment on the part of the reformers not only coincided with Pyrrhonism but actually helped to created a climate receptive to it.

Certainly other factors also contributed to the crisis of confidence in Renaissance humanist rhetoric in the later Renaissance. Since Quattrocento humanism was a civic humanism and was encouraged in part by the particular needs of the Italian city-state, the decline of the humanists' civic and rhetorical ideal in the later Renaissance can be explained in part by the different political conditions that prevailed in northern Europe. But if we limit our consideration of humanist rhetoric for the moment to the question of an available criterion of prudential judgment, then I think the more serious threat was posed by the Reformers' attack on the authority of the Church and its institutional "rule of faith."[52] This questioning of ecclesiastical authority, and of the scholastic theology that buttressed it, was undoubtedly aided and abetted by the advances in science that were undermining the accepted medieval hierarchical cosmology. For many writers of the Northern Renaissance, these advances in science and the Reformers' substitution of the subjective certainty of faith for the institutional rule of the Church meant precisely this: that skepticism and faith were no longer allied, but that faith itself had become an object of skepticism, and along with faith, the possibility of practical certainty.

47

The factors contributing to the renewed interest in classical rhetoric are thus in part the reasons for the humanists' eventual susceptibility to the negative effects of Pyrrhonist skepticism. The "crisis" in medieval thought, which Eugenio Garin and others have described, involved a breakdown of traditional social, political, and religious authorities that at first led to a more flexible sense of human potentiality and a more positive sense of the human realm of contingency in which persuasion and action could take place. (Pico's *Oration on the Dignity of Man* is emblematic of this new sense of possibility.) But while this crisis created the conditions that were favorable to the renewed interest in classical attitudes toward rhetoric, it also contained the seeds of the eventual decline of this classical ideal.[53] This dialectic is particularly clear in the humanists' relation to scholasticism: while in criticizing the natural theology of the scholastics, the humanists first made room for a practical and rhetorical theology[54] and for an emphasis on practical rather than theoretical reason, they also prepared the way for the eventual questioning of their own practical criterion of truth. A brief look at the humanist critique of the scholastic project of natural theology will provide an example of the way in which the humanists' pragmatic critique of medieval notions of authority undermined the authority of their own pragmatism.

The possibility of natural theology depends on the analogy between God and the world. As elaborated by Thomas Aquinas, the doctrine of analogy includes several kinds of analogical relation, all of which are based on the fundamental analogy of the likeness of effect to cause or of Creation to the Creator.[55] It is thus the hierarchical structure of the theological universe, culminating in the authority of God, that guarantees the rationality or legibility of the created world. Human judgment in such a world is either tautological or catachrestic, for predication, or the attribution of certain qualities to God on the basis of observed effects (the natural world), "either presupposes proper knowledge previously obtained of how God is related to His effects and properties or lacks such knowledge and so remains in ignorance of what the divine reality hidden behind the figure really is"(81). The assumption of natural theology, of course, is that human judgment is not catachrestic, but rather enables us to accede to genuine knowledge of God. Theological judgment is in turn paradigmatic of all judgment for the natural theologian, since the authority of predication depends on the same powers of reason, as well as on the hierarchical structure of the sign that functions in theological analogy.

The humanist critique of reasoning by analogy ultimately affected the humanist critic as well who, if he attacked the causal analogy of the scholastic, could not entirely abandon reasoning by analogy (in fact, it is impossible to imagine what this would involve). Rather, he transferred it to the concept of the literary and ethical decorum that is the achievement of practical, not theoretical, reason. But the notions of practical reason and practical certainty eventually raised the same doubts about the availability of a criterion of judgment as did the Reformers' notion of the subjective certainty of faith.

That the concept of literary decorum is intimately related to that of analogy was recognized by Puttenham:

> The Greekes call this good grace of every thing in his kind *tò prépon*, the Latines [*decorum*] we in our vulgar call it by a scholasticall term [*decencie*] our owne Saxon English terme is [*seemelynesse*] that is to say, for his good shape and utter appearance well pleasing the eye. . . . Now because his comelynesse resteth in the good conformitie of many things and their sundry circumstances, with respect one to another, so as there be found a just correspondencie betweene them by this or that relation, the Greekes call it *Analogie* or a convenient proportion. This lovely conformitie, or proportion, or conveniencie between the sence and the sensible hath nature her selfe first most carefully observed in all her owne works.[56]

Just as decorum presupposes a standard of judgment that allows one to determine what is appropriate in each case, so the perception of analogy presupposes a faculty of judgment that will enable one to determine the existence of likeness. Thus, Annabel Patterson, commenting on an earlier passage from Puttenham on the necessity of good judgment or "discretion" for the achievement of decorum, remarks: "The talent which Puttenham describes is one that any author would be glad to assume, but it is absolutely essential to the student of Renaissance decorum, since the subject depends for its very existence on 'reasonable and wittie distinction.' At the same time the subject calls equally on the capacity of the student to draw things together, to make analogies as well as distinctions, because decorum of style is based on analogy."[57]

The same equation between the possibility of analogy and the assurance of decorum is implicit in the medieval doctrine of analogy, though in the latter case analogy is conceived of primarily in terms of causal analogy. But whether analogy is thought of in terms of the relation of cause and effect or of simple likeness, in either case the availability of a standard of judgment (divine or the divine internalized as reason or natural law) is presupposed. The medieval doctrine of analogy can then be seen not only to provide an interpretive model and a standard of decorum for theological speculation, but also to reveal the theological presuppositions underlying the more secular or the more conventionally literary notions of decorum and of analogy. When the possibility of the one is put in question, skepticism about the other is not far behind.[58]

The humanists' rhetorical criterion of truth eventually undermined itself in yet another way. In rejecting natural theology, the humanists returned to the Augustinian and nominalist emphasis on man as a creature of volition; but while the will was the faculty which enabled man to respond freely to the contingencies of everyday life, it also proved to be a source of contingency itself. Like the arguments of Academic and Pyrrhonist skepticism, the concept of the will proved to be divided and to function *in utramque partem* within the humanist tradition.[59]

For the nominalist, man is not capable of achieving knowledge of God by the independent exercise of reason, with the result that doing the good is no longer identified with knowledge of the good. Accordingly, the will is no longer seen as the servant of the cognitive faculty of reason but as "separated from and elevated above reason."[60] As we have seen, this skepticism about the legislative and cognitive powers of reason was reflected in the humanists' emphasis on the superiority of rhetoric to theoretical philosophy: as William J. Bouwsma has written, "like Scripture, rhetoric recognized the weakness of reason and spoke to the heart"(37). But it is precisely this analogy between Scripture and rhetoric, between faith and the irrationality of the will, that threatens to undermine the authority of practical reason. If the will is recalcitrant, then the possible unity of theory and practice in the faculty of practical reason is subject to doubt. Thus, the works of Saint Augustine and some of the nominalists, while contributing in many ways to the voluntaristic cast of humanist rhetorical thought,[61] could also be used to undermine the belief in the possibility of a community established and secured in the rhetorical appeal to a shared practical reason or common sense. Along with the new translations of Sextus Empiricus, Augustine's theology of grace[62] made available an argument that contributed to the questioning of humanist faith, faith in the assumptions of the classical rhetorical tradition and in the subservience of skepticism, Academic or Pyrrhonist, to those assumptions.

The problem for the Christian humanist is that, in a Judeo-Christian world, even the limited freedom presupposed by prudence is problematic; there is, in theory, no contingency in a divinely ordered universe. Fate is man's name for his incomprehension of God's providence; and if we say that grace is precisely that which cannot be understood, we are asserting not simply man's freedom but also his absolute dependence on God. Are we not tempted to argue, as Kant did later, that the church fathers' concept of a relative freedom (man is free according to his own inner determinants) is a mere subterfuge?[63] On the other hand, a will that is only intention, that is forever possible but never actual, seems not properly to be a will at all. The will, to make any sense, must be able to provide a liaison, effect a transfer, not simply pre-form but per-form an action, negotiate a passage; in Rousseau's words, "donner un sens à ce mot 'est.'"[64]

These problems of persuasion are intrinsic to Christianity, but they are particularly aggravated in the Renaissance, when the seductiveness of classical notions of rhetoric was so powerfully felt. Erasmus's definition of free will in his *Diatribe* is just such an attempt to give meaning to the word *est*, for in his analysis of the three moments of action (corresponding to the three kinds of grace), he concentrates on the middle term or moment of assent as that which links operative grace, which invites the sinner to repent, to the grace which allows us to carry our actions to conclusion. Yet this middle point will prove to be rhetorical in more than one sense of the word, thereby revealing that rhetoric, like the word *est*, is a concept that may contradict and undermine itself. For the act of assent presupposes a rhetorical plea, but rhetoric itself is required because the effectiveness of our intention has been tainted by the Fall. An effective Christian rhetoric (if it is really rhetoric and not simply the predestination of grace) would seem to be impossible precisely because it is necessary. Or again, assent would seem to presuppose some recognition of that to which we are assenting, but we cannot recognize or judge until we have in some sense assented. This Christian paradox recalls classical debates about whether rhetoric is to be defined as the art of speaking well or the art of persuading:[65] is the excellence of the speaker to be judged in itself or by its effect on others? Is the speaker to be blamed for the obtuseness of his audience? And yet, what kind of rhetoric is it that does not persuade?

While skepticism and Christian faith were allied in the rhetorical theology of Salutati, Valla, and Pontano, a more radical skepticism about the claims of a Christian humanist rhetoric is, as we will see, something that Erasmus, Montaigne, and Hobbes share to different degrees. But they respond to this skepticism in different ways. Erasmus engages in a typical Renaissance "critique of reason" to the extent that he rejects scholastic logic and its assault upon heaven,[66] but he does so in order to save appearances,[67] to secure a realm of action for the will in the phenomenal world. To the degree that the notion of prudence that he adopts implies a certain integrity of reason, Erasmus would seem to have interiorized the medieval natural theologian's faith in the possibility of mastery. In this internalization of hierarchy and the positive consequences for prudence of a critique of theoretical reason, Erasmus follows in the tradition of Nicholas of Cusa (*docta ignorantia*)[68] and those thinkers of the early Italian Renaissance who believed in the harmony of man and nature as founded in their shared principles of order and proportion. There is no steady climb up the medieval hierarchical ladder, but experience still offers a genuine if limited kind of knowledge. Just as the goodness of nature is evidenced in man's innate ideas and natural reason, so it is apparent for Erasmus in the Ficinian doctrine of eros, according to which God's descent to man signifies not our depravity and need but rather our dignity.[69] Accordingly, Christ becomes a figure of decorum who saves us for this world rather than from it.

And yet, it is finally this ethical interpretation of Christ that threatens the uniqueness of the incarnation, for it places the burden of prudence both as interpretation and as action on the individual human subject. In saving us for appearances, Erasmus also condemns us to a merely apparent certainty with regard to the ethical postulates of free will and responsibility, and indeed, with regard to his own ethical interpretation of Scripture; and this is a certainty that bears a remarkable resemblance to the skeptic's doubt. Chapter 4 argues that Erasmus's awareness of the tensions in his own ethical interpretation of Christianity leads him to adopt a poetic and defensive strategy of argumentation in the debate on free will, according to which he can never be charged with lying because he never asserts. But if the defense of free will is a defense of the rhetorical efficacy of hypothetical arguments, the *Encomium moriae* is Erasmus's commentary on this procedure, as if to acknowledge that, like the *Encomium*, his praise of appearance is a very paradoxical encomium.

This paradox can serve to illuminate the work of Montaigne and Hobbes, for when we turn to their work we see a questioning of the early humanist belief in the compatibility of skepticism and prudence, cognitive doubt and practical certainty. While Erasmus and many of his followers share a concern with persuading the reader to right action, Montaigne is both critical of the humanist rhetorical tradition and skeptical of its claims to persuasion. He is concerned instead to develop a new practice of writing, one that will effectively dramatize his own Pyrrhonist version of prudence.

Like Montaigne, Hobbes is sensitive to the arguments of Pyrrhonist skepticism and critical of the rhetorical tradition for its failure to respond adequately to those arguments. His response, however, is not to give up the humanist concern with persuasion, but to systematize it in the form of a logically compelling political science: one that will enable the reader to convert the "truth of Speculation into the Utility of Practice" (*L* 31.408). With Hobbes, we see a new concept of practice and a new notion of political philosophy. It is no longer prudence but science that provides the "standard and measure" of political action. With this shift one can say that Renaissance humanism comes to an end.

Yet for all their criticism of the humanist rhetorical tradition, Montaigne and Hobbes are still working within that tradition. For while it is possible to question the existence of an authoritative faculty of practical reason, it is not possible for them to escape the realm of rhetoric.[70] Montaigne's *Essais* embrace the contingency of this realm, and in so doing offer us a rhetorical practice of Pyrrhonist skepticism, while Hobbes in the *Leviathan* aims to persuade us that we can escape from this realm of contingency by constructing the powerful rhetorical fiction of a political science.

The three later writers I have chosen to discuss were thus all familiar with the Quattrocento ideal of the orator as civic and Christian humanist, but they were also, in their different ways, increasingly skeptical or critical of this ideal. They questioned whether there is a common sense or natural reason shared by all individuals that informs our speech and action, that founds our communities and commonplaces, and in so doing, they were forced to consider the relation between cognitive and affective moments in the acts of persuasion and of reading, and the consequences of a skeptical epistemology for these activities. Their works dramatize a renewed concern with what it means to make a prudential judgment—a judgment of decorum that results in action, whether in the realm of politics or in the practice of the literary text.

For Erasmus, Montaigne, and Hobbes, the fact that praxis cannot be without being moved to practice is not the solution to the problem of ethical instruction, but precisely the problem itself. Accordingly, in Erasmus's *Encomium*, Montaigne's *Essais*, and Hobbes's *Leviathan*, the arguments of the Quattrocento humanist rhetorical tradition, and in particular the humanist emphasis on discursive activity as constitutive of moral philosophy, are used to question that same tradition. Rhetoric becomes the means by which the *possibility* of rhetoric is itself put in question. In these later texts, the authors are finally less concerned with moving the reader to action, or even to a particular attitude (with the possible exception of Hobbes), than with forcing the reader to reflect on how praxis can be and, in some cases, *whether* it can be.

3 The Quattrocento

Sic verissime . . . manifeste sequitur vitam activam . . . tam in vita quam in patria speculationi modis omnibus preferendum. [So it clearly follows that the active life, both in this life and the next, is to be preferred in all ways to the contemplative.]
—Salutati, *De nobilitate legum et medicine*

Is habitus [prudentiae] exercitatione comparatur, rerumque humanarum usu. [The habit of prudence is acquired by practice and by familiarity with human affairs.]
—Pontano, *De prudentia*

Coluccio Salutati: Prudence and the Active Life

The *De nobilitate legum et medicine* (1399) is Salutati's most elaborate defense of prudence and the active life.[1] As such, it is crucial to understanding the influence Salutati had on the Quattrocento humanists' prudential conception of reading.[2] Yet this work also reminds us why Salutati has so often been viewed as a transitional figure between the medieval scholastics and the Renaissance humanists; sometimes adhering to earlier values, sometimes to later, not entirely aware of the conflict, and so never offering his own synthesis.[3] The work, which was conceived in reply to a treatise by a Florentine doctor named Bernardus, is part of a long tradition of the *disputatio artium*.[4] Its division into thirty-nine chapters dealing with the origin, nature, application, and relative virtues of law and medicine (12) suggests that it has something in common with the scholastic treatise as well. Yet there is no obvious logical development from one chapter to the next, nor is the approach the same throughout. A single chapter may be devoted to discussing the usage of a single term (e.g., chapter 1 on "nobilitas"), while another may simply list the results of the argument up to that point. As Lynn Thorndike has remarked with exasperation, Salutati "employs over and over again the same arguments to reach what are supposed to be different successive conclusions" (34). In short, the work is not rhetorically innovative; it seems to reflect no consciousness that the defense of prudence and the active life might best be conveyed by means of a new genre or a new rhetorical strategy. How then can we turn to this text for evidence of the way in which the humanists' rhetorical practice reflects a new concern with the alliance of rhetoric, prudence, and skepticism? And if we do find such evidence, how can we reconcile it with Salutati's defense of the monastic life and of contemplation in the *De seculo et religione* and some of his letters?

An answer to the second question will help us with the first. When we consider Salutati's work as a whole we see that he often argued for and against a single position. The *De tyranno* defends the compatibility of freedom and monarchy while the public and private letters ardently defend Florence's republican form of government. There are, in addition to this, two extant speeches arguing for and against monarchy "quod melius est regnum successivum quam electivum . . . quod regnum melius sit electivum quam successivum" [that a monarchy is better than a republic; that a republic is better than a monarchy].[5] In one of Salutati's private letters (*Ep.* 1.156) we learn that he is planning to write a work entitled *De vita associabili et operativa* (On the social and productive life), which, had it been completed, clearly would have been the companion piece to the *De seculo et religione* (On worldliness and religion). Finally, in other letters Salutati defends the claims of both the active and the contemplative life, arguing in one case (*Ep.* 3.307–8, to Zambeccari) against his friend's retreat to a monastery, but insisting, should he retreat, that he take Salutati with him.[6] Clearly, this does not mean that Salutati is insincere or noncommittal, or that his position in each case is *merely* rhetorical. Rather, whatever the position he is espousing or defending, however apparently contradictory his work as a whole, this fact of contradiction is itself evidence of Salutati's prudential conviction that it is necessary to respond in different ways to different circumstances.

That the Quattrocento humanists interpreted Salutati's rhetoric *in utramque partem* as a defense of the active life is apparent in Leonardo Bruni's characterization of Salutati in his *Ad Petrum Paulum His-trum dialogus* (1401).[7] In the opening of book 1, "Salutati" chides the younger generation of Florentine humanists for neglecting the "dis-putandi usum exercitationemque" (the custom and practice of dis-putation) and goes on to praise the effect of such exercise:

> What restores and refreshes the mind, tired and weak and loathing these studies which require long and assiduous reading, more than those disputations which take place in company, and which excite you—by glory if you overcome others or by shame, if you are over-come—to further reading and learning? What sharpens the mind more, makes it more skillful and more clever than disputation, which requires that you apply yourself to the thing in a moment, that you reflect, consider different possibilities, compare and conclude? Thus, you can easily understand how, by this exercise, the mind becomes quicker in discerning other arguments. [*PLQ,* 48][8]

Disputation recreates and sharpens the mind, and inspires us to further learning. Its results are practical, not theoretical; rather than providing us with a set of theoretical principles it engages us in a reflexive activity of practical reasoning, and it is this *activity* rather than the subject matter under discussion that is of primary impor-tance, for it refines the faculty of judgment that will enable us to reason appropriately in each particular case. Furthermore, both in origin and effect the *usus* or activity of disputation is a social one: it requires an interlocutor (*PLQ* 48–50) and results in a socially useful skill ("there is great usefulness in disputation"; cf. 52).

Bruni's account of Salutati can serve as a cautionary tale for read-ers of the *De nobilitate.* If we judge the treatise by scholastic stan-dards, as Thorndike does, Salutati is a failed scholastic; but to the extent that the form and vocabulary of the treatise invite this judg-ment, we are forced to conclude that Salutati is not quite a humanist either. The problem is that both conclusions require that we imagine a Salutati who is rhetorically inept, one who does not see that "nova res novum vocabulum flagitat" (a new subject requires a new vocab-ulary).[9] Salutati himself, however, warns us against this conclusion when he tells us that the form of the treatise has been dictated by Bernardus's own. He suggests, in other words, that the *De nobilitate* deliberately offers us a defense of prudence and the active life in terms of the very concepts that are being contested. In so doing, Salutati adopts the time-worn rhetorical strategy of using enemy weapons to combat the enemy (cf. *Ep.* 3.539, 4.183, 4.212). Yet at the same time that he accepts Bernardus's vocabulary and logical procedure, he introduces a more obviously humanistic dimension by appealing to the consensus of classical and Christian authors, most notably Augustine and Aristotle, to prove the superiority of law to medicine, of practical consensus to theoretical truth.

Finally, even if we do not heed Salutati's remarks about the form of his treatise, his thematic defense of prudence or law as that which combines theory and praxis, the divine rule of action and the individual decorous act, should itself alert us to the way in which Salutati's own decorous rhetorical practice exemplifies his theoretical argument: it is in the form of Salutati's treatise even more than in the commonplaces he marshals that the real argument for prudence is played out. Similarly, it is in the way in which he reads Aristotle and Augustine, more than in the simple fact of citing them, that Salutati demonstrates his own prudential abilities as a reader. Quite aware that the same text can be interpreted as defending different positions, Salutati is concerned to appropriate the authority of the ancients for his own purposes.

The treatise is thus not only part of a dialogue or disputation with Bernardus; it also dramatizes this debate by setting forth both sides of the question, by using Bernardus's own arguments and sources against him, by pitting Aristotle against Augustine, and finally by counterpointing different styles of argumentation: scholastic and humanist. Furthermore, since, as Salutati tells us, disputation is itself governed by law, we can say that in defending law against medicine Salutati is not defending the legal profession so much as the activity of defense itself. Finally, this defensive activity comes to stand for all human activity that is, by definition, rule governed, that is, lawful. While Salutati's sense of the dialogical and dialectical possibilities of the text are not as sophisticated as, for example, Pontano's, in a very real sense his rhetoric can be said to anticipate that of the *De fortuna* and the *De prudentia*. As with these later works, the dialogical form of the *De nobilitate* and the prudential practice of interpretation which Salutati exhibits in his independent readings of Aristotle and Augustine provide the best evidence—and the best defense—of Salutati's prudential conception of rhetoric.

If we begin, then, by considering the status of medicine as a theoretical or speculative science, we see that in the course of the treatise Salutati argues that medicine is both less speculative than it claims to be, and more. He claims first of all that even if we grant to medicine some reliance on speculation, it is still not primarily speculative, since speculation is concerned with universal principles and is an end in itself (20, 40, 110, 130, 134; *NE* 1139b 20–25, 1140b 31), while medicine subordinates these principles to the practical end of curing the individual patient (98, 180, 252, 264). Furthermore, medicine is not properly speaking even partially speculative (30, 32, 176), because there can be no science of particulars (40, 92, 110). The doctor has no God-given standard of judgment on which to base his decisions; he deals with contingent empirical evidence and his art is correspondingly limited to provisional and pragmatic formulations.

The claims of the doctor to theoretical superiority are undermined by the fact that truth as the perfect knowledge of universal first principles is not accessible to the individual human consciousness (114, 164). Law, however, is not vulnerable to this objection, since the activity of the lawmaker is informed by the God-given faculty of practical reason (a faculty that Salutati interprets both in terms of Aristotle's "agibilium recta [ratio]" [214] or "regula practice rationis" [14], and Cicero's "semina innata virtutum" [16]). Thus, while medicine is faced with the insoluble problem of finding a general rule by which to judge the particular, contingent facts of bodily illness (92), there is no similar discrepancy between general and particular in the case of law. The individual can acquire certainty with respect to his own particular actions (108ff.) because the general principles governing the realm of law are available in his own soul (14, 118, 124, 134–36).

Having proved the superiority of law to medicine in terms of its guiding first principles, Salutati now wants to defend the superior *usefulness* of law. In order to do this he has to de-emphasize the pragmatic aspect of the doctor-patient relationship and argue instead that medicine really is concerned with speculation. In other words, he concedes the speculative dimension of medicine only when it is important to distinguish between the sterility of scientific speculation and the usefulness of moral speculation (136). Accordingly, Salutati now admits that both medicine and law are speculative insofar as they are informed by the divine rule of reason and seek universal first principles (134, 136), but the universals of medicine are empirically derived while those of law are immediately present to every human consciousness (124, 134). In other words, the particular object of medicine is external and contingent (68, 76), while the particular object of law is the moral *activity* of the legislator or the judging individual (94), and this activity is definitive of human nature. Thus, while medicine finally subordinates its presumed concern for truth to the end of curing the patient, law, Salutati argues, is both an end in itself and as such the end that is proper to man (94). It is for this reason that even if it were possible for medicine to be a purely speculative science it would still be inferior to law (cf. 136ff.):

> Nor would I readily concede to you that the end of speculation is nobler than the end of law. Indeed, the end of all speculation is knowledge, whose object is the truth. But the end of law is the guidance of human action. Its object is the good, not only the individual good, but, what is far more godly, the common good. Now, is not the good a nobler principle of being than the true? Not only the good by which we are good, but the good by which we become and are good. [32][10]

The first good, Salutati goes on to tell us, is merely natural, whereas the second is a product of the individual's free will and thus a specifically moral achievement.

Here we can begin to see what is at stake for Salutati in the *De nobilitate*. The defense of the superiority of law to medicine implies the superiority of the liberal arts (and Salutati's own profession as a lawyer) to the sciences. But in taking up the defense in terms of the claims that Bernardus has made for medicine, Salutati also offers us a transcendental defense of free will and prudence against the threat of relativism and Pyrrhonist skepticism. The superiority of law, in other words, is based on a practical reason that contains within itself a rule of decorum; a conception of human productivity (in action and in art, 28, 244–46)[11] that can claim some authority in interpretation. Law provides the model of hermeneutics for Salutati because it can refer at once to eternal, natural, or human law, with the result that the diversity of positive law (i.e., of individual interpretations of the law) is unified by reference to a single divine standard of judgment. This standard of right judgment in turn guarantees the possibility of right action. The unity of divine and human law in the purposeful activity of the individual precludes the traditional gap between theory and praxis, and ensures the passage from the heavenly to the earthly city, as well as from intention to action.

While the law is governed by divinely inspired rules, it is not concerned with the formulation of general scientific truths but with praxis (244), and it is precisely in the realm of praxis that it finds a new kind of generality: the generality of the common good (98) that is the social and political equivalent of charity. God has created man a "social and political animal" (162; cf. 94, 102, 104, 158, 164, 190), and given him the internal law of right reason (14, 16, 178) by which to govern society. By the observation of the laws the individual earns divine praise or blame and draws near to the final beatitude for which he was born (32).

For all these reasons, according to Salutati, legal knowledge is superior to the speculation of the natural sciences. And this superiority is also the source of its greater certainty: for the natural sciences seek cognitive truth, which can always be doubted, while the moral and legal disciplines seek the moral mean or the probable, which is, as Aristotle and the Academic skeptic tell us, of all things most certain (136; cf. *Ep.* 2.319; 3.602–3). Salutati's appeal to the Academic notion of probability in his defense of the Aristotelian active life is thematically consonant with his desire to provide a ground for ethical and religious behavior in the absence of cognitive certainty (114). But even more than this, it makes explicit the rhetorical form of his argument. For, as we have seen, Salutati, like the Academics, is eager to juxtapose different opinions in order to elicit a probable truth (*De orat.* 1.34.158–59; *De off.* 2.2.8; *Tusc.* 5.4.11). This rhetorical and dialectical strategy is apparent throughout the text, but particularly in chapters 22 and 23, which form the heart of Salutati's argument for the superiority of prudence to speculation and of the will to the intellect. Here Salutati confronts arguments from Aristotle's *Ethics* with those of Augustine in order to justify the claims of the active life to greater moral if not greater cognitive certainty.[12]

Most critics have recognized that Salutati reinterprets Aristotle's analysis of practical reason in the light of Augustine's view of the individual's relationship to God, but it is important to see as well that Salutati understands Augustine's notion of charity in terms of Aristotle's concept of moral virtue. In so doing, he not only brings philosophy back down to earth, as Socrates did, but imports the active life back into heaven. For while moral virtue or the *vita activa* as an end in itself is the human approximation of divine beatitude or charity (*Ep.* 3.307), this otherworldly end is identified with neither speculation nor contemplation, but with action. In insisting on the first point Salutati interprets Aristotle in terms of Augustine, but in insisting on the second, he criticizes Augustine with the help of Aristotle. Accordingly, while Salutati begins his discussion of wisdom in chapter 23 by approving Augustine's definition of *sapientia* as a "cognitio intellectualis" and a "videre . . . Deum" (190), by the end of the discussion the cognitive dimension of otherworldly contemplation has fallen away entirely. *Sapientia* or contemplation is a function not of the intellect but of the will or of love; and, unlike Augustine, Salutati identifies the will with Aristotle's notion of the active life, thus conflating contemplation and action, *caritas* and prudence.[13]

Even from this brief sketch it should be clear that Salutati appears to accept the terms of Bernardus's argument only in order to undermine this argument, along with the scholastic expectation of logical or cognitive certainty.[14] His goal, as he tells us in chapter 2, is not to arrive at a definitive conclusion, but rather to elicit a probable truth, one that is not stigmatized as less certain than logical truth, but is rather equated with the "lumen veritatis" (light of truth). This notion of probability then allows us to read the defense of law as a defense of rhetoric (266), for as we know from Salutati's other works and from his classical sources, it is within the realm of probability that rhetoric has a role to play (*NE* 1140b 25–30). It is fitting, then, that Salutati should begin his refutation of the claims of medicine by appealing to the rhetorical notion of the *consensus omnium* (40): that law is superior is not only his opinion but "the opinion of all races and all nations, and not of the common people only, but also of all those who shine most brightly in the literary community"(2).[15] Furthermore, if Bernardus is right, why hasn't he persuaded anyone to share his opinion (4)? Rhetoric, Salutati goes on to tell us, is subservient to law, but it also forms a large part of one's knowledge as a citizen, especially since it is concerned with legal controversy (6). Later in the treatise this relationship of subordination is less clearcut, and the lawyer and orator are described as sharing the same forensic duties, the same civic concerns (142; see *Ep.* 1.79).

This reliance on the *consensus omnium* or usage is manifest as well in Salutati's arguments by etymology.[16] For Cicero and Quintilian, and in particular for the Middle Ages, etymology was a form of argument, a means of rhetorical invention. It was assumed that if one could find the origin of a word, one would also be able to understand and utilize its peculiar force or power.[17] Accordingly, Nancy Struever has described etymological derivation as an exemplum of social responsibility, including the socially responsible use of linguistic power. In a passage particularly suggestive for the defense of law in the *De nobilitate*, she writes:

> [The etymologizer's duty] is to demonstrate specific social constraints on the individual's (reader's) use of language; he is engaged in a kind of linguistic jurisprudence. The narrative is a responsibility: when it is used as an instance of the *topos* "definition," it is a story of a word's force, to constrain forceful use in argument. . . . Etymologists as narrators cope with power, but, further, the coping activity postulates a social domain that is at the same time richly specified as a temporal domain, in which the linkages of past, present, and putative uses are forged by the etymologizer.[18]

Since etymology is frequently introduced to "prove" a foregone conclusion, it can also be seen as a peculiarly self-reflexive or self-confirming form of argument (one that Guiraud calls "retro-motivation").[19] It is thus particularly suited to illustrate the reflective dimension of prudence, that is, the way in which the prudent individual may be said to constitute himself in time through the exercise of judgment (134). For Salutati, etymological derivation, with its thematizing of historical change, confirms this, since it functions as an exemplum of the way in which concrete social activity precedes the formulation of abstract concepts of essence. Thus he writes: "It is most true that, both by nature and by derivation, the concrete precedes the abstract . . . [which we see from the fact that] the word 'justice,' which is an abstract word, is produced from the concrete word 'just'" (160).[20] A little further on, Salutati derives *ius* from "iuvando" or "Iove," and remarks that divine, natural, and human law are essentially the same:

> That which is ordered, what it tends to and what is instituted are the same. Divine law emerges and urges; natural law receives and moves; human law promulgates and obliges; because of this obligation law is derived from binding [lex a ligando]. The principle of law is fixed in eternity and, mixing with the human mind, inclines it to those things which are lawful, and persuades man to establish and promulgate the common good. . . .

> Equity was chosen, and by promulgating it and constituting themselves, they obliged themselves to observe it. It was noted down on tablets so that those who had not been present could learn by reading

what they should preserve. From "choosing," therefore, and "binding oneself," and finally "reading," we derive "law," since it is chosen, binding and legible. [ab eligendo igitur, et se ligando, tandemque legendo, lex dicta est, tamque electa, ligans atque legenda.] [160–62]

With this etymological narrative, Salutati manages to illustrate both formally and thematically the main points of the *De nobilitate*. The narrative is adduced as proof of the claims he has been making for law, but if Bernardus accepts the introduction of this kind of evidence, he has already admitted defeat; for, regardless of the content of the narrative, the appeal is to usage, which is the social and linguistic manifestation of prudence. Here we return to "Salutati's" remarks about the usefulness of the *usus* or practice of rhetorical debate. Practice in rhetoric is important because it sharpens our ability to deal with the realm of praxis, usage, *consuetudo.* Similarly, given the definition of the realm of human affairs as a contingent and practical one, only arguments that appeal to usage will have any authority.[21] Precisely because we have to use our knowledge in practical ways, that knowledge must be governed by, defined in terms of, usage. For all these reasons, rhetorical praxis, which necessarily takes account of usage, can educate to social and political praxis.

Salutati's etymological narrative also makes the rhetorical and pragmatic dimension of prudence explicit in another way: while divine law is present in the individual soul, it merely acts as a standard or rule according to which the individual *produces* the law (or engages in any other activity). Furthermore, the relation of divine law to individual activity is one of persuasion (*persuadet*); for only if the law is not compelling can the individual *bind himself* to the law and thereby constitute himself as a free agent and a moral individual. Here, as elsewhere for Salutati, it is clear that the definitive characteristic that raises man above the animals is not "ratio" but "secundum rationem *operari*" (operating or working according to *ratio,* 94).[22]

Finally, the rhetorical dimension of Salutati's treatise is apparent in still another way that suggests that Salutati's writing of the *De nobilitate* must itself be understood as a exemplum of prudence. It is true that at the end of the work Salutati characterizes the activity of responding to Bernardus as speculative, but he goes on to describe the activity of the *reader* of the *De nobilitate* in terms that recall his earlier analysis of law:

> I beg you and all who read this work, that you not be hasty in judging, nor hurried in reading, but rather that, patiently reading the whole, you weigh the individual parts, as is fitting [*sicut decet*], before you pass judgment. I hope that all who consider with due moderation what I have written, if truth is capable of anything, will disagree with nothing or little [in this treatise], if they think right. And I, ignorant as I am, am ready to correct the errors they perceive, or to clarify those [passages] in which they perceive truth and my intention. [270–72]

It is the business of law, as we have seen, to "pass judgment" (82–84); it is the office of rhetoric to determine "[quid] decet." Salutati is describing a decorous *activity* of reading, a social community of readers who will, in passing judgment on his text, help him arrive at a probable truth. This becomes clear when we remember that throughout the treatise the activity of disputation is both equated with law, or said to be governed by law (10, 134, 158); and that disputation *confirms* the superiority of law. By the exchange of contrasting opinion we arrive at a *consensus omnium*, which reflects or is evidence of our shared standard of judgment. This is not the case with medicine, since if the precepts of medicine are contradicted, medicine as a science is undermined (134, 146). Law, then, is superior to medicine because the lawful activity of debate is constituted by and therefore capable of containing contradiction.

The speech of Medicine in defense of the superiority of law in chapter 38 is illustrative of this. First of all, in speaking as an orator in defense of law, Medicine speaks against—*contra-dicts*—herself, and so is undone. Secondly, in mocking Bernardus's claim that medicine can arrive at the truth by means of speculation, she points up the central paradox of Salutati's Christian humanism, one that enables rather than disables the possibility of a humanist rhetoric *in utramque partem*: "I have always laughed at the dignity of human speculation, whose glory you exalt above the active life; and I see that the merit of the active life is placed above the contemplative by divine judgment, since God has made the wisdom of this world folly"(256). This paradox of wise folly exemplifies Salutati's humanistic belief in the compatibility of skepticism and prudence, cognitive ignorance and moral action, divine foreknowledge and free will.[23]

In other words, once we see that probability holds a greater degree of certainty for Salutati than theoretical reason because the faculty of practical reason (and with it, free will) is granted to us by God, Salutati's use of argument *in utramque partem* can be seen to be a function of this central paradox of a divinely authorized free will. It is because we have free will and are morally responsible that persuasion is necessary, and it is for this reason that it will be necessary to present different, and even contrasting, arguments at different times and to different audiences. As the faculty that unites the universal and the particular, theory and praxis, and that disarms logical contradiction with the notion of a probable truth, a practical certainty, prudence is itself contingent upon the essential paradox of Christian humanism: the coexistence of divine foreknowledge and free will. So the belief that we do indeed have free will justifies a rhetoric of contradiction as that which allows us to respond appropriately to any given situation.

The *De nobilitate* is important for our understanding of Quattrocento humanism because it expresses both formally and thematically the belief in the alliance of an Academic rhetoric *in utramque partem*, prudence and faith. This belief will inform Quattrocento conceptions of reading as a practical and persuasive activity rather than a logical or cognitive one. The defense of the active life in the *De nobilitate* both implies and enacts such a practical conception of reading. It may also help us understand the import of Salutati's conflicting attitudes toward poetry throughout his life.[24]

While in his early works (the *De laboribus Herculis* and some of the letters) Salutati often defines poetry in terms of praising and blaming, and on occasion attributes to the poet Cicero's emphasis on the civic function of the orator (*De lab.* 7–8), he does not describe the activity of reading poetry in prudential terms. Rather, he insists on the similarities between poetry and Scripture as allegorical vehicles of divine truth.[25] God has divinely inspired at least some of the poets; like Scripture, their works reveal sacred truths. The only difference between the two is that Scripture is true both on the literal and the allegorical level, while on the literal level pagan works are manifestly untrue. Later in life Salutati argues that even the Bible recounts events that are fictive; the difference now between Scripture and secular writing is that the source of truth is divine in the one case and human in the other. Thus, in his last letter to Giovanni da Samminiato (*Ep.* 4.170–205), Salutati claims that poetic truth is *produced* by the poet (4.199–200), and in his last letter to Dominici he explicitly ties his defense of the study of classical literature in this letter to his defense of the superiority of the will to the intellect in the *De nobilitate:* from the ancients we learn rhetoric and rhetoric is concerned with moving the will (4.213).[26] In both his early and later work Salutati emphasizes that poetry and Scripture persuade us to right action, but it may be only when he begins to conceive of poetry itself as a particularly human activity that reading can be conceived in these terms as well—that is, that reading as an activity that exercises the judgment can acquire its own moral force.[27]

This emphasis on the productive nature of poetry, which is anticipated by Salutati's remarks in the *De nobilitate,* will lead to an even greater emphasis by the Quattrocento humanists on the analogy between the practices of writing and reading, and practical reason. The activity of reading will not be described in terms of the pleasurable cognition of allegorical truth, as it was for example by Boccaccio and in some of Salutati's own letters, but in terms of prudential action. The text will be seen to work on us by moving us to work—in the words of the *De nobilitate* (136), "nec solummodo frui, sed operari" (cf. *Ep.* 2.295). With this active conception of reading in mind, we can turn to Giovanni Pontano's two treatises, *De prudentia* and *De fortuna.*

Giovanni Pontano: A Rhetoric of Prudence

Giovanni Pontano, who lived from 1429 to 1503, was humanist secretary to Alfonso I of Naples and diplomat for his son Ferdinand. He is perhaps best known for his dialogues—witty, urbane, polished imitations of Lucian and Cicero—and for his Latin poetry. His treatises have for the most part been ignored, but like Salutati's *De nobilitate,* they can tell us much about the humanists' prudential conception of rhetoric. Like Salutati, Pontano uses the humanist convention of argument *in utramque partem* to construct works that are logically contradictory but, precisely for this reason, rhetorically instructive and persuasive. Yet, whereas Salutati directs Medicine and the vocabulary of scholastic disputation against themselves, Pontano takes on the whole realm of contingency, that is, fortune, and turns it to an occasion for his own—and his reader's—exercise of prudential judgment.

Pontano's concern with prudence has led some readers to complain that he is not a philosopher. But these critics, like Pontano's own careless contemporaries, have failed to see the distinction between wisdom and prudence that Pontano himself insists on.[28] For if philosophy is understood as theoretical wisdom, the cognition of universal precepts that yield certain knowledge, the objection (and it is always an objection) is valid; but Pontano is not claiming to be such a philosopher.[29] Indeed, like Salutati, he thinks that this is the least interesting kind of philosophy one could engage in. He is concerned instead with a practical philosophy, similar to the one elaborated by Aristotle in book 6 of the *Ethics,* and he sees his task as making this available to his Latin-reading contemporaries.[30]

Although Pontano admits that there have been followers of Aristotle writing in Latin, he argues that their lack of eloquence only betrays the extent to which they failed to understand the true import of Aristotle's *Ethics:* the inseparability of ethical and linguistic practice.[31] The most effective communication about practical philosophy involves the recognition that this active communication is itself a form of practice. Of particular interest to the reader who is concerned with Pontano's views on practical philosophy, then, is Pontano's own practice of writing in the *De prudentia* and the *De fortuna,* the two treatises that are thematically most explicit with regard to this subject and, at least at first glance, rhetorically least interesting.

While critics have tended to ignore the *De prudentia* and the *De fortuna,* charging Pontano with simply relaying Aristotle's ideas in the *Nicomachean Ethics* or Aquinas's in the *Summa theologica* (Question 57), it is my aim to show that both Pontano's conception of rhetoric and his own rhetorical practice are essential parts of his philosophical argument.[32] Thus, for example, while it is true that Pontano refuses to attribute the vagaries of fortune to the will of divine providence, this does not amount to an insistence on the inexplicable factor of pure contingency in human life, as some critics have suggested. Rather, Pontano domesticates contingency by describing it in terms of a rhetorical praxis. By attributing the effects of contingency on human life, that is, deliberation *in utramque partem,* to the cause, he suggests that we have only to be more practiced rhetoricians in order for prudence to triumph over fortune.[33] Pontano himself is such a rhetorician, since his rhetorical arguments in the two treatises exemplify the theoretical position he is elaborating. For the notions of prudence and fortune—and indeed of rhetoric itself—are what W. B. Gallie in this century has called "essentially contested concepts," concepts "the proper use of which inevitably involves endless disputes about their proper uses on the part of their users."[34] Pontano's treatment of the concepts of prudence and fortune involves reflection on the "essential contestability" of these notions and the intrinsically rhetorical nature of that contest: it is always possible to argue—to read and interpret—*in utramque partem*.

The *De prudentia* was written either in 1496 or in 1498 and 1499, and was published along with the *De fortuna* in 1508. It was dedicated to Tristanus Caraciolus and Franciscus Pudericus, two of Pontano's friends, who had asked him to discuss the nature of prudence and happiness (2). The first two books of the *De fortuna* were written in 1500, and the third in 1501. It bears a dedication to Consalvo di Cordova, conqueror of the French at Cerignola (128) and a man of "divinaque quaedam prudentia" (a certain divine prudence).[35] The two treatises are of a piece, as the description of Consalvo suggests, for prudence is the ability that enables the individual to triumph over fortune—hence the chapter heading in the *De prudentia* with the title "De fortuna" (9), and in the *De fortuna* of "Fortunam adversari prudentiae" (Fortune opposes prudence [133]). Although these works are treatises (the *De prudentia* consisting of five books, the *De fortuna* of three), neither is organized according to the logical *sic et non* of their medieval scholastic predecessors. In the case of the *De prudentia* each book begins with a gesture toward the dialogue form of so many Quattrocento humanist works, by way of a "prooemium" that both addresses Pontano's interlocutors and comments on the circumstances and eventually the progress of the discussion. In the *De fortuna* there is no original interlocutor, but in the gap between the second and the third books one appears—Father Aegidius of Viterbo, who had read and disapproved of the first two books. Hence the third book begins with a reply to Aegidius's objections.

One cannot properly call these works dialogues, however, since the body of each treatise is taken up with Pontano's exposition of his own views in a series of short, titled chapters. While this method enables him to devote separate chapters to the differences, for example, between fortune and God, nature, intellect, and reason (the first four chapters of the *De fortuna*), and to describe the different parts of prudence (book 4 of the *De prudentia*), the effect on the whole is essayistic rather than analytical. The emphasis is on repetition and variety of argument, rather than on the logical progression of thought. It is as though he were circling around his subject, or attacking it from different angles. But within these chapters certain arguments reappear, now in the same context, now in different ones. It is to the nature of these arguments and Pontano's own rhetorical practice that I now turn.

As in Machiavelli's *Il principe*, the way to be absolutely successful in the contingent realm of human affairs is to be as flexible and capable of change as Fortune herself. On the other hand, if an individual were as flexible and as amoral as fortune, he would not be happy, since happiness depends on moral virtue; he would be a sophist—as fortune is.[36] This is particularly clear in the *De fortuna*, where Pontano goes beyond the traditional opposition of fortune and prudence when he uses the phrase *in utramque partem* to describe fortune's effects: for, while there is no personification strictly speaking in the treatise, this phrase goes a long way toward humanizing fortune.[37] Although Cicero uses the phrase in the *De officiis* (2.6.19) to describe the two kinds of fortune ("magnam vim esse in fortuna in utramque partem, vel secundas ad res vel adversas, quis ignorat" [who does not know that fortune has a great power to act in two ways, in our favor or against us]), the tag appears far more often in his works in discussions of rhetorical skill. Thus, to cite just one example, Cicero writes in the *De oratore*: "We orators are bound to possess the intelligence, capacity and skill to speak both *pro* and *contra* [*in utramque partem*] on the topics of virtue, duty, equity and good, moral worth and utility, honor and disgrace, reward and punishment and like matters" (3.27.107).[38] Yet, if fortune is an orator, she is an unscrupulous one, since her arguments *in utramque partem* are not constrained by any considerations of ethical decorum. She will "argue for" the happiness of the bad man, and the misfortune of the good, as well as for the just reward and the just punishment. She is to be judged by her effects rather than by her intention ("ab eventu," not "a ratione" [134])—just as the sophistical rhetorician desires to be. Not speaking well, but speaking persuasively is her forte. Like the orator, fortune operates in the realm of contingency—not the contingency of the natural world, but of the human sphere of deliberation, desire, and action (127–38, 142). In fact, fortune and the prudent man are engaged in a struggle for control of this sphere. Whatever occurs contrary to our intentions or beyond our expectations (including favorable events), is due to fortune (165), but without us, fortune would not exist, since fortune names our own inability to understand or determine perfectly our actions (138). Yet it is precisely because fortune is inconsistent and unpredictable, precisely because we are ignorant of it, that there is both the room and the need for the exercise of prudence.[39] Because everything is not causally determined by natural law or fate (186), there is room for the causality of free will, or for the persuasions of rhetoric.[40]

As I have already suggested, Pontano recognizes the essential contestability of the concepts of rhetoric, prudence, and fortune, and goes to some lengths to incorporate different interpretations of these notions into his treatises. Throughout the two works he tries to do justice to the intrinsic ambiguity of these notions, an ambiguity that according to some is a strength, to others a weakness (39, 71, 87–90). And he does so not only thematically, in his analysis of these notions (e.g., prudence is neither a science nor an art, fortune is granted to us by God, for the exercise of free will), but also rhetorically, by marshaling the same arguments on different sides of the question. In fact, he uses his examination of the nature of prudence and fortune as an occasion for his own rhetorical exercises *in utramque partem*. For example, at different times both fortune (*De fortuna*, 168) and prudence (*De prudentia*, 11) are described as the helmsman of human life. Poetry is invoked as analogous both to prudence (*De prudentia*, 30–31, 71 [Orpheus], 88, 91) and to the irrationality of fortune (*De fortuna*, 154). Similarly, fortune's relation to matter is seen in terms of the artist's relation to his material (*De fortuna*, 136), an analogy that Pontano employs in the *De prudentia* in order to suggest the efforts of the prudent man to impose the form of his action on the matter of his experience (18).

A more striking example of this kind of argumentation is Pontano's "Defensio fortunae" (178), which involves attacking nature with the same arguments that were earlier applied to fortune. The defense of fortune is addressed to those who blame her for every mishap. This accusation, Pontano argues, could be made against God and nature as well. While the book of Job shows that God needs no defense, Nature can be defended by pointing to the way in which she uses inequality—that is to say, diversity and variety—to accomplish her ends.

This defense of fortune then leads Pontano to consider whether he himself can be justly accused of un-Christian concerns for undertaking the defense in the first place. It leads him, in short, to a defense of his own activity as a writer. Thus, book 3 opens with Aegidius's claim that there are other subjects worthier of Pontano's time than fortune: "[Aegidius] would have wished that we had turned our thoughts to things greater and worthier of being known, things which would have been more useful either in a Christian republic or for the education of civic life and moral philosophy. He said it was to a certain extent unworthy of a Christian to reason about fortune" (182). Pontano replies that knowledge of fortune's power is useful, since it tells us what we can act on and what we must simply bear.[41] Investigation into the domain of fortune is thus, at the same time, an investigation into the question of free will (184) and divine foreknowledge. The logical conclusion of this argument, which is consistent with the earlier conflation of fortune, nature, and God, is that a realm of fortune in which events may occur *in utramque partem* exists by divine fiat, because God himself is a rhetorician with respect to man: "God alone in those things which are chosen by man considers himself as a persuader. . . . For this reason, those things of which heaven gives portents *in utramque partem* are able to be mitigated by genius or art" (188).[42]

The use of the same arguments to make different points is not the only way that Pontano emphasizes the rhetorical nature of his investigation. As Aegidius's objection illustrates, he presents us with conflicting views of fortune and prudence throughout both treatises. Thus he begins the *De fortuna* by pointing up both the essential agreement, the *consensus omnium*, regarding the power of fortune, and the essential disagreement about the nature of fortune, both between Christians and non-Christians (139), and among the pagan philosophers themselves (Plato, Anaxagoras, and the Stoics [137]). In this way he highlights the rhetorical and prudential nature of his enterprise, for no one, as Aristotle tells us in the *Rhetoric* (1357a), debates about something that is obvious to everyone. Further on, he refers to the opposing ways in which fortune, reason, and the will can be viewed. Some argue that fortune is due to God (162), others that it is not. The will is seen either as capable of doing something against fortune (188, 191) or not (175). Reason may be considered to be (naturally) moved by God or (rationally) moved by itself (171), to have power or to be impotent against fortune (175). The essential contestability of these concepts is further stressed by referring to other equally contested concepts (e.g., nature), in an attempt to clarify the first.

Clearly, we cannot simply extract a definition of prudence from Pontano's work because on the thematic level the treatises are contradictory. The definition, or rather the process of definition, is instead exemplified in the rhetorical structure of the work as a whole. Just as Pontano illustrates his own prudential reading of earlier authoritative texts, so the reader is invited to imitate the deliberative process rather than any single example in the text. The point, in short, is not that Pontano approves of one or another of these definitions, but that the very fact of diverse opinion provides us with evidence of the realm of praxis in which prudence, persuasion, and free will all have their place. The diversity of opinion suggests the possibility of persuading someone to share your opinion, and as Kenneth Burke has remarked, "Persuasion involves choice, will; it is directed to man only as he is *free.*"[43]

But Pontano is not content to rest with an exploration of the different opinions concerning fortune and prudence. He argues not only that there can be different opinions because these notions pertain to the realm of praxis but that consequently such notions must themselves be defined in terms of praxis—that is, in terms both of linguistic usage and of the *usus* or practice of the virtue of prudence. The argument from linguistic usage is both a point of departure and a goal. Like Aristotle (*NE* 1140a 25–30), Pontano appeals to the way we *use* the word "fortune" in order to get at its meaning (136, 148–149, 158–59). The authority of such common speech derives, according to Aristotle, from the fact that in some practical sense (*NE* 1139a 27), "What all believe to be true is actually true" (*NE* 1173a).[44] But proper usage is also the aim of his argument, as we see in the *De prudentia*, where he censures the contemporary use of the term *sapiens* to mean *prudens* (66–68).

This emphasis on linguistic usage finds its ethical equivalent in the notion of *usus* as experience. In the *De prudentia* we learn that the virtues are only truly realized in action, and thus that the virtues are not passions but the right *use* of the passions (44). Furthermore, the whole realm of action is described in terms of *usus*: prudence pertains "ad usum civilem," it is acquired by "usus" or experience (73, 79, 92), and it is concerned with things that regard "utilitas." It is because the passions and the goods of nature can be used well or badly, *in utramque partem*, that we can be praised or blamed for our actions.[45] And this right use involves a consideration both of one's own nature and of the context or circumstances in which one finds oneself (51). As a result, there will be different styles of prudence just as there are of speech (Seneca: "talis hominibus fuit oratio qualis vita"; cf. *De orat.* 3.7.28, 3.55.211–12; *De prudentia*, 78): "There are as many [kinds] of character as there are men. Whence it happens that in the use of prudence, each man follows his own character" (94).

This brings us finally to Pontano's use of examples in the two treatises. From Aristotle at least through the Renaissance, the example was seen as the rhetorical equivalent of induction (*Rhet.* 1356b–1357b). In the Renaissance it was also viewed as a particularly effective way of illustrating prudent or virtuous action, and inculcating it in the reader.[46] Thus, Pontano explains his inclusion of a whole book of examples in the *De prudentia*: "When these examples are understood and intelligently considered (since there is in examples a most powerful efficacy which the Greeks call *energeia*), you will easily understand what is fitting to the prudent man" (98).[47] The examples that follow include virtuous speech as well as virtuous action (126), suggesting once again that "dicere apposite ad persuadendum" (*Antonius*, 59; *De inv.*, 1.5.6) is itself a form of prudence. But the most striking example of all is the autobiographical portrait included in the first book of the *De prudentia*. Here we learn that while the life of retirement is the reward of a life of active service (31), prudent retirement will itself be active.[48] Like Cicero's (*De off.* 3.1.1), Pontano's composition of rhetorical and philosophical works in retirement is both an example of and an argument for the active life:

> Truly, since this whole discourse has been taken up concerning civic man, living in society, he who should withdraw from that society and care for nothing but the investigation of his own mind, living in solitude for himself alone, in a bestial rather than a human way, how could he ever attain happiness? [31]

> [The effect of this discourse] is for those words and things which were done or administered by others, with strength, prudence and temperance, as well as those studies and works of a contemplative nature, to be commended to posterity. [30]

It is significant, however, that Pontano's "choice" of retirement, like Cicero's, was governed by unfortunate political circumstances

(*De prudentia*, 32–33).[49] After describing his role as a counselor to Ferdinand of Naples, he writes: "For, as you yourselves know, although I have tried three times to withdraw from public service under Ferdinand, who did not agree to this, a certain enemy force [Charles VIII's invasion of Naples] granted me a divine *otium* and an end to public affairs" (33). Pontano knows how to turn this misfortune prudently to advantage. He devotes his leisure to reading and contemplation, but he also uses this learning to argue for a life of action.[50]

Fortune, then although opposed to prudence, has been incorporated into Pontano's argument less as an adversary than as the rhetorical occasion for the exercise of prudence. And if fortune is an orator *in utramque partem*, Pontano may be said to adopt fortune's own method of arguing in order to persuade us to the possibility of using fortune's means against herself. Thus, while acknowledging the essential contestability of the concepts of fortune and prudence, Pontano does not concede the truth of his opponents' arguments, but rather includes them within his own rhetorical practice. In so doing, he both exemplifies and vindicates the claims of praxis over those of scientific truth within the realm of action. The import of Pontano's argument for a rhetorical notion of truth and a prudential conception of writing in the *De fortuna* and the *De prudentia* is finally consonant with that of the most eloquent passages of his *Dialogi*: "Non ex bonorum cognitione humana existit felicitas, verum ex eorum possessione et usu" (human happiness derives not from the knowledge of goods, but from their possession and use [*Charon*, 42]).

Lorenzo Valla: A Rhetoric of Faith

Lorenzo Valla would have agreed with Pontano that happiness is a matter not of knowledge but of practice or usage. But he was also concerned to define that usage in the context of theology. In so doing, Valla reminds us more forcefully than any of his contemporaries that linguistic usage could have formidable theological implications in the Renaissance, and that philology could itself be an instrument of religious, philosophical (and potentially political) reform. All students of the Renaissance are familiar with Valla's critique of the "Donation of Constantine" on philological grounds; but this is only the most famous example of Valla's application of rhetorical analysis to questions of philosophical or theological importance. In the *Elegantiae* (*OO* 215, bk. 6, chap. 34), for example, Valla uses an etymological discussion of the word *persona* to argue for a particular conception of the trinity; and in the *Dialecticae disputationes* he attacks scholastic logic with its emphasis on the notion of substance by means of a rhetorical and pragmatic analysis of Aristotle's categories.

But Valla was not only interested in attacking the hubris of scholastic rationalism. His critique of reason extended to the Aristotelian notion of prudence as well. Charity, and not prudence, Valla argued, is the condition of the possibility of right action. While this was ultimately the position of Salutati and his humanist followers as well, to Valla's mind, his Florentine contemporaries were in danger of substituting a classical (and at times excessively intellectual) persuasion for Christian faith.[51] Hence the need for a polemical reassertion of the fundamental incomprehensibility of God's ways, an incomprehensibility that, as we shall see, is not incompatible with the belief in the existence of free will.

In a discussion of Valla's rhetorical theology, Salvatore Camporeale suggests that the incompatibility of philosophy and theology, and the humanists' subsequent reduction of theology to rhetoric, first became apparent in the Quattrocento debates on the freedom of the will.[52] The failure of the Scholastic attempt to solve the conflict of predestination and free will with the help of Boethius's theological vocabulary gave way before the rhetorical and pragmatic solutions of the Quattrocento humanists. We have seen how Salutati's and Pontano's defense of rhetoric and prudence necessarily involved a defense of free will, one that, particularly in the case of Pontano, took a very different form from that of the Scholastic debates on this problem. But even more than Pontano's treatises, Valla's *De libero arbitrio* helps us to see how it is that language itself comes to be seen as a form of action and thus provides a rhetorical and pragmatic solution to the cognitive problem of free will. Although Valla attacks the notion of prudence thematically, his practical conception of rhetoric and his own rhetorical practice turn out to have much in common with the rhetoric of his humanist contemporaries.

Finally, however, Valla's attack on the Academic skeptics in *De libero arbitrio* (an attack that, as we have seen, is uncharacteristic of the Quattrocento humanists) forces us to consider the possible antinomy of Ciceronian skeptical rhetoric and religion, prudence and faith—an antinomy that, while it is rejected by Valla and his humanist contemporaries, will become a source of increasing anxiety for Erasmus and a conviction for Luther. While Valla's work provides us with a demonstration of rhetoric *in utramque partem*, it also uses that rhetoric against itself; in so doing, it sows the first seeds of doubt regarding the humanist alliance of rhetoric and prudence.

The *De libero arbitrio* is uncharacteristic of Valla's work in many ways—not least for the humility of the speaker bearing Lorenzo's own name.[53] That humility in turn is part of a radical critique not only of Scholastic philosophy, but more important, of the traditional humanist appeal to Ciceronian skepticism in the defense of rhetoric. For when the figure of the Academic skeptic is mentioned in Valla's dialogue, he is quickly dismissed by both interlocutors. Lorenzo, who will eventually argue for the impossibility of rationally understanding divine will, says, "In brief, there are many things which are unknown. For this reason the Academic, though wrongly, nevertheless said nothing is fully known to us" (159; 528). And Antonio, who, unlike Lorenzo, is eager for a rational solution to the problem of free will, agrees in rejecting this form of skepticism: "Let us dismiss the Academics with their point of view, who, although they would put all in doubt, certainly could not doubt of their own doubts" (159; 528–30).

This conjuring away of the Academic is troublesome, not least because both Lorenzo and the Academic philosopher-orator share an interest in persuading to action in spite of cognitive uncertainty. Furthermore, as we have seen, the linguistic and rhetorical criterion of usage that Valla invokes throughout his works has much in common with the Academic criticism of authority and the appeal to the notion of consensus in ethical as well as linguistic matters.[54] Finally, Valla himself, in at least one work, claims to be arguing *in utramque partem* like the Academic skeptic, and he frequently refers to the Academic method of arguing in other works.[55] It is significant, then, that he does not ally his conception of rhetoric in *De libero arbitrio* with the skeptical notion of probability, but rather with the theological criteria of faith and charity.

A close examination of this dialogue will show just how radical Valla's conception of rhetoric is in this text, not only in comparison with that of his Florentine contemporaries, but also in comparison with Valla's other works. I will argue, however, that the rhetoric of *De libero arbitrio* is finally crucial for understanding the implications of Valla's work as a whole, since in taking up the question of free will Valla cannot avoid considering the nature and the possibility of rhetoric and of signification. This is because as an art of persuasion rhetoric appeals to the will, and thus presupposes the freedom of the listener to respond, and as an art of language, rhetoric is itself an instance of the will or, as Augustine writes in *De doctrina christiana*, of the *voluntas significandi* (the will to signify, 2.2.1). If in his other works Valla asserts the superiority of rhetoric to all other disciplines, in *De libero arbitrio* he may be said to explore the religious grounds of such an assertion.[56] But we need to know something in general about Valla's conception of rhetoric before we can begin to understand the rhetoric of *De libero arbitrio*.

In a seemingly innocuous passage in the *Elegantiae*, concerned with the correct usage of the words *suadeo* and *persuadeo*, Valla gives the classical rhetorical definition of persuasion as *facere fidem*.[57] This passage has usually, and correctly, been understood in the context of Valla's criticism of the reigning theological vocabulary and his own attempt to discuss theological questions in rhetorical rather than philosophical terms.[58] But it is important to see as well that the comparison of the notion of rhetorical proof with the religious concept of faith involves a redefinition of rhetoric as well as of theology: Valla does not simply want to redefine theological disputation in terms of rhetorical argument, in which case the traditional ties between rhetoric and Academic skepticism remain intact, but to reformulate the Academic and rhetorical notion of proof (*probatio*) in the context of Christian faith (*persuasio*). "Persuasion seems to signify what Christians call faith. Faith in Latin is, strictly speaking, proof, as I prove something through instruments, arguments, witnesses. The Christian religion, however, does not rest on proof, but on persuasion, which is superior to proof" (*OO* 1.172).

This reformulation can be further clarified by a brief look at Valla's attack on Aristotle in the *Dialecticae disputationes*. As Valla tells us in book I, chapter 10 of this work, prudence is only the intellectual virtue of deliberation ("deliberatio de futurisque consilium" [*OO* 1.663]), a kind of technical skill or cleverness ("solertia" [*OO* 1.664]), which is neither good nor bad in itself, because while it may be used for the good, it can never of itself move us to virtuous action. It is the will rather than the intellect that has the power to move, and the will

78

is identical with love of God or charity (*OO* 1.667).[59] Furthermore, it is not action but the will that is praiseworthy, since an ostensibly virtuous action might be performed accidentally or for the wrong reasons. Valla's is an ethic of intention. And this emphasis on the will as intention helps explain Valla's pragmatic "reduction" of the ten Aristotelian and Scholastic categories to *actio,* and *qualitas*—for the true and the good are not essences but qualities or aspects of human consciousness and conduct.[60]

This move from cognition to volition is characteristic of Valla's work and in particular of his emphasis on practice as definitive of meaning. Meaning, for Valla, is not simply available for contemplation; it must be produced in action.[61] Hence the importance throughout Valla's work of the notion of usage or *consuetudo,* and the insistence that the orator is the true wise man (*OO* 1.708) because, unlike the theologian, he takes account of such usage. Hence also the polemic against the syntax and vocabulary of Scholastic philosophy, which is not at all governed by the canons of everyday usage and which as a result leads to serious theological error. One example will suffice to illustrate this point and to introduce the dialogue on free will.

In book 2, chapter 19 of the *Disputationes,*[62] Valla argues that the six modalities of propositions (possible/impossible, contingent/necessary, true/false) are redundant, and should be reduced to three: possible, impossible, and true. When this reduction is made, certain theological problems are cleared up as well. For example, when the mode of necessity is done away with, one can no longer make the mistake of thinking that propositions about God are necessary and therefore that God is constrained by such propositions. Furthermore, necessity will also be seen to be inapplicable to human action: "For now I write neither necessarily nor contingently, but voluntarily and deliberately: & God made man by his will and grace, not by necessity and contingency" (*OO* 1.718). For Valla, as for Salutati and Pontano, grace and free will are not mutually exclusive—rather, it is precisely grace that saves human action from the rational, Scholastic alternative of contingency or necessity. This antirational solution to the problem of free will is dramatized in the rhetoric of *De libero arbitrio.*

At first glance, the dialogue seems to fall in with those Quattrocento dialogues that Francesco Tateo and more recently David

Marsh have discussed in connection with Ciceronian rhetoric.[63] On closer look, however, as we have seen, the Ciceronian notion of probability is precisely what is absent from Valla's discussion. At the same time, the dialogue cannot be assimilated to the late-fifteenth-century Neoplatonic or Augustinian model that Marsh opposes to the earlier Ciceronian one, since the open-endedness and genuine exchange of opinion that he attributes to the Ciceronian dialogue are characteristic of Valla's work as well.[64] The dialogue seems to have more in common with the Christian "oratorical skepticism" of Lactantius, the model that Letizia A. Panizza proposes for Valla's *De vero bono*, according to which the interlocutors argue *in utramque partem* in order to allow the truth of Christianity to emerge victoriously at the end. But there is one significant difference. For while both Lactantius and Lorenzo argue rationally in order to undermine the authority of human reason, Lactantius appeals to Academic skepticism in doing so,[65] while Valla in *De libero arbitrio* is intent on rejecting such an appeal. It is only when Lactantius criticises the Academic himself that Christian oratorical skepticism begins to sound like Valla's rhetoric in this dialogue. At such moments Lactantius is not simply arguing *in utramque partem* to suspend the validity of opposing philosophic dogmas, but to suspend the validity of the Academic-rhetorical method as well. Similarly, in the radically Christian context that Valla is elaborating in *De libero arbitrio*, it is not only philosophy that "consumes and destroys itself," but also rhetorical skepticism. As Lactantius remarks of the Academic Arcesilas: "Having dispatched all the philosophers, he pierced himself also with the same sword-point."[66] But we need to read further to understand how this dismissal of the Academic is reinforced by Valla's rhetorical practice in the rest of the dialogue.

Lorenzo prefaces the dialogue with an address to the bishop of Lerida, in which he contrasts two methods of theological inquiry, the first depending on the precepts of classical philosophy, the second on the reason—but even more important, on the authority and example—of the church fathers. Patristic thought is thus from the very beginning defined primarily in rhetorical terms: "Why, therefore, do you not walk in the footsteps of your ancestors? If not their reason, certainly their authority and example ought to persuade that they should be followed instead of your entering on some new path" (156; 523). Lorenzo then draws an analogy between these two approaches and two kinds of speech: "Formerly neither citizen nor stranger was allowed to speak in a foreign tongue in the Roman state, and only the dialect of that city could be used. However, you who could be called senators of the Christian commonwealth, are better pleased to hear and employ pagan speech than ecclesiastical" (156; 523–25).[67] This analogy suggests the fifteenth- and sixteenth-century debates about Ciceronianism—for example, the decorum of addressing God as Optimus Maximus—but it also allows Lorenzo to identify the authority and simplicity of patristic language with the pristine elegance of classical Latin.[68] Boethius, on the other hand, whose arguments about free will Lorenzo intends to refute in this dialogue, is associated with the philosophical "lingua peregrina." Lorenzo's original contrast between barbarous and persuasive discourse then informs the entire dialogue, for while he does discuss the problems of free will in the barbarous Scholastic terms that Antonio introduces (necessity, contingency, etc.), his rhetorical strategy as a whole is to suspend this theoretical issue, to drive a wedge between cognitive and practical concerns, and thereby to open up a space in which the very fact of debate can be evidence for the freedom of the will—which can never be known but which can be practiced.

Thus, when Antonio tells us how anxious he is about his failure to understand the question of free will, since "all human action, all right and wrong, all reward and punishment, in this life and the future as well" depend on the answer, Lorenzo replies: "As you say, this question is very difficult, and I scarcely know whether it has been understood by anyone. But that is no reason for you to be disturbed or confused, even if you never understand it" (158; 526)— not only because no one has solved this problem but because freedom of action does not depend on perfect understanding.

This separation between cognition and volition is particularly clear at the end of the dialogue when Lorenzo abandons the cognitive mode of teaching for the persuasive mode of exhortation. Here we return to the considerations of *Elegantiae* 5.30, for the conclusion of *De libero arbitrio* can be seen as an example of the conflation of rhetorical *fides* and Christian faith which we observed in the earlier passage: "We do not know the cause of this matter [of divine will, concludes Lorenzo]; of what consequence is it? We stand by faith and not by the probability of reason. Does knowledge do much for the corroboration of faith? Humility does more. . . . Is the fore-knowledge of divine things useful? Charity is more useful" (180; 560–62).

These remarks, in conjunction with those that introduce the dialogue, serve to bracket and effectively to suspend the rational discussion of scholastic questions concerning necessity and contingency. But in fact such a suspension has already occurred in the dialogue, so that Lorenzo's final distinction between teaching and exhortation is in one sense ironic. For the dialogue within the dialogue that Lorenzo invents to dramatize the distinctions he has been making between foreknowledge and divine power—the way, for example, in which divine will is less of an impediment to free will than divine foreknowledge (176; 554–56)—only teaches us the impossibility of rationally understanding free will. Here, the critique of Boethius is doubly forceful. To begin with, Lorenzo abandons the Scholastic vocabulary of Boethius for the narrative mode of classical mythology which, Antonio and Lorenzo both agree, is "appositum. . . et aptum ad persuadendum" (169; 544). But the further criticism is that in *visualizing* an encounter between Sextus Tarquinius and Apollo, Valla dramatizes the impossibility of our *perceiving* any answer to the question of free will. In doing so, he indirectly reminds us of Boethius's own visual illustration of his rational solution to this problem. For Lady Philosophy, there can be no conflict between divine providence and human volition because God sees all things in an eternal present; His sight can no more cause our actions than our own sight can cause the present events that we perceive.[69] Valla thus underscores the conventional metaphorical tie between intellectual and perceptual vision only to undermine this tie and with it, the consolation of philosophy.

To summarize the myth briefly: Sextus Tarquinius consults Apollo about his future, and is informed that he will die an "exile and a pauper" (170). When he complains to Apollo about the injustice of this fate, Apollo replies that "the power and decision over the fates are seated with . . . [Jupiter, the fates, and Fortune]; with me, mere foreknowledge and prediction." Lorenzo then glosses the fable in the following way: "Although the wisdom of God cannot be separated from His power and will, I may by this device of Apollo and Jupiter separate them. What cannot be achieved with one god may be achieved with two, each having his own proper nature—the one for creating the character of men, the other for knowing—that it

82

may appear that providence is not the cause of necessity but that all this whatever it is must be referred to the will of God" (174; 550). When Antonio objects that his myth simply displaces the responsibility for necessity from divine foreknowledge to the divine will, Lorenzo replies with a question: "Do I say that free will is annulled by God?" (174; 550)—thereby suspending his own responsibility for resolving this issue.

Interpreted in one way, this "solution" appears to be similar to the one proposed by Boethius in *De consolatione philosophiae*: divine foreknowledge does not prohibit the exercise of free will. But Antonio and Boethius differ profoundly in the way in which they convey this belief—and this finally makes all the difference. In fact, the myth not only exemplifies a very different kind of rhetorical practice from the discursive practice of Boethius; it may also be seen as an allegory of this difference. First of all, like Boethius, Sextus Tarquinius hopes to comprehend his future actions rationally. Then, if we return to Lorenzo's opening discussion of theological method, we see that Tarquin in exile represents the triumph of rhetoric over philosophy. Speaking of those who argue philosophically, Lorenzo cries: 'They do not realize that the most pious antiquity, which lacked the arm of philosophy in combatting heresies, and which often fought bitterly against philosophy itself—driving it forth like Tarquin into exile, never to return again—is thus accused of ignorance" (155–56; 524).

Lorenzo's mythical interlude, in illustrating the failure of reason to comprehend the divine will, is thus the ironic equivalent of the method of Boethius, who, as Lorenzo tells us early on in the dialogue, "is himself unable to complete what he undertakes and at certain points takes refuge in the imaginary and fictitious" (160; 530).

> For he says God, through an intelligence which is beyond reason, both knows all things for eternity and holds all things present. But can I, who am rational and know nothing outside of time, aspire to the knowledge of intelligence and eternity? I suspect Boethius himself did not understand them, even if the things he said were true, which I do not believe. For he should not be thought to speak truly whose speech not he himself nor anyone else understands. [160; 530]

Whereas Boethius mistakes his own barbarous, rational explanation for the truth, and so is guilty of pride, Lorenzo explicitly calls attention to the fictional nature of his refuge (174; 550), thereby demonstrating his true patristic humility.

Lorenzo's use of myth in *De libero arbitrio* should also be opposed to the function of Antonio's rhetoric in *De vero falsoque bono*. In this earlier text Antonio argues that although it is impossible for us to imagine heaven, "nevertheless it will be worthwhile to attempt to imagine it" (145): "For if we place these things which do not fall before our eyes before them by a certain imagination, will we not supply a certain great strengthening of faith and a kind of surety?"[70] While Antonio aims to present a picture of heaven that, however inadequate, will be powerful enough to strengthen the listener's faith,[71] Lorenzo's poetic interlude intends the more radical effect of undermining altogether the possibility of visualizing a solution to the problem of free will. But the ultimate intention is in both cases the same: to shift the listener's concentration from the cognitive problems of understanding to an active conception of charity.

Valla's self-consuming rhetoric has its own dangers, however. For his refusal to resolve the problem of free will in the cognitive or intellectual terms in which Antonio poses the question could be interpreted as a denial of free will—and, in fact, was so interpreted by Erasmus and Luther in the following century.[72] It is somewhat surprising that Erasmus should have read Valla's dialogue in this way for, as we will see, his own *De libero arbitrio* is similarly concerned to suspend intellectual deliberation in order to make room for an active conception of charity. However, it is not entirely surprising that Luther spoke favorably of this dialogue, for Lorenzo's fable functions in much the same way that biblical language does according to Luther in *De servo arbitrio*. While Erasmus argued that those biblical passages which literally deny free will must be interpreted figuratively, Luther insisted on the literal meaning of Scripture, including those passages in which God commands man to do good works. He then argued that although the imperative mode of these commands would seem to imply that we do indeed have free will, this is not the case; for God commands us only in order to make us realize that we are incapable of obeying Him. The effect is to make us realize our absolute dependence on God's grace or charity.

As we have seen, Lorenzo's myth and the distinctions he introduces by means of it dramatize in much the same way the impossibility of making useful distinctions with respect to the question of free will. Or, if the myth is thought of in allegorical terms, he offers us a figurative narrative whose literal referent is infinitely regressive. Yet while Luther reads the Bible as literally destroying our creaturely assumption of free will, Valla seems to go one step further by suggesting that if human reason is incapable of asserting the existence of free will, it must also be incapable of denying its existence. The question is rationally undecidable; but that is precisely why it is *practicable*. In fact, Lorenzo's own fictional practice is one locus of this potentiality. For it can just as well as not be interpreted as evidence for the existence of free will. And this possibility of practice (the evidence of things unseen) is, as we have seen from the end of *De libero arbitrio*, grounded in Christian charity.

While in his other works Valla describes language itself as a practice, it is clear from *De libero arbitrio* that this practice must be interpreted in theological rather than philosophical terms. Furthermore, this emphasis on the practical standard of usage or *consuetudo*, in conjunction with Valla's critique of the substantializing vocabulary of the scholastics, has much in common with Augustine's remarks on use and enjoyment in *De doctrina christiana*, an analogy that Valla himself suggests by his simultaneous use and conflation of these terms in *De libero arbitrio* ("utilior caritas").[73] A brief look at *De doctrina* will help us to see the way in which Valla founds the Christian rhetoric of his dialogue on charity rather than on the classical notion of prudence and the skeptical notion of probability.

Augustine tells us that God is to be enjoyed (*frui*), that is, loved, while all other things are to be used (*uti*) as a means to that end. But God himself cannot properly speaking be conceived or known. Thus, when we use the word *Deus*, "He is not recognized in the noise of these two syllables [; rather]. . . all those who know the Latin language, when this sound reaches their ears, are moved to think of [Him]" (1.6.6). Our affective relationship to God then becomes the justification for the priority of rhetoric over logic, of charity over rational understanding. In fact, charity is the condition of rational understanding, for while the Ciceronian orator is ideally guided by prudence in constructing his speech and in persuading his listeners to a prudent course of action, the Christian preacher is guided by the rule of charity. This rule informs his interpretation of Scripture (1.36.40) and is manifest, both ethically and pedagogically, in the act of preaching: he embodies the ethical imperative of charity and he instructs with respect to this same imperative. And in the case of both activities—that of interpreting and that of preaching—the possibility of charity is divinely given (3.27.38, 4.16.33). Interpreting Scripture and preaching are thus both examples of the way in which the affective and active principle of charity takes precedence over and indeed founds the possibility of any sort of intellectual deliberation or decorum.[74] Enjoyment of God is the precondition of the right use of those human institutions, including language, which are governed by the criterion of custom or usage (2.2.3; see 2.25.38). Finally, this charity is identified with Christian liberty:

> If it is a carnal slavery to adhere to a usefully instituted sign instead of to the thing it was designed to signify, how much is it a worse slavery to embrace signs instituted for spiritually useless things instead of the things themselves? [3.7.11] . . . Christian liberty freed those it found under useful signs, discovering them to be among those who were "nigh" [i.e., the Jews], interpreting the signs to which they were subject, and elevating them to the things which the signs represented. . . . Nor were they led to a servitude under useful signs, but rather to an exercise of the mind directed toward understanding them spiritually. [3.8.12][75]

When we enjoy those things that should be used, we are guilty of idolatry, just as the Scholastic theologians are guilty when they take their substances and essences as things in themselves, rather than as conventional signs.[76] But the linguistic criterion of usage does not guarantee the proper *use* of language in the Augustinian sense, for usage itself can be misused if it is not referred to charity. Like Augustine, Valla wants to demonstrate that usage must be used, and not loved for its own sake.

This question of the proper use of rhetoric, and thus of the rhetorical criterion of usage or decorum, is taken up in the famous preface to the fourth book of the *Elegantiae*. Here, Valla is careful to distinguish between rhetoric and faith in order then to redefine the proper use of rhetoric in religious rather than pagan or even secular terms. Jerome should be criticized not for reading classical authors or for admiring classical eloquence, but for reading and admiring in the wrong way: for failing to subordinate the *use* of rhetoric to the love of God.[77]

We can now see that *De libero arbitrio* stands in a kind of mirror relation to Valla's other works and to the works of his contemporaries. For while Valla himself associates his conception of rhetoric and usage with Academic skepticism in many of his works, this dialogue shows both the inadequacy of this formulation and the more radical foundation of rhetoric in Christian charity. And it does so, as we have seen, not only in the opening and concluding criticisms of philosophy and theoretical reason, but in the self-consuming artifact of Lorenzo's fictive dialogue.

The rhetorical effect of this mythical dialogue is purgative rather than simply instructive, as Antonio suggests by his complaint: "Is it thus you have defrauded me and coerced me through a deceitful promise? Promises in which deceit enters do not stand, nor do I think I have received luncheon from you if I am forced to vomit up whatever I have eaten, or, to speak more lightly, you send me away no less hungry than you received me" (174–75; 552).[78] The truth it brings to light is not cognitive, but affective. Lorenzo has played the doctor who cures his patient—not of dogmatic philosophy as in *De vero bono*, but of the desire for even the probable truth [560: *probabilitate rationum*] promised by the Academic skeptic.

Lorenzo glosses the myth with a quotation from *Romans* that serves as the visual equivalent of the earlier image of purgation: "And a little later, as if the excessive splendor of the wisdom of God darkened his eyes, [Paul] . . . proclaimed (Rom. 11:33): 'O the depths of the riches both of the wisdom and the knowledge of God! how unsearchable are his judgments, and his ways past finding out'" (176; 554).

These images of purgation and excessive light are then repeated in an inverted form at the end of the dialogue. First, Aristotle is swallowed up by his own mouth, just as Antonio could have been swallowed up by his own expectation of a rational decision about the existence of free will:

> Let us not wish to know the height, but let us fear lest we become like the philosophers who, calling themselves wise, are made foolish; who, lest they should appear ignorant of anything, disputed about everything. Raising their own mouths to heaven, and wishing to scale it . . . they were hurled down to earth by the strong forearm of God. . . . For when he could not discover the nature of Euripus, throwing himself into its depth, he was swallowed up. [181; 562][79]

Lorenzo then concludes: "To attain [God's] . . . grace I will no longer be anxious about this question lest by investigating the majesty of

God I might be blinded by his light" (181; 652).[80] Academic disputation cannot allow the truth to emerge into the light (*De off.* 2.2.8); for the light that is truth is the condition of the right use of language and thus of disputation. And right use in theological questions involves exhortation rather than debate, "not so much that I might move you," Lorenzo tells Antonio, since this is the work of God, "as that I might show my own disposition of mind" (181), *animi persuasionem* (560), which, as we know from the *Elegantiae*, is the evidence of things unseen.

It is therefore appropriate that the dialogue should end with Antonio urging Lorenzo to commit the debate to writing and thereby share it with others, for it suggests once again the active dimension of Valla's Augustinian notion of charity. Augustine, in *De doctrina*, distinguishes between natural and conventional signs on the grounds that only the latter involves a "voluntas significandi" (2.2.1)—a *will to signify*. These signs, then, in addition to conveying a particular signified, also *signify the will*. Finally, language itself becomes evidence for the freedom of the will granted us by God's charity: "The condition of man would be lowered if God had not wished to have men supply His word to men. . . . For charity itself, which holds men together in a knot of unity, would not have a means of infusing souls and almost mixing them together if men could teach nothing to men" (Prol. 6). Thus, in the very act of dramatizing the incomprehensibility of God's ways, Valla's *De libero arbitrio* can be said to illustrate the speaker's own *animi persuasionem* and, in so doing, to demonstrate both the possibility and the right use of rhetoric.

4 Erasmus: Prudence and Faith

Vide, huc perpulit Diatriben imprudentem invicibilis et potentissima veritas, et stultam fecit sapientiam eius, ut contra nos dictura, pro nobis se dicere cogeretur. [See how the invincible and all-powerful truth has cornered witless Diatribe and turned her wisdom into folly, so that while meaning to speak against us, she is compelled to speak for us and against herself.]

—Luther, *De servo arbitrio*

When Erasmus criticized Luther's decision to publish the paradox of enslaved will (*LE 41, 134*) to the world for fear of the offense it would cause "pious ears,"[1] Luther replied ironically that paradox is everywhere apparent in the argument of Erasmus's own *Diatribe*.[2] The feminine personification of Diatribe and the description of her wisdom as folly suggest that Luther is alluding to Erasmus's earlier published paradox, perhaps with the implication that the *Moriae encomium* was a true praise of Christian wisdom and the contradictory praise of prudence in the *Diatribe* merely foolish. Erasmus himself, however, did not publically distinguish between the positions espoused in the two works. And when Martin Dorp charged that the publication of the *Encomium* was an offense to pious ears, Erasmus did not insist on its offensiveness, as Luther would have, but appealed instead to the principles of decorum and prudence that were to figure so largely in the argument of the *Diatribe*. The central problem that faces readers of the *Encomium* is whether to accept the guidelines for interpretation that Erasmus offers in his letter to Martin Dorp, or to see the *Encomium* as Luther may have, that is, as an uncharacteristic exploration by Erasmus of the complexities, difficulties, and inevitable ironies of his own prudential position. While in its paradoxical form the *Encomium* is typical of Erasmus's work in encouraging the reader actively to exercise his judgment, it is also quite untypical in moving him to reflect on the possibility of such exercise. In this text, Erasmus is less concerned with persuading the reader to read or act according to a certain ethical view of Christ than to question Erasmus's own humanist assumptions about the nature of persuasion and interpretation.

Luther's remark is a useful point of departure for a consideration of the status of paradox in Erasmus's view of Christianity in general and in the debate on free will and the *Encomium* in particular. Rosalie Colie, one of the most perceptive readers of the *Encomium*, has also written of the rhetorical effect of Folly's paradox in a way that ties it to the debate on free will. Her interpretation, however, is informed by Erasmus's view of free will rather than Luther's. "[Folly] undercuts and undermines her whole argument herself, to leave each reader alone with the unpleasant realization that Folly has been consistent to the last; "on all sydes like unto her selfe," she has abandoned the reader to make his own decisions about value. True to Erasmus' principles of free will . . . Folly has left it up to each reader to interpret her words as he can and as he must."[3] But even this is too much of an assertion for the *Encomium*. Colie's later description is more to the point: "The rhetorical paradox is . . . paradoxical in its double aim of dazzling—that is, of arresting thought altogether in the possessive experience of wonder—and of stimulating further questions, speculations, qualifications, even contradiction on the part of that wondering audience" (97). Not the least of the paradoxes, I suggest, is that while the *Encomium* leaves the interpretation to the reader, it also forces him to question the possibility of an interpretation that would be grounded in the reader's prudence or a rhetoric that would appeal to the reader's free will. In order to see how the paradox of the*Encomium* encourages this kind of reflection, we need first of all to consider the assumptions that underlie Erasmus's and Luther's positions in the debate on free will.

I

As a "moderate skeptical theologian" (*LE* 116; *WA* 613), Erasmus was concerned above all with preserving the realm of prudence or responsible human action. He viewed man as a participant in the social and political realms in which things can be other than they are, and his criticism of the scholastic emphasis on reason led him to develop a model of action and reading that has much in common with classical and Quattrocento notions of prudence and decorum. Like the Quattrocento humanists, Erasmus believed that classical and patristic texts were exemplary in instructing and moving the reader to ethical practice. Furthermore, if one can be moved to praxis by the works of antiquity, then the primary responsibility of the humanist is to ensure the accuracy and reliability of these texts. Accordingly, much of Erasmus's literary activity was engaged in editing classical texts and in making a bilingual edition of the New Testament available to the reading public.[4]

But Erasmus was not only an editor, he was also an author. And it is here that we see most clearly his concern with educating his readers to a certain notion of praxis by means of the rhetorical practice of literature. Among his many efforts, the *Adages* in particular testify to his desire not only to provide his readers with the rudiments of a classical education, but also to excite them by the *form* of his text to further learning and to the application of this learning in their own lives.[5] As Erasmus himself tells us, in his comments on the adages he exemplifies the practice of interpretation or judgment[6] most appropriate to the Christian life, and in the fragmentary and essayistic form of his commentary he urges the reader to continue the activity of interpretation and scholarship that he has begun.[7]

Moreover, according to Erasmus, this ethical practice of interpretation is not only compatible with but is actually grounded in the nature of Christ Himself. In a famous passage in the *Encomium moriae* (to be examined in greater detail below), Erasmus discusses the activity of interpretation in terms of the Silenus figure, and in the *Adages* he tells us that the most perfect Silenus is Christ.

> But is not Christ the most extraordinary Silenus of all? If it is permissible to speak of him in this way—and I cannot see why all who rejoice in the name of Christians should not do their best to imitate it. If you look on the face only of the Silenus-image, what could be lower or more contemptible, measured by popular standards? . . . But if one may attain to a closer look at this Silenus-image, that is if he deigns to show himself to the purified eyes of the soul, what unspeakable riches you will find there. [79; *LB* 2.771 D ("Sileni Alcibiadis")]

It would have been easy for Christ to "set up his throne over all the earth, and to possess it" (80), but He preferred to persuade rather than to compel the faithful. And this persuasion took the form of the incarnation, the embodiment of the divine in the lowly and abject, in a Silenus figure that forces the individual to "examine more closely" (79).

The image of the Silenus is misleading, however, if it suggests that Erasmus's own works are structured allegorically, that is, according to the inside/outside dichotomy of the grostesque figurine. As his comments on the form of the *Adages* testify, Erasmus is less concerned with the product of interpretation than with the process—less concerned, that is, with presenting a kernel of doctrinal truth than with educating his readers to an activity of judgment and to the exercise of that judgment in their own lives. In a certain sense, then, we can say that for Erasmus the *absence* of Christ is required in order to make room for the practice of interpretation and the ethical praxis that constitute the true *imitatio Christi*. This is clear from the following passage in the *Enchiridion*, where Erasmus comments on the disciples' lack of faith.

> After the performance of so many miracles, after years of teaching straight from His holy lips, after so many evidences of His resurrection, did He not at the final moment when He was to be received into heaven chide them for their lack of faith? Then what was the reason? *Assuredly the flesh of Christ stood in the way.* So it is that He says, "Unless I go away, the Comforter will not come. It is best for you that I go." The physical presence of Christ is useless as far as spiritual health is concerned. . . . Paul had seen Christ in the flesh. What do you consider more important than this? But he is indifferent to the fact. "Even if we have known Christ in the flesh," he says, "we know Him no longer." Why not? because he had achieved more satisfying gifts of the spirit.[8]

Similarly, it is the *absence* of any fixed interpretation of Scripture which necessitates an interpretive activity on the part of the reader. As Erasmus wrote to Luther during the exchange on free will, "The authority of the Scripture is not here in dispute. The same Scriptures are acknowledged and venerated on either side. Our battle is about the meaning of Scripture" (*LE* 43). This activity of interpretation is, correctly understood, an *act* of faith. As Erasmus tells us in the *Paraclesis*, the effect of meditation on Scripture is spiritual transformation, and the activity of reading and carrying its teaching into effect is the true *philosophia Christi*. "Let us all, therefore, with our whole heart covet this literature [Scripture], let us embrace it, let us continually occupy ourselves with it, let us fondly kiss it, at length let us die in its embrace, let us be transformed in it, since indeed studies are transmuted into morals [*abeunt studia in mores*]."[9]

These passages from the *Adages* and the *Paraclesis* indicate Erasmus's interest in editing and composing texts that persuade the reader actively to assume the ethical burden of interpretation and imitation. But Erasmus was also sensitive to the claim that the notion of interpretive and ethical praxis must be modified within the context of Christianity, that is, in relation to an omniscient and omnipotent God. It may have been for this reason that Erasmus felt obliged to phrase his own moderate views about the possibility of prudence in *De libero arbitrio* in skeptical terms: within a Christian framework any assertion of human capability apart from divine grace must be heretical. Here his famous "So far am I from delighting in assertions that I would readily take refuge in the opinion of the skeptics" (*LE* 35; *LB* 9.1215D) would be a prudential, in the sense of a cautious, move. In fact, Erasmus is doubly cautious, since he qualifies in the second half of this sentence even his right to skepticism: "whenever this is allowed by the inviolable authority of Holy Scriptures and the decrees of the Church." He thus acknowledges, as will Montaigne in a very different context, that any skeptical statement, and particularly one whose function is to secure the realm of phenomena for human action, may be interpreted as an assertion of knowledge and therefore as hubristic.

Yet while Erasmus may have been a skeptic about the possibility of human knowledge of God, he was not skeptical about the necessity of responsible human action. He wanted, on the contrary, to argue for an independent realm of praxis or prudence, for which the skeptical suspension of theoretical assertions in *De libero arbitrio* would provide an acceptable Christian formulation. The attempt to save the realm of practice from the contamination of skepticism in the *Diatribe* is typical of Erasmus's work as a whole. In general, the doubts he felt about reason's capacity to know God or to have access to a reliable standard of judgment seem only to have confirmed him in his commitment to a *theologia practica* and the restitution of *bonae litterae* in which he was engaged.[10] The response to Luther's denial of free will was thus an attempt to argue in the subjunctive about Scholastic questions and thereby suspend both the theoretical argu-

93

ment and any accusations of presumption. But this skeptical suspension is itself a rhetorical invitation to the reader to imitate Erasmus's moderation on issues of dogma and, more important, to abandon speculation for the practice of a Christian life. Not surprisingly, however, Luther in particular failed to be convinced by Erasmus's attempt to suspend the epistemological paradoxes of Christianity by means of a practical theology. And the objections of this reader suggest that, in at least one text, Erasmus too may have been questioning his own presuppositions about prudence and persuasion.

II

If Erasmus's *Diatribe* is an attempt to navigate a passage (what he himself refers to as a *transgressus*)[11] between epistemological skepticism and ethical practice by means of a hypothesis or faith in the possibility of free will, Luther's response attacks both the hypothetical nature of this defense and the considerations of decorum and prudence by which it is governed. While the impossibility of knowing divine will makes Erasmus cautious about assertions, Luther views this caution, or prudence in the modern sense of the word, as an all-too-human (*LE* 125) and hubristic attempt to bind God to the rule of decorum and to mitigate the uncompromisingly offensive meaning of Scripture. "He is God," Luther declares, "and for his will there is no cause or reason that can be laid down as a rule or measure for it, since there is nothing equal or superior to it, but it is itself the rule of all things" (*LE* 236; *WA* 712). And when Erasmus argues that it is not always expedient to speak the truth, Luther inquires: "Who has empowered you or given you the right to bind Christian doctrine to places, persons, times, or causes when Christ wills it to be proclaimed and to reign throughout the world in entire freedom? 'The word of God is not bound,' says Paul [2 Tim. 2:9]; and will Erasmus bind the Word?" (*LE* 132; *WA* 628).

Throughout *De servo arbitrio* Luther criticizes Erasmus for his reliance on the protean rhetorical standard of decorum. He refers to Erasmus's "highly decorative arguments" (*LE* 103) and his "seductive charm" (102); he calls him a "distinguished rhetorician" (117) and a "fluent orator" (127) and remarks on the prudence of his definition of free will: "It is very prudent [*prudenter*] of you to give only a bare definition and not to explain (as others usually do) any part of it—perhaps because you were afraid you might be shipwrecked on more than one point" (*LE* 170; *WA* 661–62). Elsewhere Luther is more abusive: he accuses Erasmus of defiling his "very elegant and ingenious style with . . . trash," and of conveying "utterly unworthy matter . . . in such rich ornaments of eloquence, like refuse or ordure being carried in gold and silver vases" (*LE* 102; *WA* 601). Furthermore, Luther argues, the excessive concern with persuasion, with the rhetorical concessions that the language of the Bible must, according to Erasmus, make to its human readers, leads one to conceive of God Himself as a rhetorician: "To talk as you do, one must imagine the Living God to be nothing but a kind of shallow and ignorant ranter declaiming from some platform, whose words you can if you wish interpret in any direction you like, and accept or reject them according as ungodly men are seen to be moved or affected by them" (*LE* 135–36; *WA* 631).

While it is obviously not true that Erasmus sees God as a "shallow and ignorant ranter," he does, like his Quattrocento predecessors, conceive of Him as a rhetorician. His further presupposition is that as creatures of the phenomenal world we can only justify our interpretations in the context of that world. In this life all conclusions will be provisional and pragmatic, since the only authentic judgment is the Last Judgment. It is because of these human limitations, according to Erasmus, that God speaks to man in figurative language and that the reader of Scripture is obliged to exercise a prudential and reflective judgment by drawing analogies between clear passages and unclear ones (*De doctrina* 2.6.8, 3.26.37; *LE* 36, 47). But Luther cannot accept the dangerous and all-too-human instability of this method of interpretation. He cannot accept the view that Scripture requires any human interpretation at all. Thus, when Erasmus's *collatio* (comparison) ends with the formal *contuli* of the Sunday conference, "I have completed my discourse," Luther puns on this "conclusion" by claiming that he has made assertions, not comparisons:

> And it is not difficult to suppose that you, since you are human, may not have rightly understood or observed with due care the Scriptures or the sayings of the Fathers under whose guidance you think you are attaining your goal; and of this there is more than a hint in your statement that you are asserting nothing, but have only "discoursed."

95

No one writes like that who has a thorough insight into the subject and rightly understands it. I for my part in this book *have not discoursed, but have asserted and do assert* [NON CONTULI, SED ASSERVI, ET AS-SERO], and I am unwilling to submit the matter to anyone's judgment, but advise everyone to yield assent. [*LE* 334; *WA* 787]

Thus, while Erasmus writes that it would be harmful to assert the absence of free will, Luther claims that this assertion "is not irreverent, inquisitive, or superfluous, but essentially salutary and necessary for a Christian" (*LE* 116).

For the skeptic who is uncertain, it may be possible to argue *in utramque partem* and to suspend one's judgment (105), but "the Holy Spirit is no Skeptic" (*LE* 109). Again Luther insists:

Nothing is better known or more common among Christians than assertion. Take away assertions and you take away Christianity. Why, the Holy Spirit is given them from heaven, that a Christian may glorify Christ and confess him unto death—unless it is not asserting when one dies for one's confession and assertion. Moreover, the Spirit goes to such length in asserting, that he takes the initiative and accuses the world of sin [John 16:8], as if he would provoke a fight; and Paul commands Timothy to "exhort" and "be urgent out of season" [2 Tim. 4:2]. But what a droll exhorter he would be, who himself neither firmly believed nor consistently asserted the thing he was exhorting about! (*LE* 106, *WA* 603)

If assertions are necessarily part of Christianity, then any assertion to the contrary will also be an assertion. Thus, when Erasmus argues that it is not necessary to know that which is impossible to know (whether we have free will), Luther points up the assertion consequent upon Erasmus's skepticism: "Contrary to your natural bent, and with an assertion unprecedented for you, you declare that those things are not necessary; whereas, unless they are necessary and known with certainty, then neither God, nor Christ, nor gospel, nor faith, nor anything is left, not even of Judaism, much less of Christianity" (*LE* 114; *WA* 610).

But Luther does not simply object that skepticism about free will is itself a kind of assertion. He also argues against Erasmus's attempt to separate pedagogical exhortation from the act of cognition, or the persuasive from the cognitive function of language, on the grounds that the possibility of persuasion is undermined by the skeptical assertion of the impossibility of knowledge. In so doing, he offers an epistemological critique of the Quattrocento humanists' assumptions about the possibility of prudence:

> But when you tell Christians themselves to become reckless workers, and order them not to be inquisitive about what they can and cannot do in the matter of obtaining eternal salvation, this is beyond question the truly unforgivable sin. For as long as they are ignorant of what and how much they can do, they will not know what they should do; and being ignorant of what they should do, they cannot repent if they do wrong; and impenitence is the unforgivable sin. This is what your moderate Skeptical Theology leads to. [*LE* 116; *WA* 613: "tua illa moderata Sceptica Theologia"]

Erasmus and Luther seem to agree that rhetoric is concerned both with persuasion and with tropes. But for Luther the latter are defined by their deviance from the proper or literal expression that allows the cognition of an external or a priori referent, whereas for Erasmus the reader who recognizes a figurative dimension to the language of the Bible will always be compelled to be an interpreter, to make a decision about or distinction between the literal and figurative uses of language. But, Luther argues, if tropological language is radically unstable according to the skeptical critique of judgment, how is it possible to be persuaded to anything? Or, in the words of Augustine, "Who is moved if he does not know what is being said?" (*De doctrina* 4.26.58). Luther then objects to Erasmus's practical theology both by insisting that the persuasive function of language depends on the tropological and by calling attention to the fact that the very notion of metaphor presupposes the availability of the literal meaning. In so doing, he suppresses the role of the interpreter: *scriptura sui ipsius interpres* (scripture is its own interpreter).[12]

Beginning, then, with the assumption that God's word is known and can only be salutary, Luther is forced to condemn Erasmus's strategy, whether it is one of indirection or indecision: "For if you think that free choice is a subject we need know nothing about, and one that has nothing to do with Christ, then your language is correct [i.e., conforms to your thought], but your thought is impious. If, on the other hand, you think it is a necessary subject, then your language is impious [because indirect], though your thought is correct" (*LE* 107; *WA* 604).

If a skeptical distrust of assertion is, within the context of faith, the most dogmatic of positions, then the attempt to separate epis-temology and ethics, to draw an analogy on the basis of an amphi-boly, and to preserve the realm of responsible human action from the consequences of this skepticism will be merely contradictory. Thus, Erasmus's statement that he is arguing in order to engender such a distrust in his reader provokes this characterization of his unwitting self-contradiction:

> It is, you say, irreverent, inquisitive, and superfluous to want to know whether our will does anything in matters pertaining to eternal salva-tion or whether it is simply passive under the action of grace. Yet now you contradict this by saying that Christian godliness means striving with one's powers, and that without the mercy of God the will is not effective. Here you plainly assert that the will does something in mat-ters pertaining to eternal salvation, when you represent it as striving, though you make it passive when you say it is ineffective apart from mercy. You do not, however, state precisely how this activity and passivity are to be understood, for you take good care to keep us in ignorance of what God's mercy and our will *can* achieve, even while you are telling us what they actually do. Thus that prudence of yours makes you veer about, determined not to commit yourself to either side, but to pass safely between Scylla and Charybdis; with the result that, finding yourself battered and buffeted by the waves in the midst of the sea, you assert everything you deny and deny everything you assert. [*LE* 114–15; *WA* 611]

This, Luther would seem to be arguing, is indeed a new kind of prudence, which is merely indirection and inconsistency, and a new rhetoric, whose paradigmatic topos is aporia and whose place is utopic. While Erasmus expresses his reluctance to "publish the par-adox of enslaved choice to the world," the paradox, Luther com-plains, is everywhere apparent in the *Diatribe*. It is a function of Erasmus's attempt to make human sense of God, to master Chris-tian folly by the foolishness of reason (232). For although Erasmus himself is critical of the attempt to "measure God by human reason" instead of "reverencing the secrets of his majesty" (*LE* 229), he is guilty of just that when he refuses to accept the paradox of the enslaved will or tries to "make excuses" for God by explaining the paradox away. Diatribe is falsely constrained by human notions of consistency when she argues that "Absurdity . . . is one of the prin-ciple reasons for not taking the words of Moses and Paul [about enslaved will] literally" (229).

But what article of faith does this absurdity sin against? [Luther retorts.] Or who is offended by it? Human Reason is offended, who although she is blind, deaf, stupid, impious and sacrilegious with regard to all the words and works of God, is brought in at this point as a judge of the words and works of God. . . . Let us therefore invent some tropes with the Arians to prevent Christ from being literally God. Let us invent tropes with the Manichees to prevent his being truly man. . . . That will be a fine way for us to handle Scriptures!

But tropes are no use, and there is no avoiding absurdity. For it remains absurd (as Reason judges) that a God who is just and good should demand of free choice impossible things. [LE 229–30; WA 707]

The very fact that Luther engages Erasmus in debate, it could be argued, means that he believes in the value of rhetoric: there would be no point in arguing if there were no chance of persuading one's interlocutor. Furthermore, this possibility of persuasion (the classical *movere*) is what Luther seems to presuppose when he points up the dangers of Erasmus's teaching (LE 116). On the other hand, both Erasmus and Luther are concerned with redefining the notions of persuasion and debate as they are commonly understood. Just as Erasmus engages in a skeptical effort to suspend argument by means of argument, so Luther has his own way of doing away with the conditions of legitimate disagreement. Whereas Erasmus separates the authority of Scripture from the reader's grasp of its meaning, Luther refers the reader to a principle of interpretive authority so transcendent that it is immanent.[13] Although God is obscure to human knowledge, he argues, the meaning of His Scripture is perfectly accessible to man (110–11). There is no need for skeptical moderation when one has access to the truth of the Bible—though Luther is careful to define this truth not as perfect understanding, which belongs only to God, but as certainty (LE 108).

The exegetical consequences of this are important, for the gift of certainty is the gift of a monological or literal meaning. The self-evidence of Scripture means that Luther can reject the tradition of patristic hermeneutics as a supplementary kind of authority required by those for whom the authority of the Bible is primarily formal. The amphiboly or obscurity that Erasmus finds in Scripture Luther then attributes to Erasmus's own "darkened heart" (LE 112). As Luther was to say in the *Tischreden*, "Erasmus ist rex amphiboliarum" (Erasmus is the king of amphibolies).[14]

Luther's insistence on a literal reading of the Bible could prompt one to object with Erasmus that God's exhorting man to do good

99

works implies that we *can* indeed do them. But here the subtlety of Luther's reading comes to the fore: he does not deny that these commands and exhortations should be understood literally, but he does deny the all-too-human inference.[15] While in an interpersonal context we command or urge others on the assumption that they can obey or respond to our urging, Luther argues, God commands precisely in order to destroy this creaturely understanding. In other words, He uses our literal reading to destroy our literal reading, or, in more familiar theological terms, He uses the law to destroy the law. In *Von der Freiheit eines Christenmenschen* Luther tells us that the Bible consists of two kinds of speech: "Commands or the laws of God, and promises or agreements." The first exists only "so that man will recognize his inability to do good and learn to despair of himself. . . . From this he learns to deny himself and to seek help elsewhere, that he may be without evil desires and fulfill the command through another which he cannot do by himself. So are all other commands impossible for us."[16]

Luther insists that this destruction of the law or of the old man must not be understood as the simple replacement of the law by grace, or of the letter by the spirit (his charge against Erasmus for relying on figurative interpretation in the manner of Origen and Jerome). We are no longer operating with the distinctions of literal and figurative (144) or even of cognitive and persuasive, since we must understand God's commandments literally, yet at the same time outside of any human context; and the commandments persuade us to something, but only because we wrongly assume that they are assertions.

There are many points of agreement between Luther and Erasmus, as Erasmus indicated when he wrote that he feared Luther's enemies more than Luther himself.[17] Critics have argued that a close examination of the debate on free will shows many of the disagreements to be terminological, since ultimately both men agree that we have free will in affairs not pertaining to God, but no independent power to affect our own salvation. Thus Gerhard Ebeling writes, "The point at issue between Erasmus and Luther does not lie in the first instance in the evaluation of the free will itself, but in the value of posing the question at all."[18] But this point finally makes all the difference. It is the difference between Erasmus's desire to be prudent even about asserting the possibility of prudence, and Luther's assertion of the impiety of such a desire.[19] It is a difference that is owing finally not to disagreement about whether one interprets Scripture literally or figuratively, but rather to where one locates and how one understands the authoritative standard for interpretation, or the relationship between authority and interpretation, authority and meaning.

Luther believed that God guaranteed the meaning of Scripture. Although the Bible is written in the language of men, God speaks through it incontrovertibly and univocally. Such an intersection of the divine and the human, or eruption of the absolute into the phenomenal context of our lives, cannot help but have a violent effect. To Erasmus's desire for peace Luther objects:

> You do not read or do not observe that it is the most unvarying fate of the Word of God to have the world in a state of tumult because of it. This is plainly asserted by Christ, when he says: "I have not come to bring peace, but a sword" (Matt. 10:34). . . . The world and its god cannot and will not endure the Word of the true God, and also the true God neither will nor can keep silence; so when these two Gods are at war with one another, what can there be but tumult in the whole world? [LE 128–29; WA 626]

Erasmus also believes that God speaks to man in human words, but unlike Luther he holds that man is not capable of a complete or unequivocal understanding of these words, not so much because it is God Who is speaking but because it is man who is interpreting—a distinction Luther would not have allowed insofar as it suggests the reader's participation in deciding the meaning of the text. Amphiboly is not simply brought about by carelessness or ignorance on the part of the reader: it is unavoidable, precisely because there is no authoritative criterion for distinguishing between literal and figurative language. Luther accuses Erasmus of being merely rhetorical and merely prudent: his dislike of assertion betrays an irreligious caution. But Erasmus is prudent in this cautious sense because he does not *know* whether man can exercise the prudence that is right judgment. In the absence of this knowledge, assertion is not only violent but also unjustified; and this, according to other works of Erasmus, is precisely Christ's lesson. For His adoption of human form was not so much the eruption of the absolute into the phenomenal, as a reconciliation of the two through the humble human acknowledgment of our inability to know God. Christ's message is one not of violence but of peace.[20]

In Erasmus's theology, theoretical wisdom or contemplation is supplanted by prudence as an ethical practice that can praise God but cannot conceive Him. With Augustine he says, "I know the love by which I love better than that which I love." The human approximation of Christ's example of accommodation, the *imitatio Christi*, entails the now divinely sanctioned rhetorical principle of decorum, for it is decorum that enables us to accommodate ourselves to different circumstances as Christ accommodated Himself to this world. And just as Erasmus viewed the authority of Scripture as primarily formal, so the authority of Christ's example lies in the formal principle of the *à propos*. *Kairos* is not only the moment of epiphany, but every moment ever after that demands a new response to, and interpretation of, Christ's example. The *Encomium moriae* is just such an act of interpretation. But it is one that in reinterpreting Christ's prudential example, causes us to rethink Erasmus's praise of prudence in the *Diatribe* on free will.

III

Most readers of the *Encomium* agree that the work falls roughly into three parts. The problem is to determine the relation of these sections to each other. And this is not an interpretive problem that can be solved easily, for the shifting tone of the speaker and the changing object of her praise and her irony preclude any simple allegorical translation of her discourse. Nor can we look outside the *Encomium* for an authoritative standard of interpretation, for while Erasmus tells us in the prefatory letter that the *Encomium* should be read as though it were the *Enchiridion*, in the adage *Ollas ostentare* he reminds us that the *Encomium* must be judged by "the fitness of the speech to the speaker." It is not Erasmus who is speaking, but Folly.[21] The question, then, is whether the antinomies of the three parts of this paradoxical encomium can be resolved dialectically—whether, in short, it is possible to give a unified interpretation of the text. In order to begin to consider this question we need to take a closer look at Folly's attitudes toward prudence in each of the three sections.

In the first section, Folly appears as an amiable goddess and rhetorician who praises her followers and the natural and social forms of accommodation that constitute society. It is at the end of this part that she humorously redefines the prudent man as "the fool, who is never restrained from any undertaking whatsoever, neither by modesty (because he has none), nor by danger (to which he pays no attention)" (42).[22] As most critics have noted, this redefinition gains a kind of seriousness when Folly proceeds to criticize the common definition of prudence as good judgment. At first the famous description of human affairs in terms of the Sileni of Alcibiades (42–43; *LB* 4.428 A) suggests that a single reversal of terms will enable us to determine the contents of the box, the truth of the figure, or the true form of prudence. It suggests, in short, that it is possible to read the *Encomium* as *Enchiridion*. But Folly's concept of figuration or indirection is complicated both by the subject of accommodation and by the further analogy she introduces to clarify her point:

> Listen, then, to how I will develop the argument. If someone should try to strip away the costumes and makeup from the actors performing a play on the stage and to display them to the spectators in their own natural appearance, wouldn't he ruin the whole play? Wouldn't all the spectators be right to throw rocks at such a madman and drive him out of the theatre? . . . To destroy the illusions in this fashion would spoil the whole play. [43–44; *LB* 4.428 BC]

With the introduction of the theatrical metaphor the reader is directed to the surface rather than to the inside of the Silenus box, for if the search for the kernel of meaning beneath appearances is indecorous and imprudent, then it is only by the prudent crediting of appearances that consensus and social harmony can be maintained.[23]

If the *Encomium* is (at this moment) a praise of accommodation and prudence, then the description of the wise man anticipates Luther's behavior toward the *Diatribe*:

> If at this moment some wiseman, dropped down directly from heaven, should suddenly jump up and begin shouting that this [theatrical] figure whom everyone reverences as if he were the lord god is not even a man because he is controlled by his passions like an animal . . . or if he should turn to another man who is mourning the death of his parent and tell him to laugh instead because the dead man has at last really begun to live, whereas this life is really nothing but a sort of death . . . what would he accomplish except to make everyone take him for a raving lunatic? [44; *LB* 4.428 D–429 C]

103

Folly's defense against the wise man's charge that theater is an illusion or that consensus is a mere fiction can then be seen to prefigure Diatribe's defense against the hypothesis of free will: "True [Folly admits], all these images are unreal, but this play cannot be performed in any other way" (44; 4.428 D). It is a "false" conception of wisdom to insist on the "truth": "Why keep still," she inquires, "[about a thing which] is 'truer than truth itself'" (45; LB 4.429 D). Folly's summary remarks on prudence in this first section of the Encomium could then be read as a defense of Erasmus's moderate skeptical theology, in which she opposes the accommodation of the prudent man to the assertions of the "wise." The former makes no assertions not simply because to do so would be destructive, but also because he has no basis upon which to make them. As Folly has remarked, the person who tries to do away with illusion is rightly called a madman, since to see life as it really is is to be left with nothing. "True prudence [vere prudentis est]," she concludes, "recognizes human limitations and does not strive to leap beyond them" (44; LB 4.429 C).[24]

While the concern with prudence and decorum carries over into the middle section of the Encomium, the form this concern takes is at odds with Folly's earlier praise of prudence. For in engaging in a medieval satire of ecclesiastical and secular authorities and professions, Folly adopts the stance of the critical wise man she earlier mocked. In the final third of the Encomium Folly's attitude changes once again: far from attacking her followers, as in the second section, or praising them, as in the first, she is concerned with persuading them to accept her claim to authority. She begins by citing proverbs and classical authors, but she is gradually led, by considerations of decorum, to an examination of Scripture: "But perhaps the authority of these [classical] writers is not highly respected among Christians. Therefore, if you please, let us support (or as the learned say, 'ground') our praises from Holy Scripture" (118; LB 4.488 E). After quoting a number of biblical passages, Folly introduces Christ as yet another example of her omnipresence. As a good orator she knows that the example of Christ is the most persuasive one she can present to the Christians in her audience. At the same time, Christ's accommodation offers another instance of Folly's rule of decorum:

Christ, though he was the wisdom of the Father, became somehow foolish in order to relieve folly of mortals when he took on human nature and appeared in the form of a man. . . . Just as he became sin in order to heal sins. Nor did he choose any other way to heal them but through the folly of the cross, through ignorant doltish apostles. For them, too, he carefully prescribed folly, warning them against wisdom, when he set before them the example of children, lilies, mustard seed, and sparrows—stupid creatures lacking all intelligence, leading their lives according to the dictates of nature. [130; LB 4.498 AB]

There is a tension throughout Erasmus's work between Christ as the unique instance of accommodation that sanctions and enables all others and the fact that, as the incarnation of *decorum*, he renders the uniqueness of the metaphysical event less important than its force as an ethical example.[25] Folly's discussion of Christ as *one more type* of accommodation, the one most appropriate for the Christians in her audience, calls attention to the paradox implicit in Erasmus's ethical interpretation of the incarnation. In making Folly refer to Christ as an example of decorum and then portraying the followers of Christ in their refusal to accommodate themselves to this world, Erasmus seems to be acknowledging the force of Luther's radically uncompromising denial of prudence and free will. Thus, while Folly's mock definition of prudence in the first part of the *Encomium* turned out to contain an element of truth, if only because the grounds of truth had themselves been undermined by a skeptical critique of appearance, here Folly's skeptical and prudential authority comes into conflict with an example that is Truth itself. It is an example that affects the second part of the *Encomium* as well, for whereas the satire of professionals and social classes had seemed to preserve the possibility of the sort of accommodating posture adopted by Erasmus and More, in this last part the ideal of prudence as worldly-wise accommodation is put aside:

Paul testifies very clearly on this point when he says "What is foolish to the world, God has chosen," and when he says that God was pleased to save the world through folly because it could not be redeemed by wisdom. Indeed, God himself makes the same point clear enough when he cries out through the mouth of the prophet, "I will destroy the wisdom of the wise and the prudence of the prudent I will reject," and again when he gives thanks that the mystery of salvation has been hidden from the wise and revealed to the simple, that is, to fools. [128–29; LB 4.497 A]

In recalling us to the natural folly of the first section, the analogy between the Christian and the simpleton suggests momentarily another principle of structural and semantic unity: if not prudence then the natural and supernatural rejection of prudence. But a few pages later, even this analogy between Christian and natural folly is revealed to be merely apparent. The natural fool, at least as he is portrayed in the first part of the *Encomium,* is the slave of his bodily needs and passions, while the pious man "flees from whatever is related to the body and is carried away in the pursuit of the eternal and invisible things of the spirit. Hence, since these two groups are in such utter disagreement on all matters, the result is that each thinks the other is insane—though that word applies more properly to the pious man than to ordinary men, if you want my opinion" (136; *LB* 4.502 D). The madness of the Christian fool, who strives to contemplate and enjoy "things as they truly are" (133), sounds remarkably like the uncompromising position of the (Lutheran) critic of prudence, whom Folly describes as "a raving lunatic" (44). Yet, whereas the critic was a spectator (136) of the earthly comedy, the foolish Christian is a participant in spiritual ecstasy. There is nothing compromising, tentative, or prudent about this state.

Readers have had some difficulty reconciling Folly's praise of Christian folly with her earlier praise of natural folly and of prudence, though in recent years a number of critics have interpreted her contradictions dialectically. Although these critics differ about the degree to which the possibility of this dialectical progression is itself finally questioned, they seem to agree on the dialectic itself. Geraldine Thompson writes: "The wisdom of one part is repeatedly made the folly of the next—or, if we use Moria's inversions, the follies of each part become the wisdom of the next. In the last third of the book, the folly of the cross is to resolve the contradictions arraigned in the preceding cycles."[26] Wayne Rebhorn, in an article entitled "The Metamorphoses of Moria: Structure and Meaning in *The Praise of Folly,*"[27] argues for a similar sort of progression. According to Rebhorn, the third section of the *Encomium* is "a direct response to the shifting vision of life presented in the first two sections," one that offers us "a new perspective . . . which transcends the illusory hope of the first section and the horrifying 'reality' of the second. Note that Folly no longer claims man's worship, for Christian folly clearly means worship of God, trust in that which alone is good, stable, and immutable" (471). Rebhorn concludes that "The meaning of the *Praise* . . . does not reside in the complex irony of the first part or the straight invective of the middle or even the

106

Christian transvaluation at the end. The meaning is the total structure, the process of movement itself, which leads from comedy to tragedy and then beyond" (472). This interpretation makes both the portrayal of Christ's humble accommodation and the ecstatic movement of the third part reconcilable with the prudence of the first: the Christian would live prudently by playing the comedy of life while recognizing its limitations.[28]

Finally, while W. David Kay does not make the same points about the progress of the *Encomium* as Thompson and Rebhorn, he shares their willingness to determine the unified meaning of Erasmus's "learned joking."[29] Kay argues that Folly's deliberate perversion of familiar classical and humanist arguments allows the reader to perceive Erasmus's unambiguous intention behind her intentional ambiguities: "Folly's misuse of humanistic learning continually encourages an evaluative response, and it is not the least of the work's paradoxes that her foolish praise of irrationality is responsible for exercising the reader's own reason" (260). Although Kay admits that Folly's discussion of the foolish prudence of accommodation makes the choice of higher folly "far more complicated than it seems in the *Enchiridion*" (261), he concludes that the portrayal of More in the prefatory epistle is Erasmus's "way of reminding his readers that we need not choose, as Folly insists we must, between wisdom and our humanity, but can hope to combine them both as his friend More has done" (263).

This remark returns us to the problem of interpretation posed at the beginning of this chapter, that is, whether we are to take the references to prudence and decorum in the prefatory letter and the letter to Dorp as a model of interpretation or as an expression of Erasmus's reluctance to publish his paradox to the world. On the basis of Erasmus's own view of interpretation,[30] we might well credit this letter with authority without assuming that it offers us the key to interpreting either it or the *Encomium*. Why, Folly might inquire, should we trust the prudential figure that Erasmus impersonates in this letter any more than we would trust the critic of prudence in the *Encomium*? Yet to the extent that the critics I have cited propose a dialectical synthesis for the *Encomium*, they are guided by the considerations of prudence that Folly praises in the end of the first part of her speech. They assume that because Erasmus speaks for prudence in the majority of his works, he must really intend to speak on its behalf in the *Encomium* as well. Yet, as Clarence H. Miller writes in his introduction to the new Latin edition of the *Encomium*, "When Folly uses the same [Platonic] ideas [as Erasmus does in the *Enchiridion*] in the last part of the *Moria* to explain the notion of the Christian fool, our experience of her ironical and inconsistent use of Plato ought to alert us not to take her idea of Platonic love and of the Christian fool as absolutely identical with Erasmus's" (20).[31] It is true that the fictional persona of Folly is not identical with Erasmus, but the more pressing question for the interpreter is whether Erasmus is identical with himself. Why should we assume that he was always comfortable with or confident of his moderate skeptical position? As he tells us himself in the *Diatribe*, the dislike of assertions necessarily involves the willingness to examine one's own views along with those of others.

On the other hand, if we cannot rely on Erasmus's letters, neither can we appeal to Folly to resolve the problem of interpretation, since she is, by her own admission, an unreliable narrator. In the satirical middle section of her speech Folly turns into a critical "wise man," disrupting the illusion of harmony she had created in the first section; and in the final section she attacks both the hubris of that critical stance and the accommodating prudence of the first section. But, although she presents herself as a very Erasmian figure of accommodation and learned ignorance, her final examination of Christian folly destroys the possibility of totalization that the dialectical progression of her speech has seemed to promise. To view this final criticism as the dialectical synthesis of the previous two sections is to absolve Erasmus of blame at the very moment when Folly is most accusatory, and prudently to resolve the paradox of Christ at the very moment when Folly is most insistent upon it. It is here that the principle of decorum breaks down—both in terms of the relation of this praise of Christian folly to the rest of Folly's speech and in terms of the peculiar sort of unworldly accommodation that Christian folly involves. The simile of common folly and divine madness is a trope whose place or common ground is utopic, as Folly herself may indicate in several genealogical clues (her home is the Blessed Isles); and the failure of a peaceful resolution of the two makes the *Encomium* symptomatic of the greater difficulties of Erasmus's Christian humanism.[32]

The problems involved in the *Encomium*'s analogy of natural and Christian folly take the form elsewhere in Erasmus's work of an attempted reconciliation of piety and learning. In the *Encomium*

Erasmus partially signals his awareness of these difficulties by having Folly satirize the scholar who, like Erasmus, defends the Christian faith with humanist weapons. A. H. T. Levi writes in his introduction to the *Encomium moriae*: "Folly proclaims the virtues of the religious ideal in which Erasmus was brought up, in terms which exclude the possibility of defending it in the way Erasmus had dedicated his life to defending it."[33] In light of what Folly actually says, this may be true; but when we consider the way in which she speaks, the issue becomes more complicated, since the wealth of classical and Christian allusion testifies to a great deal of learning on Erasmus's part (as he does not hesitate to tell us in the prefatory letter and the letter to Dorp): it is itself an emblem of *docta ignorantia*. The problem is not one of exclusion but one of contradictory inclusion, since the conflict between Christian folly and the classical ideals of decorum and prudence is apparent not only in the thematic ridicule of the scholar but, more important, in the form of the work, which forces us to examine the appropriateness of the choice of a figure of decorum to expound, at least in part, the teaching of Christ.

Yet while in the last third of the *Encomium* Folly seems to anticipate Luther's criticisms of the *Diatribe*, it is impossible to say that this self-castigation is the meaning of the *Encomium*. The juxtaposition of the Christian wise fool and the folly of classical prudence in a single figure works to create a skeptical logic of contradiction rather than Luther's monologic discourse of assertions. One could argue that, like Quintilian's rhetoric,[34] Folly cannot contradict herself because she is herself the figure of contradiction: "I am no counterfeit," she informs us, "nor do I carry one thing in my looks and another in my breast. No, I am in every respect so like myself that neither can they dissemble me who arrogate to themselves the appearance and title of wise men."[35] Thus, although Folly seems at several points to be speaking in the medieval tradition of the wise fool—the fool who can speak the truth without recrimination because she is by definition not taken seriously—in the long run neither the structure of the *Encomium* nor the figure of Folly can be understood, like the Silenus box, as a simple strategy of indirection according to which, by a final ironic twist, a mock encomium (of human folly) is turned into a real encomium (of Christian folly). For if the mock encomium in the end self-destructs, the question is still whether it does so in the way Christ takes leave of his disciples in the *Enchiridion,* in order to make the prudential, ethical task more apparent, or in a way that dramatizes the impossibility of prudence and the superfluousness of letters, not least of all the letters of the *Encomium.* If the former is the case, if the *Encomium* is read as *Enchiridion,* then Folly's learned joking will have served not to castigate learning but to exalt it; will Erasmus then, ironically enough, have effected the reconciliation of sacred and secular scriptures, piety and prudence, truth and appearance, that Folly criticizes in her praise of Christianity?

Folly does direct us back to the world of appearance in her peroration, but she can do so only because she has forgotten the Lutheran absolutism of her final praise of Christianity. Similarly, one could argue, the critic who effects a reconciliation of the different parts of her speech must forget that they are irreconcilable. And he forgets because this return to the realm of appearance is characteristic of Erasmus's work as a whole, that is, of the attempt to reconcile Christianity with classical letters. In a different context, Montaigne has described a structurally similar task as "faire valoir la vanité" (to show vanity to advantage).[36] From the "perspective" of the absolute, secular literature and human activity are vanity.[37] From the perspective of reason, sacred Scripture is foolish. To "faire valoir" sacred Scripture is hubristic, while the same attempt with respect to secular scripture is necessarily self-defeating: pagan literature is useful only insofar as it is transcended.[38] Enjoyed for itself, it is a form of vanity, although appropriate to the vanity of this life. But just as fideism frees reason for secular speculation that may ultimately oppose its own conclusions to the resolution of faith, so, Folly implies, the peaceful coexistence of Christian and classical letters, of piety and prudence, may finally prove to be a subtle form of violence.[39]

The difficulties of Erasmus's ideal of reconciliation can be further exemplified on the microcosmic grammatical level by comparing the subjective and objective genitive of the *Moriae encomium* to Luther's very different understanding of the genitive.[40] For Luther was also aware of the theological and ontological implications of this grammatical hinge. In the famous introduction to his Latin works, he writes that he could not understand the passage in *Romans* (1.17)[41] concerning the justice of God until he realized that justice was not to be thought of in human terms as the meting out of punishment and reward according to one's deserts, but rather as the justifying of man by God (*WA* 54.165–66). The correct reading of *iustitia Dei* then led to a similar understanding of *virtus Dei*, *gloria Dei*, and so on, that is, to an understanding of the subjective genitive in theological discourse, which meant, paradoxically, an understanding of the incomprehensibility of God's ways.[42]

Erasmus's customary reading of the genitive was completely contrary to Luther's radical isolation of man in the face of God and his refusal of human intellection. In the best of all possible worlds (of all possible *words*), the "of" in the *Praise of Folly* would function temporally and copulatively to permit a response to and integration of the classical tradition, a response that would be appropriate to our inescapably human and temporal existence. We need all the help we can get; it would be foolish indeed to reject both the recreative and authoritative resources of the past.

But to Luther it is precisely this utopian suspension bridge that betrays the hubris of Erasmus's skepticism, for the power of attribution (of "of") belongs properly to God alone. This power is the crux of the debate on free will, where the issue is whether free will can be attributed to man without God's grace, whether man can attribute free will to himself. Luther challenges Erasmus to prove this attribution:

> If from such a series of ages, men and everything else you have mentioned, you can show one work (if only the lifting of a straw from the ground), or one word (if only the syllable "my"),[43] or one thought (if only the faintest sigh), arising from the power of free choice, by which they have applied themselves to grace or merited the Spirit or obtained pardon or done anything alongside God, however slight . . . then again you shall be the victors and we the vanquished. (*LE* 147–48; *WA* 643)

For Luther, however, post-lapsarian man no longer has the power to attribute predicates freely to himself. He is subject to the Devil, bound by his own sinful nature, and incapable of affecting his own salvation in any way (*LE* 175). In this world the words "free will" no longer have a referent: their proper meaning is nowhere realized among men. It is for this reason that Luther accuses Erasmus over and over again of employing a meaningless term, "a voice and nothing more," an "empty name" (*LE* 175–76, 181). Thus, when Erasmus writes "I shall make full use of the authority [*abutor*] of the Fathers who say that there are certain seeds of virtue implanted in the minds of men by which they in some way see and seek after virtue" (*LE* 76), Luther retorts that this authority by consensus is as catachrestic, as abusive and utopian as the "neutral ground" (*LE* 294) that Erasmus claims for human judgment: "'Meanwhile' you seek to 'make full use of' [*vis abuti*] the authority of the Fathers who say that 'there are certain seeds of virtue implanted in the minds of men.' First, if that is what you want, as far as we are concerned you may use or abuse [*abutaris*] the authority of the Fathers; but you should take note of what you believe when you believe men who are expressing their own ideas without the word of God" (*LE* 277; *WA* 744–45). There is no neutral ground for Luther, there is only the paradox; there is no rule of the appropriate (*LE* 132–33), but only Christ's exhortation to be "urgent out of season" (*LE* 106).

By insisting on the absolute difference between God and man, and the absurdity and offensiveness to reason of the incarnation (*LE* 230–31), Luther implies the sacrilege of those prudential fictions (*LE* 177) which are designed to reconcile men in and to this world by obscuring the folly of the next. And in pointing up the contradictions in Erasmus's argument for free will (the embedding of a discussion of the hypothetical value of free will within an assertion of the dangers involved in such a discussion; claiming that free will has no power and can yet do something), Luther also comments on the self-destructing operation of Folly's praise of prudence.

This turn to the debate on free will in a discussion of the *Encomium* is suggested not only by Luther's characterization of witless Diatribe, but also by the structure of Erasmus's argument in the two works. Both the *Encomium* and the *Diatribe* are examples of the kind of argument by contraries that Henri Estienne proposed in his 1562 preface to *Hypotyposes pyrrhoniens* of Sextus Empiricus. The Christian apology for the publication of this pagan work was that the believer could counter the excesses of dogmatic philosophy with the deliberately excessive logic of skepticism (which argued by contraries) and thus make room for faith. So, if we can believe the prefatory letter, the *Encomium* fights folly with folly (4) just as the *Diatribe* would ideally fight its own assertions as well as Luther's with its praise of skepticism, and in both cases this rhetoric is defended as that which is most appropriate. If the *Encomium* is read as the *Enchiridion*, all three works could then be considered as Erasmian imitations of Christ, Himself interpreted as a figure of rhetorical argumentation and decorum: Christ too argues by contraries, whether in taking on sin to rid us of sin, or in absenting Himself from His disciples in order to make Himself more forcefully present. And just as Estienne's "cure" destroys itself, so does Christ's incarnation. He takes on sin because this is the most appropriate way to set an example, and He leaves his disciples because this too is the most appropriate way to persuade us to action. But as a figure of decorum, Christ calls attention to the difficulties and dangers of (our) imitation. How do we know, both Luther and Folly seem to be asking, that this kind of argumentation necessarily results in faith? If Christ, according to the *Enchiridion*, urges us by a self-destructing rhetorical proposition to realize prudence in our own lives, what is there to keep us from understanding that what is most appropriate to human existence is that all propositions, even that of our imitation of Christ, necessarily self-destruct? One reading of the *Encomium* might then argue that while the speech is structured by contraries, the effect is not to preserve the realm of prudence and decorum, but to destroy it altogether.

The *Encomium* is finally the dialogic text par excellence, though in a sense that forces us to question the assumptions of the Quattrocento humanistic dialogue. Read in one way, the natural folly of the first section and the Christian folly of the third are alike in criticizing and containing the delusions of the middle. Read in another, these two sections represent the antinomy of rhetoric and religion, prudence and faith. For although the work is described in the letters to More and Dorp as though it were a Silenus figure that concealed a religious truth, it turns out that when the figure is destroyed (as it seems to be in the third section), so is the message of reconciliation or accommodation. But natural folly does not then give way to Christian folly, nor false encomium to real (which would presume that the praise of natural folly was not serious); the analogy of decorum and folly is not structured according to the medieval analogy of cause and effect (which would allow us to privilege one term, the cause, as ontologically superior), but as an apparent likeness, the perception and evaluation of which depends on the reader. There is no consensus of interpretation for the *Moriae encomium*.

The similarity of Christ and Folly, according to this reading, is that both are figures of contradiction, which can be interpreted either as figures of reconciliation or as paradoxes. Folly thus becomes a figure for the paradox at the very heart of the project of reconciliation that informs all of Erasmus's work. For the problems of choosing a figure of prudence and decorum to eulogize Christian folly are analogous to those of using classical letters as a propaedeutic to faith. The problem is not simply that Folly's classical perspective acts as a solvent on Christian values, and therefore implicitly questions the usefulness of classical letters, but also that, in speaking as Folly, she ironizes the classical patrimony of such ideas as prudence and the *consensus omnium*. The paradoxical structure of the *Encomium* points to this abyss between the sacred and the profane that generations of theologians before Erasmus, and Erasmus himself in most of his lifework, had tried to bridge, and that is itself a function of the paradox of the incarnation at the center of Christianity. Thus, ironically, to interpret Christ as the paradigm of decorum, to understand Christ formally, at least in part, as a figure of reconciliation between God and man, allows for the suspension of conclusions that we know as Pyrrhonist skepticism. Similarly, one might argue, the interpreter's effort to maintain the analogy between natural and Christian folly forces him to adopt Erasmus's own moderate skeptical viewpoint. But Folly's Lutheran critique of skepticism argues as well that in refusing to provide a univocal meaning, to fix the object (or subject) of the encomium, Folly has indirectly illustrated Luther's view of Christ: as an example that cannot be imitated, or an interpretive paradox that cannot be prudently resolved.

5 Montaigne: A Rhetoric of Skepticism

Sin aliquis exstiterit aliquando qui Aristotelio more de omnibus rebus in utramque sententiam possit dicere et in omni causa duas contrarias orationes praeceptis illius cognitis explicare, aut hoc Arcesilae modo et Carneadis contra omne quod propositum sit disserat, quique ad eam rationem adiungat hunc usum exercitationemque dicendi, is sit verus, is perfectus, is solus orator. [If there has really been a person who was able in Aristotelian fashion to speak on both sides about every subject and by means of knowing Aristotle's rules to reel off two speeches on opposite sides of every case, or in the manner of Arcesilas and Carneades argue against every statement put forward, and who to that method adds the experience and practice [*usum exercitationemque*] in speaking indicated, he would be the one and only true and perfect orator.]

—Cicero, *De oratore*

Montaigne's *Essais*[1] provide us with one of the most forceful sixteenth-century critiques of the humanist faith in the power of rhetoric to persuade to the good. Yet while readers of Montaigne are familiar with his characterization of rhetoric as "un'art piperesse et mensongere" (a lying and deceitful art [1.51.292]), as well as with his disparaging remarks about Cicero's verbiage (2.10.393) and about the specialized and barren knowledge of rhetoricians and grammarians, the more interesting and more radical criticism of rhetoric is not found in these thematic statements, but in the form and practice (the *exercitation*) of the essay itself. For while Montaigne borrows the *in utramque partem* method of arguing from the Academic skeptic and the classical orator, he does not share their conviction that this form of argument will allow one to arrive at some approximation of the truth.[2] Neither is the training in this method of arguing simply preliminary to being able to argue most effectively with respect to a given case. Montaigne's usual practice is rather that of the Pyrrhonist who argues both sides of a case in order to suspend the possibility of judgment or persuasion to action altogether. It is this skeptical practice of writing that redefines the possibility of prudence as it was classically and humanistically conceived.

Consider, for example, Montaigne's most famous skeptical text, the "Apologie de Raimond Sebond." Sebond claimed to defend natural theology, to prove the legibility of the created world on the basis of natural reason. Montaigne's apology for this claim, like so many apologies, is both a defense of and a defense against his subject since, according to Montaigne, Sebond's arguments can only be supported by being suspended. Accordingly, Montaigne first argues against those critics of Sebond who claim that reason has no role to play in Christian apologetics, then against those who claim that Sebond's reasons are not good, but ultimately against both Sebond and his critics by undermining the claims of reason altogether. Arguments are being marshaled in service neither of the truth nor necessarily of Christian faith, the possibility of which, as befits a Pyrrhonist mode of argumentation, is usually referred to in the conditional or the subjunctive (e.g., 2.12.418, 421). This desperate strategy (*un coup desesperé* [2.12.540]) of a defense that succeeds only by destroying the very possibility of defense is one of the most obvious examples of the skeptical rhetoric that Montaigne was attempting to practice in the *Essais*. That he was not unaware of the difficulties of this practice is clear from the following passage in the "Apologie":

> Our speech has its weaknesses and its defects, like all the rest. Most of the occasions for the troubles of the world are grammatical. Our lawsuits spring only from debate over the interpretation of the laws, and most of our wars from the inability to express clearly the conventions and treaties of agreement of princes. How many quarrrels, and how important, have been produced in the world by doubt of the meaning of that syllable *Hoc!* Let us take the sentence that logic itself offers us as the clearest. If you say "It is fine weather," and if you are speaking the truth, then it is fine weather. Isn't that a sure way of speaking? Still it will deceive us. To show this let us continue the example. If you say "I lie," and if you are speaking the truth, then you lie. The art, the reason, the force, of the conclusion of this one are the same as in the

other; yet there we are stuck in the mud. I can see why the Pyrrhonian philosophers cannot express their general conception in any manner of speaking; for they would need a new language. Ours is wholly formed of propositions, which to them are utterly repugnant; so that when they say "I doubt," immediately you have them by the throat to make them admit that at least they know and are sure of this fact, that they doubt. [2.12.392; 508]

Since someone is bound to interpret the form of the proposition logically, and thus as an assertion of knowledge, the Pyrrhonist cannot state his doubt "directly." One is tempted to say that the use of grammar involves him in an inescapable contradiction between grammar and meaning, and renders his sentence meaningless, or at least subverts his apparent intention so that his meaning can only be secured indirectly or figuratively. And yet it is not so much that the language itself is assertive as that it is interpreted this way, that priority is given to the form of the proposition. The skeptic is thus forced to "clarify" his meaning, not by denying the contradiction between the assertive form of the proposition and the meaning of his statement, but by making it even more obvious: by insisting on the rhetorical dimension of his sentence by recourse to a more recognizable figure: "Thus they have been constrained to take refuge in this comparison from medicine, without which their attitude would be inexplicable: when they declare 'I do not know' or 'I doubt,' they say that this proposition carries itself away with the rest, no more nor less than rhubarb, which expels evil humors and carries itself off with them" (2.12.392–93; 508).[3] Yet, if this is metaphor, it is a metaphor that transports itself. The phrase "I doubt" is not simply a figurative statement that indirectly represents another signified, and so it cannot be clarified by recourse to a comparison. The apparent contradiction between grammar and meaning forces us to seek an interpretation of a seemingly straightforward sentence; and yet the contradiction, rather than generating some new, indirect significance (such as the skeptic knows he doubts), seems to swallow up the possibility of any such inference. Insofar as the skeptic knows nothing, there is nothing he can name; and all the names he uses name nothing. The image of the rhubarb is in one sense a figurative use of language, since it depends on our ability to perceive the analogy between the purgative effects of rhubarb and the correct reading of the skeptic's proposition; but it is a self-destroying or self-purging figure, for even as it relies on the notion of a literal meaning

117

and the trope of analogy, it figures the skeptic's proposition and so the impossibility of naming that which would be indirectly signified. In short, the skeptic's proposition is not literal, since this would presuppose the possibility of knowledge, but it is also not figurative, since there can be no literal meaning to which the figure refers.

Montaigne offers his own solution to the problem: "This idea is more firmly grasped in the form of interrogation: 'What do I know?'—the words I bear as a motto, inscribed over a pair of scales" (393; 508). At first glance the balance or scale appears to be an example of figurative language: it stands for the activity of judgment, and it is the traditional understanding of judgment as the adequation of a statement to an objective state of affairs that enables us to justify this interpretation. Yet as all of the *Essais* redefine this activity, so the image of the balance destroys both the traditional idea of judgment and its own rhetorical function as an illustration of that judgment.

The image of the scale is an ambiguous one. On the one hand it belongs to the scientific world of quantitative measurement (the weight of the objects themselves would incline the scale one way or another); hence the use of the scale to symbolize the impartiality of justice. Yet in Montaigne's scheme, inclination can only be the result of human prejudice. Thus, the figurative understanding of the scale is misleading, for in the binary opposition of the two objects to be weighed, it neglects the third term, which is consciousness. It is not the intrinsic properties of the objects that incline the scale one way or another, but the individual who judges. In this way the normal function of the scale (precisely *to* incline) becomes a sign of its malfunction. The two sides will remain equal only if one doesn't attempt to measure.

It is at the end of the "Apologie" that Montaigne meditates on the consequences of the skeptic's denial of an authoritative standard of judgment for the practice of rhetoric and of his own narration:

> Finally, there is no existence that is constant, either of our being or of that of objects. And we, and our judgment, and all mortal things go on flowing and rolling unceasingly. . . .
> But together with its *being the same*, it also changes its simple *being*, from one thing always becoming another. And consequently the senses of nature are mistaken and lie, taking what appears for what is, for want of really knowing what it is that *is*. But then what really is? That which is eternal. [2.12.455–56; 586–87]

Since being is eternal, temporality is a condition only of that which is not: narrative and identity for Montaigne are mutually exclusive: "And as for these words, *present, immediate, now,* on which it seems that we chiefly found and support our understanding of time, reason discovering this immediately destroys it; for she at once splits and divides it into future and past, as though wanting to see it necessarily divided into two. The same thing happens to nature that is measured, as to time that measures it" (2.12.456–57; 588). With these remarks in mind, we can turn to the narrative of "De l'exercitation" (2.6), an essay whose very title suggests all the various kinds of exercise, practice, or experience that go into the making of a good orator—the exercising of one's natural faculties of reason, judgment, and memory through the practice of reading and writing, and through those preliminary Academic exercises of arguing on both sides which Cicero describes in *De oratore.* The reading of this essay will in turn affect our understanding of the *Essais* as a whole, for it is precisely the extent to which the central part of "De l'exercitation" is taken up with the narration of a single event— Montaigne's violent fall from his horse—that it dramatizes, more strikingly than any other essay, both the criticism of Ciceronian rhetoric and the skeptical practice of narration that follows from the Pyrrhonist epistemology of the "Apologie."

I

It will be helpful to begin with a brief discussion of the two related assumptions about language that Sextus criticizes in the *Outlines of Pyrrhonism,* since they go a long way toward explaining the various rhetorical strategies of the essay.[4] According to Sextus's account of the Stoic theory of language, signs may be either associative or indicative. The first represent things that are only temporarily nonevident (as smoke signals the existence of fire); the second things that can never be evident, such as abstract ideas. The examples Sextus gives of the indicative sign are those bodily motions which serve as signs of the soul. He tells us, furthermore, that the indicative sign can be viewed as an effect that is the sign of its cause.[5] "A theory of signs," for the Stoic, "is thus analogous to a doctrine of evidence. It furnishe[s] a way of proceeding by inference from what is immediately given to the unperceived."[6] (The same structure of causality which informs this view of the indicative sign allows the reader to posit the author as the cause of the text and to conceive of the passage of time as a continuous chain of consequences in which practice can be a progressive activity—a notion very much at odds with Montaigne's own remarks about the passage of time at the end of the "Apologie.")

The Pyrrhonist offers a number of arguments against the Stoic theory of the indicative sign, claiming among other things that an antecedent cannot be known unless its consequent is known at the same time (117); an argument that also applies to the notion of cause and effect. That which is nonevident cannot be a sign, because it will always need an apparent sign in order to be apprehended, but the apparent sign can never designate the nonevident unless the non-evident appears along with its sign.

Sextus's skeptical critique of causality and of the indicative sign as an effect of a hidden cause is instructive with respect to Montaigne's essay, since what is most striking about Montaigne's narration is his concern with the physical effects of his accident, and the interpretation to which those effects are subject. But what interests us in the pages that follow is not only Montaigne's implication of Sextus's arguments against the indicative sign and causality in his thematic remarks on the involuntary movements of the body, but also the way in which Montaigne's own writing becomes a body as well, one that literally embodies this skeptical critique. If we remember that Cicero spoke of vigorous rhetoric in terms of a strong and healthy body (*Brutus* 9.36, 16.64, 17.68; *Orator* 23.76), Montaigne's essay reads as an attack on the metaphorical body of rhetoric by means of a Pyrrhonist account of the rhetoric of the actual body.

The first sentences of the essay seem to be in agreement with Cicero's assumptions about the nature and necessity of practice, not only with respect to rhetorical excellence but also with respect to excellence in one's life, for Montaigne begins by asserting that the feebleness of our reason necessitates our learning by experience: "Reasoning and education, though we are willing to put our trust in them, can hardly be powerful enough to lead us to action, unless besides we exercise and form our soul by experience to the way we want it to go" (2.6.267; 350). The insistence is on the active life and on the necessity of training the will by repeated exercise. But there is one thing for which we cannot prepare ourselves by practicing, and that is death: "But for dying, which is the greatest task we have to perform, practice [*l'exercitation*] cannot help us. . . . We can try [*essayer*] it only once" (2.6.267; 350). Death is the limit of experience. We may approach the experience of it, Montaigne tells us, in thinking about sleep or about a violent accident, but the "passage" itself (see 3.2.611; 782) cannot be conceived or expressed, not only for the obvious reason that no one has returned from death to tell us about it, but also because language by its very nature articulates its subject in a syntactical and temporal line. We can experience only that which we can be conscious of, and this experience involves the discursive activity of the imagination. Hence Montaigne rightly says that it is not death itself that we fear, but our imaginative approximation of it.

But if death cannot be practiced in the rhetorical sense, it can nevertheless be approached or anticipated: "It seems to me, however, that there is a certain way of familiarizing ourselves with death and trying it out to some extent. . . . And if we do not penetrate as far as its fort, at least we shall see and become acquainted with [*prattiquerons*] the approaches to it" (2.6.268; 351). As Seneca writes, "For by looking forward to whatever can happen as though it would happen, . . . [one] will soften the attacks of all ills."[7] Here the rhetorical notion of practice merges with that of the Stoic meditation on death. In both cases the assumption is that virtue and judgment can be perfected by continual exercise, and that the two are inseparable.[8] But as we shall see, the interest of Montaigne's narrative strategy is that, unlike Seneca's, it takes the form not of a meditation on or anticipation of his future death, but rather of an anticipation of the past. For while the closest approximation of death, as Montaigne tells us, is a violent accident, the paradox of such an accident is that it cannot, properly speaking, be experienced when it occurs: it can only be experienced retrospectively, not literally but figuratively, as the use of the word *tomber* in the following lines reveals:

But those who by some violent accident have fallen [*tombez*] into a faint and lost all sensation, those, in my opinion, have been very close to seeing death's true and natural face. For as for the instant and point of passing away, it is not to be feared that it carries with it any travail or pain, since we can have no feeling without leisure. Our sufferings need time, which in death is so short and precipitate that it must necessarily be imperceptible. It is the approaches that we have to fear; and these may fall [*tomber*] within our experience. [2.6.268; 351–52]

In this essay, death apparently has the status that the external world has for the skeptic. It is that which can never be known but which, according to the Academic skeptic (and to Montaigne at this point in his narrative), can be approximated. If we cannot have access to the truth, we can have access to some likeness of it. And yet, if everything is always changing for the skeptic—always "autre d'un autre," as he tells us in the "Apologie" (587)—then, contrary to what Montaigne says in the beginning of "De l'exercitation," death can have no special privilege in only being able to be tried (*essayé*) once. The repetition of "l'exercitation" can never be cumulative, and cannot lead to greater experience or self-knowledge, and this will prove to be as true of narration as it is of death; for the fact that death cannot be practiced but can be essayed suggests that the impossibility of narrating one's death may provide the model for the practice of writing which is the *essai*.

Montaigne begins his story proper by telling us how he was thrown from his horse when he was overturned by another horse and rider, "so that there lay the horse bowled over and stunned, and I ten or twelve paces beyond, dead, stretched on my back" (2.6.269; 353). If it is true that experience requires time, then it would seem that one could only experience such an accident after the fact, when one had regained consciousness and the power of reflection. Montaigne suggests as much in the course of his narration. Still, since he tells us early in the essay that no one has returned from death "nous en dire les nouvelles" (to tell us news of it," 350), we suspect even at this point that it is only in the role of a *revenant* that he could describe his actions at the time.

He then tries to explain the way he felt before having regained complete consciousness—a state that might be described as the somatic equivalent of the Pyrrhonist skeptic's rhetoric *in utramque partem:* suspended halfway between life and death, between presence and absence of mind (353). As though to signal his lack of consciousness or of judgment at the time of the event, he momentarily cedes the authority of narration to Tasso by inserting two quotations that not only suspend the author's own discourse but also describe his dubious state:

> Perche, dubbiosa anchor del suo ritorno,
> Non s'assecura attonita la mente.
> [Because the shaken soul, uncertain yet

122

Of its return, is still not firmly set;]

come quel ch'or apre or chiude
Gli occhi, mezzo tra'l sonno e l'esser desto.
[as one 'twixt wakefulness and doze,
Whose eyes now open, now again they close (269; 353)]

Shortly after this, there is a digression on the subject of the uncon-scious movements of those who are "prostrate and comatose as their end approaches" (270; 354). In a paragraph that recalls Sextus's critique of the indicative sign, Montaigne argues that these wounded and dying individuals gives the signs (*signes*) of con-sciousness (271; 354) but are not conscious. They sigh and groan, their limbs move, and they even on occasion give forth "short and incoherent words and replies" (271; 355), but none of this is evi-dence that they are fully awake. Further on he tells us: "Thus those who are falling throw out their arms in front of them, by a natural impulse which makes our limbs lend each other their services and have stirrings apart from our discourse [des agitations à part de nostre discours]" (2.6.271, 355).

By the time we have arrived at this last mention of *discours* we know that the agitations we have apart from the *discours* that is reason may include the *discours* that is speech. Thus Montaigne, returning home in a stupor after the accident, orders that a horse be brought for his wife, without being conscious of so doing: "It would seem that this consideration must have proceeded from a wide-awake soul; yet the fact is that I was not there at all. These were idle thoughts, in the clouds, set in motion by the sensations of the eyes and ears; they did not come from within me. . . . These are slight effects which the senses produce of themselves, as if by habit [ce sont des legiers effects que les sens produisoyent d'eux-mesmes, comme d'un usage]" (2.6.271–72; 356). By this account, when intention no longer governs the body, the body itself becomes the producer of meaning or of the effects of intention: "les sens [se] produisoyent d'eux-mesmes."[9]

That the external signs of consciousness (including the written signs of the essay) are not evidence of consciousness is apparent not only in the events following the accident but also in Montaigne's *narration* of the accident. He has already written a full page before he comes to his first thought: "The first thought that came to me was that I had gotten a harquebus shot in the head; indeed several were being fired around us at the time of the accident" (269; 353–54). And he eventually tells us, "I do not want to forget this, that the last thing I was able to recover was the memory of this accident" (272; 357). But there are earlier moments where the authority of the narration is revealed to be "autre." While describing how he demanded a horse for his wife, Montaigne remarks that he knows this from others ("They say . . ." [271; 356]). And he finally confesses, "I had people repeat to me several times where I was going, where I was coming from, at what time it had happened to me, before I could take it in" (272; 357). Although the syntax of this last sentence would seem to suggest that Montaigne's memory of the accident was only confirmed by its subsequent narration by others, the final clause reveals that memory is an effect rather than a cause of narration. The narration of the accident can then be seen as a variation on reported speech, an ironic version of the rhetorical *exercitatio* that may involve the repetition of another's words.[10] In short, Montaigne does not recognize or remember the events of the accident, but anticipates them retrospectively, as it were, on the basis of its effects (on others at the time, and on him through their narration).

Montaigne's "forme d'escrire douteuse" (doubtful form of writing [2.12.489]) is thus not only apparent in the subject matter of his narration and in his practice of citation (a practice that includes his own words to the extent that "ils ne venoyent pas de chez moy" [they didn't come from me]). His ironic embodiment of the skeptic's arguing on both sides of the question (if the question here is understood to be that of the epistemological and temporal status of the accident) is evident as well in a curious ambiguity of syntax and temporality: "Cette recordation que j'en ay fort empreinte en mon ame, me representant son visage et son idée si près du naturel, me concilie aucunement à elle" (This recollection, which is strongly implanted on my soul, showing me the face and idea of death so true to nature, reconciles me to it somewhat [353, cf. 357–58; 269]). In one interpretation, remembrance and representation have effected some kind of partial reconciliation with death, which is mentioned in the previous sentence. But in the present sentence the grammatical subject of "me representant son visage et son idée si près du naturel" is ambiguous (an ambiguity that is necessarily lost in English translation); and the absence of a direct reference to death in this sentence makes us question whether the "naturel" that Montaigne has drawn near to is death or the accident itself, which he is only now remembering. The narrator seems to be describing an event that is located properly speaking neither in the past nor in the present. He can only draw near to the event from the distance of reflection—a narrative distance in this case, which is the temporal equivalent of our inability to know "le naturel." A little further on Montaigne writes of the accident, "Or, à present que je l'ay essayé par effect, je ne fay nul doubte que je n'en ay bien jugé jusqu'à cette heure" (Now I have no doubt, now that I have tried this out by experience, that I judged this matter rightly all along [355; 271]),[11] situating the moment of consciousness in the present of writing; and later, in describing the way in which he remembers the collision, he imagines how it would have seemed had he been able to experience it:

> But a long time after, and the next day, when my memory came to open up and picture to me the state I had been in at the instant I had perceived that horse bearing down on me (for I had seen him at my heels and thought I was a dead man, but that thought had been so sudden that I had no time to be afraid), it seemed to me that a flash of lightning was striking my soul with a violent shock, and that I was coming back from the other world. [2.6.272; 357]

Here once again it is hard to know whether the flash of lightning that struck him down was due to the original collision or to the act of memory, but this uncertainty is precisely the point. It is only in the *essai* that the accident can be experienced.

The effect of Montaigne's narration up to this point is to induce a suspension of judgment in the reader about the truth value of the extratextual event, or of the essay as an accurate representation of Montaigne's own intention as a writer. But if Montaigne cannot claim authority for the narrated events, he can at least claim a kind of value for their repetition: "This account of so trivial an event would be rather pointless, were it not for the instruction that I have derived from it for myself. . . . And yet it should not be held against me if I publish what I write. What is useful to me may also by accident [*par accident*] be useful to another" (2.6.272; 357). We are reminded here of the conclusion of "De la force de l'imagination," an ironic defense of poetry (which anticipates the concluding pages of "De l'exercitation") where Montaigne refuses to take responsibility not only for the moral interest of his tale (1.21.104), but also for its truthfulness. He claims only his faithful representation of another text, another writer's account of fabulous events, and even then he cannot guarantee the truth of this claim. Like a true skeptic, he can only say that it appears this way to him: "In the examples that I bring in here of what I have heard, done, or said, I have forbidden myself to dare to alter even the slightest and most inconsequential circumstances. My conscience does not falsify one iota; my knowledge, I don't know" (1.21.76; 104).

And yet it is just this skeptical suspension of the claim to truth that allows for Montaigne's ironic defense of the poetry of the *Essais*. Truthfulness, we discover, is irrelevant to moral profit: "Fabulous testimonies, provided they are possible, serve like true ones" (1.21.75; 104). Thus, although Montaigne also refuses to assume responsibility for the *possibilité* or likelihood of the events he recounts, this is something the reader may assume for himself. The epistemological question of truth or falsehood gives way to Sextus Empiricus's practical criterion.[12] Verisimilitude becomes a function of or metaphor for a different kind of possibility: that of the reader's own commentary, his reading of the text in whatever way he finds useful: "Si je ne comme bien, qu'un autre comme pour moy" (If I do not apply them well, let another apply them for me [104; 75]).

In "De l'exercitation," however, while Montaigne's own claim that he has learned something by relating his accident suggests that instruction is simply a function of the effort to attain self-knowledge ("la suffisance de s'espier de près" [the capacity to spy on himself from close up], 357; 272), the use of the word "accident" in the passage just quoted threatens the notion that the reader's intention has anything to do with the productiveness of his reading. In an ironic adverbial phrase, "par accident," the narration of Montaigne's accident is described as having only accidental value for another reader of the *Essais*—not only because Montaigne denies responsibility but because the reader himself is not responsible. If we read the sentence, "What is useful to me. . . ," on the analogy of Montaigne's physical accident, we would have to say that the accident of reading the *Essais* is like "these passions which touch only the rind of us [and which] cannot be called ours" (271; 356). The reader is cast in the role of the injured man who, like Montaigne trying to approach "de chez [soi]," discovers only "idle thoughts, in the clouds," which are not, properly speaking, his own. Like death or an accident, Montaigne's *Essais* also can't be practiced, it seems, in the sense of the reader's becoming more experienced or acquiring a body of knowledge.

Yet Montaigne's ironic defense of the *Essais* in terms of a pedagogical value for which he will make no claims is only one of the defenses he offers at the end of this essay. As justification for speaking of himself in public he invokes the ethical notion of self-examination, and this defense seems to be straightforward. Montaigne tells us that, as with poetry, speaking of oneself may be abused, but "on ne peut abuser que des choses qui sont bonnes" (We can misuse only things which are good[358; 273]). Writing ideally allows for the exercise and progress of self-knowledge. In invoking this ideal of practicing oneself ("se hanter et prattiquer" [to frequent and associate with oneself, 360; 274]), Montaigne might appear to be returning to the rhetorical tradition he had seemed to deny.[13] In this case the project and epistemology of the *Essais* would be the internalized version of the preliminary rhetorical exercises the orator must engage in, with their presupposition of a faculty of judgment which ensures the possibility of decorum. "I hold that a man should be cautious [*prudent*] in making an estimate of himself, and equally conscientious in testifying about himself—whether he rates himself high or low makes no difference" (274; 359). Montaigne's final insistence on self-knowledge through contemplation rather than action would also be consistent with this internalized version of prudence. And yet, it is just at this point that Montaigne returns us to the problems of effects by speaking of the difficulty of embodying his "cogitations, subject informe."

> Je peins principalement mes cogitations, subject informe, qui ne peut tomber en production ouvragere. A toute peine le puis je coucher en ce corps aërée de la voix. Des plus sages hommes et des plus devots ont vescu fuyants tous apparents effects. Les effects diroyent plus de la Fortune que de moy. Ils tesmoignent leur roolle, non pas le mien, si ce n'est conjecturalement et incertainement: eschantillons d'une montre particuliere. Je m'estalle entier: c'est un *skeletos* où, d'une veuë, les veines, les muscles, les tendons paroissent, chaque piece en son siege. L'effect de la toux en produisoit une partie; l'effect de la palleur ou battement de coeur, un'autre, et doubteusement. [359]

> [What I chiefly portray is my cogitations, a shapeless subject that does not lend itself to expression in actions. It is all I can do to couch my thoughts in this airy body of the voice. Some of the wisest and most devout men have lived avoiding all noticeable effects. My effects would tell more about fortune than about me. They bear witness to their own part, not to mine, unless it be by conjecture and without

certainty: they are samples which display only details. I expose myself entire: my portrait is a cadaver on which the veins, the muscles, and the tendons appear at a glance, each part in its place. One part of what I am was produced by the effect of a cough, another by a pallor or a palpitation of the heart—in any case dubiously. (274)]

This description recalls an earlier passage in the essay where Montaigne is describing the behavior of persons who are addressed while sleeping and who reply "à la suitte des dernieres paroles qu'on [leur] . . . a dites, qui ont plus de fortune que de sens" (following the last words spoken to us, we make answers that are more random than sensible" [355; 271]). Montaigne's metaphor of the body is just such a response to classical metaphors of the body of speech, for the "apparents effects" that the wise man flees must be the inevitable effects of writing over which the writer has no control. In denying his own authoritative role, Montaigne undercuts the authority of the quotation from the *Ars poetica* preceding these remarks: *In vitium ducit culpae fuga* (Flight from a fault will lead us into crime [273, 358]) which in Horace's text refers to the necessary exercise of judgment in the realization of decorum. He also mocks, as I suggested earlier, the Ciceronian analogy between persuasive speech and a healthy body. While in the *Brutus* Cicero speaks of the "marrow" (15.59) of persuasion, and in commending the Attic style to his contemporaries writes, "I would that they might imitate not its bones only, but its flesh and blood as well" (17.68), Montaigne presents us with a skeleton and a dissected body. Furthermore, the different parts of the body are themselves viewed as effects of contingent effects of the body: "L'effect de la toux en produisoit une partie." According to this (skeptical parody of Stoic) logic, if the voice is a body ("corps aërée") which produces a text, then the textual effect ("l'effect de la toux") is really that which produces the effect of the voice. Yet, if the subject's contribution is "conjectural and uncertain," so the effect's production is described as "doubtful." Thematization of the body means the suspension of (authorial) meaning.

It is not surprising, then, that the essay concludes with the image of Socrates—the sage who wrote nothing and who made himself known—or, what comes to the same thing, unknown—"par sa bouche" (by his own mouth): "Because Socrates alone had seriously digested the precept of his god—to know himself—and because by that study he had come to despise himself, he alone was deemed worthy of the name *wise*" (275; 360). Far from providing the occasion for the authoritative exercise in self-knowledge either for the author or the reader, Montaigne's *Essais* involve a practice of writing that aims to suspend the claims of knowledge altogether. If there is a rhetoric of the essay, it is a Pyrrhonist rhetoric; one that is not in the service of persuasion to the good, though it does not deny the possibility of such an effect. But it is an effect over which Montaigne has no control. One could argue that the true figure of the author in this essay is not Montaigne alive and writing ("à cette heure"), but Montaigne "ten or twelve paces beyond, dead"—whose essays live after him and have effects apart from his discourse, effects that must appear as accidents to the skeptical reader who, it seems, if he has learned anything from the *Essais*, has learned that Montaigne is the "true and perfect orator."

II

Je ne suis excessivement desireux ny de salades, ny de fruits, sauf les melons. [I am not excessively fond of either salads or fruits, except melons.]
—Montaigne, *Essais*

Erfarung ist/ wenn einer wol versucht ist/ und kan davon reden als einer der dabey gewesen ist. [Experience occurs, if someone is tempted, and can speak about it as someone who was there.]
—Luther, marginal gloss on *"Die Epistel an die Römer"*

Montaigne's criticisms of the naive acceptance of the *consensus omnium* as evidence of the integrity of reason and its foundation in natural law are frequent in the *Essais*. With Augustine he constantly remarks on the hubris of a Ciceronian decorum or Stoical prudence that refers to the authority of innate ideas or the integrity of the will (2.12.479). We cannot know or believe in God by means of our own prudence, and there are no grounds for accepting the rhetoric of consensus:

Let us confess frankly that God alone has told us so, and faith; for a lesson of nature and of our reason it is not. And whoever will test his nature and his powers again and again, both inside and out, without this divine privilege; whoever will see man without flattering him, will see in him neither efficacy nor any faculty that savors of anything but death and earth. The more we give, and owe, and render to God, the more like Christians we act. What this Stoic philosopher says he holds from this accidental consensus of the voice of the people, would it not have been better if he had held it from God? *"When we discuss the eternity of souls, the agreement of men who either fear or honor the infernal powers is of no small moment to us. I adopt this public belief* [Seneca].*"* [2.12.415; 536]

Montaigne's creed of learned ignorance is a continual exercise (Augustine's *exercitatio* [2.12.535]) in contraries, for the genuine skeptic does not deny the (desire for the) possibility of knowledge, and therefore keeps searching. But this leads to a new kind of prudence, one that can only be understood in terms of Montaigne's skeptical practice of rhetoric. The following pages aim to clarify this new kind of prudence through an examination of Montaigne's practice of interpretation in "De l'experience," that essay which takes as its subject the traditional source and object of prudential judgment. As Hobbes, speaking for all of his humanist predecessors, writes in the *Leviathan:* "Prudence is a *Praesumtion* of the *Future,* contracted from the *Experience* of time *Past"* (*L* 3.98). As we shall see, Montaigne elaborates his conception of the prudential contract with experience in this last essay by means of the rhetorical variations he works on the topos of taste. Focusing on Montaigne's transformations of this traditional humanist metaphor for literary imitation and assimilation will thus help us to understand his new practical conception of rhetoric and of experience.

Toward the beginning of "De l'experience" Montaigne describes the *Essais* as a record of his past experience: "J'ay assez vescu, pour mettre en compte l'usage qui m'a conduict si loing. Pour qui en voudra gouster, j'en ay faict l'essay, son eschançon" (I have lived long enough to give an account of the practice that has guided me so far. For anyone who wants to try it I have tasted it like his cupbearer [3.13.1057; 827]). At first reading this metaphor of tasting or *gouster* appears to function like many of those classical metaphors of taste and digestion that refer to the judgment and possible appropriation of another text or another's ideas. The reasoning behind these metaphors seems to go as follows: the mouth is our first organ of perception and taste our first sense. It enables us to appropriate the external world, literally to ingest it. Thus by metaphorical extension the sense of taste can refer to the process of learning—physical ingestion is like mental ingestion—or to the faculty of judgment. We might then paraphrase Montaigne's sentence as "I have tried or attempted various things in my life and present them to you for your sampling and delectation." But more interesting than this apparent commonplace of taste as reading is the implicit equation of tasting and writing, for the juxtaposition of *gouster* and *essai* activates one of the original meanings of the word *essai*. The word comes from the Latin *exagium* meaning "weighing, weight, or balance" (*Lewis and Short*), hence the primary definition of the essay as the activity of weighing or judging, an attempt or trial. But the second definition that *Littré* gives is that of tasting, in particular the tasting of the king's food or wine.[14] Hence the appearance of the *eschançon* or cupbearer in Montaigne's sentence, a word that Florio translates as "taster." The essay then seems to involve a kind of tasting both for the author and his reader, and on the part of the author for his reader.

The application of gustatory or digestive metaphors to imply the notion of practical reason or prudence and to invoke the epistemological assumptions of a certain rhetorical tradition (e.g., Seneca's "talis hominibus fuit oratio qualis vita") is something that Montaigne would have found in many of his favorite classical texts. Thus, in a discussion of the activity of judgment that is involved in reading and writing, Seneca remarks:

> The food we have eaten, as long as it retains its original quality and floats in our stomachs as an undiluted mass, is a burden; but it passes into tissue and blood only when it has been changed from its original form. So it is with the food which nourishes our higher nature,—we should see to it that whatever we have absorbed should not be allowed to remain unchanged, or it will be no part of us. We must digest it; otherwise it will merely enter the memory and not the reasoning power. Let us loyally welcome such foods and make them our own, so that something that is one may be formed out of many elements.[15]

For Seneca the proper digestion of received ideas both educates and is the result of an independent faculty of judgment, and this in turn is the precondition of right action, whether of the reader as citizen or as poet. Thus the active intervention of judgment in the process of literary imitation is frequently described in classical literature in terms of digestive metaphors: it is not enough to swallow the tradition whole; it must be transformed. This activity of digestion is crucial for the orator as well who, like the poet, imitates and alters his predecessors by incorporating their work into his own.

In another of his letters (114) Seneca explicitly ties the metaphor of taste as judgment to the discipline of rhetoric, by speaking of the decline of rhetoric as analogous to and partially dependent upon a decline in taste, both social and gustatory. The excesses of style in rhetoric are

> due sometimes to the man, and sometimes to his epoch. When prosperity has spread luxury far and wide, men begin by paying closer attention to their personal appearance. Then they go crazy over furniture. . . . After that, they transfer their exquisite taste (*lautitia*) to the dinner table, attempting to court approval by novelty and by departures from the customary order of dishes. . . . When the mind has acquired the habit of scorning the usual things of life, and regarding as mean that which was once customary, it begins to look for novelties in speech also. [3.307]

Here the physical sense of taste functions as a synecdoche for the moral health of the whole man. The explanation of their simultaneous decline depends on the conviction that a "man's speech is just like his life," and this in turn refers to the classical belief that the good orator is necessarily a good man: the exercising of taste as sound judgment is as much a necessity in the practice of rhetoric as it is in academic training.

It is not surprising, then, that when Montaigne undertakes to rewrite or interpret Seneca, his practice of interpretation also redefines the possibility of the judgment of taste. In the essay "De l'institution des enfans," Montaigne alludes to Seneca when he advises the tutor to exercise his pupil's judgment, "making it taste things, choose them, and discern them by itself. . . . It is a sign of rawness and indigestion to disgorge food just as we swallowed it. The stomach has not done its work if it has not changed the condition and form of what it has been given to cook" (1.26.110, 111; 149, 150). Even when Montaigne begins to elaborate his own notion of education, he reminds us of Seneca's ideal program of liberal studies:

> Truth and reason are common to everyone, and no more belong to the man who first spoke them than to the man who says them later. It is no

more according to Plato than according to me, since he and I understand and see it in the same way. The bees plunder the flowers here
and there, but afterward they make of them honey, which is all theirs;
it is no longer thyme or marjoram. Even so with the pieces borrowed
from others; he will transform them and blend them to make a work
that is all his own, to wit, his judgment. [1.26.111; 150–51]

This is one version of the classical doctrine of imitation, according to
which the student assimilates and transforms the arguments of his
predecessors in order to form his own text (Montaigne's own act of
transformation in this case is to emphasize the formation of one's
judgment rather than the creation of a work of art).[16] While Montaigne at first seems to be authorizing the judgment of the individual
on the basis of a shared standard of natural law or reason ("truth
and reason are common to everyone"), he gradually moves to a
more subjective view of interpretation. Speaking of the student of
history he says: "Let him be taught not so much the histories as how
to judge them. That, in my opinion, is of all matters the one to
which we apply our minds in the most varying degree. I have read
in Livy a hundred things that another man has not read in him.
Plutarch has read in him a hundred besides the ones I could read,
and perhaps besides what the author had put in" (1.26.115; 155–56).
Finally the natural world, which is to serve as the occasion for the
exercise of judgment, becomes the book in which we read about the
imperfection of this faculty: "In short, I want it [nature] to be the
book of my student. So many humors, sects, judgments, opinions,
laws, and customs teach us to judge sanely of our own, and teach
our judgment to recognize its own imperfection and natural weakness, which is no small lesson" (1.26.116; 157). Predictably, Socrates
enters the picture shortly after this.

Socrates, . . . [the] prime favorite [of virtue], deliberately gives up his
strength, to slip into the naturalness and ease of her gait. She is the
nursing mother of human pleasures. By making them just, she makes
them sure and pure. By moderating them, she keeps them in breath
and appetite [goust] (unless perchance we want to say that the regimen
that stops the drinker short of drunkenness, the eater short of indigestion, the lecher short of baldness, is an enemy of our pleasures).
[1.26.120; 161]

With this emphasis on the intrinsic goodness of physical pleasure,
we have come a long way from Seneca's traditional reading of the

metaphor of taste. In fact, we have come full circle, for by tasting and digesting Seneca's ideas, Montaigne has returned us to the physical pleasures of taste. In short, he reads Seneca's metaphor literally, and in so doing raises the question of whether there can be a reading or judgment that is grounded in the authority of natural reason, a sense of taste that refers us to a common sense.

This interpretation is supported by Montaigne's description of his skeptical "new language" in the "Apologie," a description that reads as a gloss on the two meanings of the word *essai:* to taste and to judge. For as we saw, Montaigne does not use the faculty of taste as a metaphor for the Senecan exercise of one's own judgment in assimilating another's ideas. On the contrary, the effect of the metaphor in the rhubarb passage is, both thematically and rhetorically, to destroy the very possibility of appropriation or assimilation, and in so doing to resist the claims of common sense and the naive reading of the skeptic's sentence as proposition. The form of the skeptic's judgment is self-reflexive, as is the form of purgation, indicated by the reflexive verb *s'emporter*, to transport itself. But in the moment of self-reflection the specular model of consciousness and the distinction between the literal and figurative uses of language are themselves destroyed. For if the skeptic knows nothing, he can be neither certain nor uncertain of the "I" that does not know. So the "I" of the judging subject is subject to the same kind of suspension of any claim to authority as is the skeptic's proposition. Thus, whereas the Senecan version of taste as a faculty of judgment suggested an unproblematic concept of knowledge and of reading, Montaigne insists on the physical sense of taste—eating the rhubarb—in order to put these traditional notions into question. According to one writer this skeptical sort of self-reflection is characteristic of Socratic irony. In a passage reminiscent of the "Apologie" we read:

> It has been shown . . . that when Socrates said he was ignorant, he was nevertheless in possession of knowledge, for he had a knowledge of his ignorance. This knowledge, however, was not a knowledge of something, that is, it had no positive content, and to this extent his knowledge was ironic. . . . To know that one is ignorant is the beginning of wisdom, but if one knows no more than this it is only a beginning. It is this knowledge which holds Socrates ironically aloft.[17]

This last phrase refers to Aristophanes' depiction of Socrates in *The Clouds*, suspended in a basket between heaven and earth—an accurate if ironic representation of the way Socrates spoke ironically. He did not descend from theoretical considerations to concrete examples, but rather "through the immediately concrete . . . cause[d] the abstract to become visible" (284). In other words, Socrates did not illustrate theoretical points by reference to actuality, but made actuality itself a theoretical construct. So, too, Montaigne attempts to speak in the subjunctive by beginning with the concrete in order "constantly to arrive" (284) at the abstract. This is the function of Montaigne's increasingly frequent references to his body, as well as of many of the citations and figures in the *Essais*. Whether or not these references or figures are thematically concerned with the sense of taste, they are part of an epistemology of taste, a practice of reading and writing, which becomes more abstract and hypothetical as it becomes more concrete.

To become abstract in this skeptical sense is to have no pedagogical value, no practical application. For pedagogy, like an ethic of decorum, depends on the authority or at least on the legibility of the example: it depends on our ability to conceptualize experience, to render the concrete abstract—not in the sense of suspending all claims to instruction but rather in the sense of formulating the rules of instruction. Yet the epistemology of taste destroys the validity of examples just as the skeptic's proposition, in destroying itself, also destroys its exemplary or emblematic privilege. "L'exemple est un miroüer vague, universel et à tout sens. Si c'est une medicine voluptueuse, acceptez la" (Example is a hazy mirror, reflecting all things in all ways. If it is a pleasant medicine, take it [3.13.1067; 834]). It is appropriate, then, that Montaigne's refusal of exemplarity in the later essays should be accompanied by frequent references to the pleasures of the physical sense of taste, and by the insistent mention of his own bodily functions. The criticism of exemplarity and the sense of taste are in fact inseparable, for just as Montaigne's sense of taste is quite literally the individual palate, so it is this aesthetic moment, in the original sense of *aesthesis*, that undermines the general claim of the example.

Thus, from taste as a self-destructing metaphor for the skeptical sort of judgment we pass to a new emphasis in "De l'experience" on that sense of taste which resists any metaphorical translation. For the impossibility of examples is the impossibility of exalting a disinterested pleasure at the expense of an interested one. (Hence the numerous instances of the variety of custom and habit in and within different individuals and different countries, not a few having to do with food.) The skeptic's rhubarb potion becomes Circe's brew; for taste is the curious coincidence (in one sense) of opposites, about which there is no arguing:

> It is for habit to give form to our life, just as it pleases; it is all powerful in that; it is Circe's drink, which varies our nature as it sees fit. How many nations, and three steps from us, regard as ridiculous the fear of the night dew, which appears so hurtful to us; and our boatmen and peasants laugh at it. You make a German sick if you put him to bed on a mattress, like an Italian on a feather bed, and a Frenchman without curtains and a fire. A Spaniard's stomach cannot stand our way of eating, nor can ours stand to drink Swiss fashion. [3.13.827; 1058]

But Montaigne's observations are not limited to remarks about the cultural relativity of taste. He tells us that he is not "excessivement desireux ny de salades, ny de fruits, sauf les melons" (1082), and that his father "hated all kinds of sauces" but he likes them all. Furthermore, even his own taste is unpredictable: "Radishes, for example, I first found to agree with me, then to disagree, now to agree again. In several respects I feel my stomach and appetite vary that way" (846; 1082). These remarks, I suggest, do not point beyond themselves to any greater significance. They resist translation, sublimation, or incorporation into a system or a comprehensive reading. They are an attempt at purgation, on the thematic level, of the generalizing claim of the example.

This mediation on the taste of rhubarb and the variety of tastes, in the sense both of digestion and of judgment, will perhaps already have suggested to the reader Socrates' famous comparison between cooking and rhetoric; an analogy, indeed, that Montaigne would seem wholeheartedly to accept. Yet while Socrates opposes these pseudoarts or "routines" to the genuine art of medicine, Montaigne conflates the two. His own skeptical version of prudence or healthy judgment ("la veuë . . . purgée" [purged sight]; 3.12.1013) is achieved not only medicinally and rhetorically in the continual purgation of the skeptic's proposition, but also in the enjoyment of those naturally and conventionally variable pleasures of the body. Just as the credo of *docta ignorantia*—acceptance of one's limits, whether of the body, one's country, or culture—guarantees the pleasures that are accessible only within those limits, so rhetoric can have a medicinal effect, whether in purging itself of its claim to general and conclusive persuasion or in momentarily consoling or deceiving. Thus at the same time that Montaigne criticizes rhetoric as "un'art piperesse et mensongere" (1.51.292), worse than the "masques" and "fard [des femmes]," he recognizes its potential utility in his commerce with himself: "Now I treat my imagination as gently as I can, and would relieve it, if I could, of all trouble and conflict. We must help it and flatter it, and fool it if we can. My mind is suited to this service; it has no lack of plausible reasons [d'apparences] for all things. If it could persuade as well as it preaches, it would help me out very happily" (3.13.836; 1068).

Rhetoric allows for some kind of illusory conservation of the body. Thus while Socrates opposes medicine to the pseudoart of rhetoric (Gorgias, 464b–465e), Montaigne refuses the pseudoart of medicine for the comforts of rhetoric: "Would you like an example? It tells me that it is for my own good that I have the stone; and that buildings of my age must naturally suffer some leakage. It is time for them to begin to grow loose and give way. It is a common necessity—otherwise would it not have been a new miracle performed for me? Thereby I pay the tribute due to old age, and I could not get a better bargain" (836; 1068).

Even the second nature of habit has a rhetorical structure—not only because the same arguments can be used to defend different customs (1058), but because at the same time that we are passive before them, consciousness arrogates the right to criticize and assent (to define the authority of these customs as pragmatic or merely rhetorical rather than grounded in natural law). Montaigne tries to minimize the contention between consciousness and will (or of the divided will) by acknowledging that consciousness can only maintain its "magisterial seat" (1052) by abdicating its legislative powers and accepting the laws that nature or habit give us.

There is an obvious connection between Montaigne's discussion of the impossibility of recognizing natural law and of being willing to conform to that law. But Montaigne treats the problem of the will not simply as logically consequent, but also as analogous to that of the understanding. He often seems to suggest that the laws that nature gives us are no less valid for being humanly understood, and that we have only to act accordingly to achieve the virtue of moderation. These laws are referred to as "des plaisirs naturels, et par consequent necessaires et justes" (natural and therefore necessary and just pleasures [1088]), "les voluptez naturelles . . . [et] humaines" (natural and human pleasures [1086]), "les actions . . . voluptueuses" (voluptuous actions [1088]).

Finally, we might say, the function of the will is less to execute the commands of the intelligence than to conform to a kind of intelligence that is intrinsic to the will. This other kind of nonrational intelligence Montaigne calls *prudence,* and in so doing suggests one interpretation of the Aristotelian idea of *phronesis.* Commenting on the Delphic inscription, "Know thyself," Pierre Aubenque writes in *La prudence chez Aristote:*

> Contrary to all of the modern interpretations which have seen this as an invitation to man to discover in himself the power of *reflection,* this formula has never signified anything, up to Socrates and even including Plato, but this, which is entirely different: know your abilities, which are limited; know that you are mortal, and not a god. The "know yourself" . . . is the most exalted formula of Greek *prudence,* that is to say, knowledge of limits.

Montaigne's remarks support this equation of prudence with a continual profession of ignorance rather than with a specular act of self-reflection:

> The advice to everyone to know himself must have an important effect, since the god of learning and light had it planted on the front of his temple, as comprising all the counsel he had to give us. Plato also says that wisdom [*prudence*] is nothing else but the execution of this command, and Socrates, in Xenophon, verifies it in detail. . . . I, who make no other profession, find in me such infinite depth and variety, that what I have learned bears no other fruit than to make me realize how much I still have to learn. [3.13.823; 1052][18]

Prudence in the sense of acknowledging one's limits means at the same time accepting, and in accepting enjoying, one's self. Thus, while his frequent criticisms of the presumptuousness of human science have something in common with Luther, who has been described as adhering to "a mystical epistemology, a fundamental skepticism immediately rescued by grace,"[19] Montaigne does not escape from skepticism into faith, but rather in skepticism finds a new faith in the peculiarly human.

The difference between the Aristotelian version of prudence and Montaigne's seems finally to be that Aristotle slips from a descriptive to a prescriptive virtue,[20] while Montaigne is ever wary of the difficulties of legislating, either to himself or to others. If Montaigne sometimes refers to this "mesnage" as a kind of prudence, it is important to recognize that his prudence is founded not so much on natural law (however formally that may be conceived) as in the avowed ignorance of that law. While Aristotle is aware that prudence requires continual vigilance and exercise, Montaigne seems to dwell on the impossibilities of such discipline. His prudence might be more adequately described as the grace of nature—for it is a grace that, like its divine counterpart, engenders its own volitive dilemma. Of "[les] plaisirs . . . necessaires et justes," he writes: "We should neither pursue them nor flee them, we should accept them [il les faut recevoir]" (849; 1086). But acceptance too (as the imperative *il faut* indicates) is predicated on the will, and is as difficult as any other attempt at mastery: "Popular opinion is wrong: it is much easier to go along the sides, where the outer edge serves as a limit and a guide, than by the middle way, wide and open, and to go by art than by nature; but it is also much less noble and less commendable. Greatness of soul is not so much pressing upward and forward as knowing how to set oneself in order and circumscribe oneself" (3.13.852; 1090).

This is not the Renaissance commonplace that fallen man needs art in order to regain or realize his true nature, nor is it simply that man has no fixed nature and may become anything he wishes (Pico), but the more difficult problem that man has a nature that he cannot become, even with the aid of art. *Jouyssance* and *mesnage* (1092) are not opposed, as they seem to be, for example, in "De la vanité," since the second is both the necessary condition of the first and that which prevents the perfection of our self-appropriation. Thus, perfection loses its aesthetic and moral connotations of integrity or wholeness (perfect as accomplished), and comes to signify the perfection of a method that cannot be transcended (and that is, therefore, ultimately no method at all).

In one way, then, Montaigne can be read as a kind of secularization of Luther, for whereas the Christian discovers the hubris of pretending to free will, and the limits of human nature, by being tempted (*versucht*) to try (*versuchen*) to obey the Old Testament law and failing, for Montaigne this experience of the feebleness of our will and intellect is itself the unending trial of the "humaine condition" (1.20.89). Acceptance of our passivity (as in the passive: *ist versucht*), of our inability to determine the outcome of our actions or even to understand them completely—Montaigne's prudence, in short—is his version of Luther's faith.

Finally, if Montaigne's thought is a secularization of Luther, it is also a new version of Erasmian decorum. Erasmus spoke from within the confines of Christian dogma, and was forced to claim the usefulness of skepticism and moderation, not only to himself, but to the Christian community at large. His project was essentially pedagogic and persuasive, his protoessayistic *Adages* a classical and moral education in little. If he shared with Montaigne a belief in the healthiness of human nature and, most important, of accepting the limits of that nature, this was all the more incitement to inform and reform—to educate (*former* [3.2.782]) others. And this project of reform was in turn grounded in the *consensus omnium* of natural law informed by Christ. Montaigne, on the other hand, doubts the possibility of recovering a shared natural law and the kind of prudence that would simply conform to that law; he is satisfied to be temperate by (his own) nature. The difference might finally be expressed in terms of grammatical mood—for Erasmus writes of the hypothetical in the indicative, in, at least ideally, subordinating skepticism to faith, while Montaigne writes of the hypothetical in the conditional: "For in what I say I guarantee no certainty except that it is what I had at the time in my mind, a tumultuous and vacillating mind. I talk about everything by way of conversation, and about nothing by way of advice. *Nor am I ashamed, as those men are, to admit that I do not know what I do not know* [Cicero]. I would not speak so boldly if it were my right to be believed" (3.11.790; 1010–11).

III

Montaigne's interpretation of the classical notion of prudence can give us some insight into the nature of the written essay, for *phronesis* is, in Aubenque's interpretation, a concept that—like the essay—reestablishes the unity of theory and practice. The Aristotelian concept of prudence involves a criticism of the Platonic sovereignty of *nous* (reason that intuits Ideas) over *phronesis* (reason that performs the executive function in action), and as such "represents less of a dissociation between theory and praxis, and the revenge of praxis on theory, than a rupture within theory itself" (19). Aristotle's originality, according to Aubenque, lies in his discovery of this division internal to reason, and in "the recognition of this division as the condition of a new practical intellectualism" (143).

While Aristotle often discusses *phronesis* in terms similar to those he uses to describe *poesis*, there is an important distinction between the two. Although both operate within the domain of the contingent, with "things that can be other than they are," *poesis* is a mode of production, while *phronesis* is concerned with action. With this distinction in mind, Montaigne's criticism of artifacts and of the "finished product" leads us to consider the *Essais* as a form of action (I write of myself and my writings as of my other actions [3.13.818; 1046]), or at least to interpret the insistence on the identity of the book and the author or reader as an absorption of the subject into the predicate, the work into the process or "chasse de cognoissance" (chase after knowledge [1045]). And just as the classical idea of *poesis* is revised in the *Essais* to approximate that of *phronesis*, so the Aristotelian notion of *phronesis* is revised to the extent that there is no other kind of intellection besides that which is afforded by the poetic *process*. It is no surprise, then, that Montaigne's skeptical notion of prudence should be most fully revealed not in theoretical and thematic statements, but in his practice of writing and in particular his practice of citation.

As with the thematic references to the body, the body of citations is part of Montaigne's ironic or truly skeptical epistemology of taste. Because he refuses to render the concrete abstract in the sense of conceptual, he necessarily renders it abstract in another sense. He dramatizes the resistance of matter—whether as actual body or the foreign body of another text— to human intention, as well as dramatizing the questionable nature of intention itself. The wealth of the classical patrimony seems constantly to be turning into something other than either the donor or the beneficiary intended, though the exposure of this inversion or perversion of wealth is paradoxically part of Montaigne's stated intention. As he himself says, he is not responsible for what other readers find in his text. Neither can he predict what his own later self will find there. This criticism of reading as cognition of the author's intended meaning is effected through a demonstration of reading as a practice, but a practice that proves to be an ironization of the notion of prudence as correct judgment. For this prudence depends on the authority of the judging subject, and for Montaigne this authority is precisely what the practice of interpretation undermines.

In the beginning of "De l'experience" the differences of taste find

141

a kind of natural equivalent in the variety of the phenomenal world: "Nature s'est obligée à ne rien faire autre, qui ne fust dissemblable" (Nature has committed herself to make nothing separate that was not different [1042, 815]). This maxim, which appears in the text as though it were composed by Montaigne, is really an allusion to Seneca's Epistle 113, where we read: "And among the other reasons for marvelling at the genius of the Divine Creator is, I believe, this,—that amid all this abundance there is no repetition; even seemingly similar things are, on comparison, unlike" (3.291). In Seneca's letter this observation is part of an argument about virtue: living things are not alike, but virtues are all alike, and therefore not living things. Just as the function of comparison in Seneca's passage is to discover unlikeness, so in comparing the Senecan text and context with Montaigne's, we discover their difference. Seneca begins with a proposition that becomes the basis of a rhetorical syllogism, but Montaigne arrests the process of argumentation at the first stage: the observation of differences. This observation then leads to a reflection on the incommensurability of man-made laws with the human actions they are supposed to govern. Here we have moved from difference as a fact to difference as a problem—notably a problem of interpretation. But in the process of commenting on this problem, Montaigne makes the difficulty a positive source of fertility:

> Who has seen children trying to divide a mass of quicksilver into a certain number of parts? The more they press it and knead it and try to constrain it to their will, the more they provoke the independence of this spirited metal; it escapes their skill and keeps dividing and scattering in little particles beyond all reckoning. This is the same; for by subdividing these subtleties they teach men to increase their doubts; they start us extending and diversifying the difficulties, they lengthen them, they scatter them. By sowing [*semant*] questions and cutting them up, they make the world fructify and teem [*fructifier et foisonner*] with uncertainty and quarrels, as the earth is made more fertile the more it is crumbled and deeply plowed. *Learning makes difficulties.* [3.13.816; 1043–44]

The simile of the fertile earth is a C addition, a marginal comment in Montaigne's own copy of the 1588 Bordeaux edition. And it is an addition that by elaborating on the *semant*, *fructifier*, and *foisonner* of the earlier text, makes a difference in the original, for the proliferation of language begins to undermine the 1588 argument about the negative effects of making differences and distinctions, of increasing doubts. The addition also makes a difference with respect to the original Quintilian from which the Latin quotation is drawn. There the phrase Montaigne cites appears in a conditional clause, in the context of a discussion about judgment and decorum.

> It is not merely practice [*exercitatio*] that will enable us to write at greater length and with increased fluency, although doubtless practice is the most important. We need judgement [*ratio*] as well. So long as we do not lie back with our eyes turned up to the ceiling, trying to fire our imagination by muttering to ourselves . . . but turn our thoughts to consider what the circumstances of the case demand . . . we shall acquire the power of writing by rational means. . . . That is the reason why peasants and uneducated persons do not beat about the bush to discover with what they should begin, and our hesitation is all the more shameful if it is simply the result of education [*si difficultatem facit doctrina*]. [10.3.16][21]

Montaigne's context requires that this last phrase be read in the indicative since his point is precisely the impossibility of prudence in the sense of right interpretation or of the judgment of decorum. The very effort of interpretation fractures the object of interpretation into a thousand questions, each of which in turn requires the same interpretive effort.

Shortly after this passage on the fertility of differences, Montaigne again emphasizes the disruptive and divisive consequences of commentaries, but this time he also comments explicitly (rather than merely implicitly, as in the earlier simile) on the necessity of this activity: "Do we therefore find any end to the need of interpreting?" (817; 1044). This question then receives its own commentary:

> Men do not know the natural infirmity of their mind: it does nothing but ferret and quest, and keeps incessantly whirling around, building up and becoming entangled in its own work, like our silkworms, and is suffocated in it. *A mouse in a pitch barrel* [Erasmus]. It thinks it notices from a distance some sort of glimmer of imaginary light and truth ["je ne sçay quelle apparence de clarté et verité imaginaire"]; but while running toward it, it is crossed by so many difficulties and obstacles, and diverted by so many new quests, that it strays from the road, bewildered. Not very different from what happened to Aesop's dogs, who, discovering something that looked like a dead body ["quelque

apparence de corps mort"] floating in the sea, and being unable to approach it, attempted to drink up the water and dry up the passage, and choked in the attempt. To which may be joined what a certain Crates said of the writings of Heraclitus, that they needed a good swimmer for a reader, so that the depth and weight of Heraclitus' learning should not sink him and drown him. [817; 1044–45]

The intersection of these stories is itself a fruitful one. The reader, like the Aesopian dog, has to learn not to drown in the text by trying to swallow or engulf it all in a commentary. Similarly, the writer must learn to recognize that the appearance of clarity and imagined truth in an earlier text may be only a dead body, or even that the desire for truth, on the part of either the author or the reader, will be fatal to one or both. The only way to be supported rather than drowned by the watery weight of the text is not to read its affirmations as conclusions. Thus, the text continues: "It is only personal weakness that makes us content with what others or we ourselves have found out in this hunt for knowledge. An abler man will not rest content with it" (817; 1045).

In other words, the reader must be precisely like that man who sets out in pursuit of some *apparence de clarté* only to be deflected and intoxicated by a roadside distraction. He must not reach the *corps mort* of the Aesopian dog, because if he does he will have swallowed a deadly amount of water. He must swim on top of the text rather than drink it. The very activity of or desire for interpretation proves to be that which sustains the reader—and here we return to the metaphor of taste: "A spirited mind ["un esprit genereux"] never stops within itself. . . . Its pursuits are boundless and without form; its food is wonder, chase, ambiguity" (818; 1045). As in the case of the rhubarb, this food metaphor is then itself compared to language—not to a question this time, but to something equally unsatisfying: "Apollo revealed this clearly enough, always speaking to us equivocally, obscurely, and obliquely, not satisfying us, but keeping our minds interested and busy. It is an irregular, perpetual motion, without model and without aim. Its inventions excite, pursue, and produce one another" (818; 1045). The generous spirit of the beginning of this passage refers to the earlier description of quicksilver, a generous metal which eludes the grasp of children just as truth eludes the interpreter. But in this later description of the generous spirit, the subject, whether author or reader, has himself become what was earlier an image for the elusiveness of truth.

144

Yet the allusion is intertextual as well. Montaigne is probably referring to yet another of Seneca's letters, this time 114, which in the Loeb translation bears the title "On Style as a Mirror of Character." Here again Seneca is discussing the quality of rhetoric in terms of the whole man. Describing Maecenas, he writes:

> Does not the looseness of his speech match his ungirt attire? Are his habits, his attendants, his house, his wife, any less clearly marked than his words? He would have been a man of great powers, had he set himself to his task by a straight path, had he not shrunk from making himself understood, had he not been so loose in his style of speech also. You will therefore understand that his eloquence was that of an intoxicated man—twisting, turning, unlimited in its slackness. [3.303]

The echoes in Montaigne's own text are obvious. And, as is the case frequently in the *Essais*, the subtext is drawn from a classical work on rhetoric, in particular a passage on the direct relation of speech to the body. But the function of tbe allusion is not to support a present claim by reference to an authoritative precursor, but rather to undermine the authority of the classical work, and even more significantly to undermine the idea of authority itself. In other words, Montaigne is not simply praising what Seneca dispraises, since this would be to propose his own view as authoritative. The praise of the generous spirit is not an *alternative* to Seneca's straight and narrow path, because the discovery of the inevitability and endlessness of interpretation depends on precisely this Senecan desire for a fixed itinerary. The wish for a straight and narrow path is itself the condition of the possibility of this endless activity, and necessarily inscribed within it. Thus Montaigne agrees with Seneca about what is in itself desirable—a straight path, a text without an infinite number of possible interpretations. He tells us furthermore that the intoxication of commentaries is owing to a sickness of the mind (1044). But lest we think that the truth would be accessible if we would only refrain from commenting on it, he adds: "Ordinarily I find subject for doubt in what the commentary has not deigned to touch on. I am more apt to trip on flat ground, like certain horses I know which stumble more often on a smooth road" (817; 1044). The ideal of the Senecan text is not contested in principle, but what *is* contested is the possibility that its moral imperative could effect a safe passage between intention and right action, or between reading and a determinant understanding.

145

I do not want to claim that all of Montaigne's citations work in this particular ambiguous or ambivalent fashion, or that a classical passage is never cited to support a single point of view. My point is rather that while Montaigne does sometimes cite classical authorities simply to contradict them or sometimes to agree with them (whether explicitly or by the new context in which he places them), he will also in the course of any one essay contradict whatever statement he had seemed to support. These statements cannot be read simply thematically. The contradictions between them force us to read them as self-negating or skeptical propositions. This, of course, is an assertion that cannot be proved; it can only be practiced. Still, one more "example" can serve as a final illustration. In the fifth essay of the first book ("Si un chef d'une place assiégée doit sortir pour parlementer" [Whether the governor of a besieged place should go out to parley]), Montaigne opposes "truly Roman ways" to "Greek subtlety and Punic cunning, according to which it is less glorious to conquer by force than by fraud" (16; 27). Then, to clarify this point about Roman military virtue, he says that the Romans did not know the sentence *"dolus an virtus quis in hoste requirat?"* (Courage or ruse—against an enemy, who cares?). But the context of this line in the *Aeneid* (2.390) describes Aeneas's soldiers engaged in the trickery of donning the armor of the Greek soldiers they have killed in order to insinuate themselves into the Greek camp and wreak havoc in disguise. The reader who does not know the context of the quotation will be tricked since, like Aeneas's soldiers, it will appear in the text in Greek rather than Roman garb; yet for the reader who does, Montaigne will have defeated the Stoic idea of Roman virtue, which he seemed to be supporting, not by trickery but by "valliance . . . in a fair and just war" (16; 27). But finally even this momentary dispraise of the Romans and the Greeks cannot be interpreted as though it were a proposition or a statement, since Montaigne goes on to paraphrase Polybius to the effect that "The Achaeans . . . detested all manner of deceit in their wars, seeing no victory except where the courage of the enemy was subdued" (16; 28).

The effect of Montaigne's citations is not only or finally to refer outside Montaigne's text to his pre-texts, whether these are conceived of as classical authors or his own authorial intention, but to create an intratextual web: "ses inventions s'eschauffent, se suyvent, et s'entreproduisent." The juxtaposition of citations does not create a conclusive third term or authoritative proposition but suspends this kind of referential movement and lets the passage—in both senses of the word—remain hanging in midair. It also encourages the reader to ring his own metaphorical changes on the text, as I illustrated earlier with the passage on the Aesopian dog.

But these metaphorical changes are not properly metaphorical, just as the rhubarb passage could not be described adequately in terms of metaphor. We can provisionally redefine them in terms of metalepsis, though even this term is inadequate insofar as, like metaphor, it presupposes the distinction between the literal and figurative uses of language. Blair's *Rhetoric*, cited in the *Oxford English Dictionary*, says metalepsis occurs when a trope is founded on the relation of antecedent and consequent. For example, the Aesopian dog is trying to reach the dead body, and becomes one himself; the cause of his desire, the dead body, turns out to be the effect: another dead body. But even more to the point is the first definition the *Oxford English Dictionary* gives of metalepsis: "transumption, a rhetorical figure mentioned by Quintilian, consisting in the metonymical substitution of one word for another which is itself figurative." On the basis of this definition we can say that Montaigne implicitly acknowledges the metaleptical nature of interpretation when he dismisses the possibility of arriving at a proper or fixed meaning, at the truth of any author's text. The question of interpretation, he writes, "is one of words, and is answered in the same way. 'A stone is a body.' But if you pressed on· 'And what is a body?'—'Substance.' 'And what is substance?' and so on, you would finally drive the respondent to the end of his lexicon" (818–19; 1046). But Montaigne insists on the metaleptical nature of interpretation not only thematically but also rhetorically by his references to his own body and by the insertion of the foreign body of citations in his text: by two bodies or two kinds of figures, neither of which holds out the promise of a literal truth.

Finally, Quintilian writes that metalepsis provides a transition from one trope to another. "It is the nature of *metalepsis* to form a kind of intermediate step between the term transferred and the thing to which it is transferred, having no meaning in itself, but merely providing a transition" (8.6.38). Thus, metalepsis is both the figure of a figure and a figure that is elided. Here we return to the skeptic's proposition, the rhubarb, and Montaigne's medallion, since the medallion serves as a figure for the rhubarb, which is a figure for the skeptic's proposition, which depends on the notion of a figure in order to suspend it. Furthermore, in Montaigne's text the two definitions of metalepsis (the relation of antecedent to consequent, and the figure that is an elided transition) collapse within themselves and each other. In the rhubarb passage the cause of the purgation, the rhubarb, is destroyed by its effect, at the same time that the rhubarb is a figure that is elided. And the further consequence of this figuration is to collapse the distinction between literal and figurative, terms that have a hierarchical relation to each other much like that of cause and effect. In other words, the rhubarb is a metaphor for the skeptic's proposition, and in transporting or destroying itself it destroys the very nature of metaphor, which is to transport or transfer meaning.

But even within the medallion we see the figure of metalepsis, for the skeptic's act of judgment is the middle term between the two sides of the scale, just as the reader's act of judgment is the invisible figure that articulates the relation of figures in the text. According to this reading, metalepsis is the skeptical figure par excellence, the figure of the (literally) excluded middle. Consider, for example, this familiar quotation: "To compose our character is our duty, not to compose books, and to win, not battles and provinces, but order and tranquillity in our conduct. Our great and glorious masterpiece is to live appropriately [Nostre grand et glorieux chef-d'oeuvre, c'est vivre à propos]" (850–51; 1088). The function of *is* in this last sentence is not at all the equation of two known quantities, but rather a kind of rhetorical positing of two unknowns. It narrates a passage that, for the skeptic, cannot be narrated (between subject and object, subject and verb), and when we arrive, as it were, on the other side, we discover that the bridge has been burned behind us. Hegel describes an apparently similar experience in the *Phenomenology:* "Starting from the subject, as if this were a permanent base on which to proceed . . . [conceptual thinking] discovers, by the predicate being in reality the substance, that the subject has passed into the predicate, and has thereby ceased to be subject." Hence "the nature of judgment or the proposition in general, which involves the distinction of subject and predicate, is subverted and destroyed by the speculative judgment."[22] So in Montaigne's passage the noun, the work of art, Being, our greatest achievement, *is* the verb, living appropriately. But this injunction has no content, for as the first part of the sentence anticipates a judgment, a determination of value, the second part reveals grammatically and thematically that judgment is an activity. To determine what is apropos it is necessary to make an essay of consciousness, but it is precisely the activity of the essay rather than its determinate content which is appropriate.

Montaigne's proposition is, however, an ironic or skeptical version of the speculative judgment. Unlike Hegel's dialectic, Montaigne's sentence is not the discovery of the identity of two terms, but a narration of the rhetorical structure of equivalence, or of the failure of dialectic. It does not reveal the "profound tautology of all thought,"[23] but rather that an equation is authoritative only because it is apropos. In short, it is the copula itself that is the most appropriate, that is to say most useful, because finally the most pleasurable and inevitable of human fictions. We can say, then, that the sentence is a kind of rewriting of Montaigne's medallion and of many of the familiar Renaissance analogies of art and life. At first glance it seems to be a simple analogy between the mastery of art and life, or between rhetoric and prudence. But closer examination reveals that analogy is a process, that it is constructed and destroyed in the continual essay of the apropos. The essay as scale turns out to be a very dubious form of judgment, and this turn or passage can be discerned in Montaigne's rhubarb passage, and in the historical passage that is etymology, since to taste is to essay.

The skeptic knows that all judgments are reflexive, but what he does not know is what they reflect or refer back to; so he at once knows and does not know. Even more than the notion of the apropos or of decorum, the "I" is a shifter. As Montaigne writes, "Moy à cette heure et moy tantost, sommes bien deux" (Myself now and myself soon after are indeed two [3.9.941]). Just as the rhubarb destroys itself in the reflexive activity of transporting itself so the I destroys itself in the specular activity of self-reflection. The writing that was ostensibly to provide some kind of fixed image of the self for Montaigne (as he says so many places in the *Essais*) only renders explicit the impossibility of such an economy. For this reason Montaigne can only be skeptical of the classical conception of prudence and of the effectiveness of rhetoric as a technique of persuasion. If the self is not consistently one, how can the self be appealed to as the locus of a consistent moral behavior? How can it even assent wholeheartedly to any specific appeal? The recalcitrance and divided nature of the will as a volitive faculty and as physical desire is the subject of many pronouncements in the *Essais*. Just as the metaphor of taste in the rhubarb passage contradicts its classical application and serves to suggest a new kind of reading and writing by rendering these processes simultaneously more concrete and more abstract, so the waywardness of the body in the *Essais* stands both for itself and for those impersonal contingencies that infect the will or judgment.

Finally, as we say, Montaigne is doubtful not only of the appeal of rhetoric to the will, but of prudence itself as a faculty of interpretation. Yet to the reader who objects that Montaigne *does* in fact imitate and emulate his classical predecessors, that he *does* read and interpret them, Montaigne must answer in the same way that the skeptic replies to the critics of the proposition "I know nothing." In short, Montaigne recognizes that in criticizing the notion of prudence or of common sense or of the authority of judgment, he cannot avoid the same pretensions to prudence. He knows that the Senecan or Ciceronian prudent man and the writer appear alike in claiming authority. Similarly, both might be condemned for hubris when compared to the divine writing that is Scripture, that is the only true writing, and reduces all others to an abuse of God's word. Montaigne was sensitive to this view, and alludes at several points in the *Essais* to the controversies about interpretation raging at that time between the reformers and their adversaries. Thus in the "Apologie" he quotes *Corinthians* 1, 19–20: *Perdam sapientiam sapientium, et [prudentiam] prudentium reprobabo* (I will destroy the wisdom of the wise, and will bring to nothing the understanding of the prudent [2.12.535]). Or, in the translation by Florio: "For (as it is written) *I will confound the wisdome of the wise and destroy the understanding of the prudent, where is the Wise? Where is the Scribe? Where is the disputer of this world?* Hath not God made the wisdome of this world foolishnesse? For seeing the world by wisdome knew not God in the wisdome of God, it hath pleased him, by the vanity of preaching, to save them that beleeve."[24]

The question that Montaigne then seems to imply in the *Essais* is whether a form of writing that pretended to self-destruct, like Christ, *das Wort vom Creutz* (the Word from the Cross) in Luther's translation of the passage preceding the one Montaigne cites, would not be the most hubristic of all? A writing that pretended to silence, the most pretentious? A writing in which the writer asserted his will to nonsignification, to absolute self-referentiality (i.e., nonreferentiality)—the form of writing to which Flaubert aspired, where the writer would be everywhere and nowhere like God—would not this be the most blasphemous of all? As Montaigne does not pretend to "save them that believe," neither can he pretend to the perfect vanity of his work.

Montaigne's recognition of our inability to suspend the activity of judgment in a single and fatal dismantling of the architectonic self that judges is at the same time a recognition of our inability to suspend entirely the claims of language, if not to refer to some external thing-in-itself, at least to generate the common sense that is meaning. As long as we (claim to) communicate, (the presupposition of) analogy is inescapable: we sacrifice it at the price of speech and reason. We escape from it, Montaigne tells us, into the madness of Tasso or into silence (2.12.472). In this sense the analogy between God and the writer is not the exception but rather the rule: it is a kind of allegorical representation of the theological and legislative pretensions of all language, of its claim to a common sense that is finally the belief in common "insightes or insets,"[25] in a shared divine right or writing inscribed in the human mind. With this inevitability in mind, Montaigne can only try to write and be read in such a way that the proposition suspends the proposition, the citation suspends the citation, the self suspends the self. So he does not offer us a text that says nothing, but one that must always, for any one reader—that is, for any one reading—say too much.

6 Hobbes: A Rhetoric of Logic

It thus appears that rhetoric is an offshoot of dialectic and also of ethical studies. Ethical studies may fairly be called political: and for this reason rhetoric masquerades as political science, and the professors of it as political experts.

—Aristotle, *Rhetoric*

Now therein of all sciences (I speak still of human, and according to the human conceits) is our poet the monarch. For he doth not only show the way, but giveth so sweet a prospect into the way, as will entice any man to enter into it.

—Sidney, *An Apology for Poetry*

Thomas Hobbes shares with the sixteenth-century authors we have examined a concern with the conditions of the possibility of persuasion: with how interpretive and ethical praxis can be. Like Erasmus and Luther, Hobbes confronts the need for an authoritative standard of interpretation in matters of Scripture and in the Christian commonwealth. Like Montaigne's, Hobbes's quest for such a standard is complicated by his essentially nominalist and skeptical epistemology. Furthermore, like Sidney in describing the ideal poet, Hobbes wants to overcome this skeptical threat by turning the sovereign into a technician of praxis. Yet the text in which Hobbes discusses these problems is very different from those of his predecessors.

It is precisely because Hobbes shares certain concerns with the humanists but proposes different solutions that he is a critical figure for understanding the decline of humanism. He looks back to the humanist rhetorical tradition as well as forward to the new scientific model of knowledge and cognition that was to prevail in the seventeenth century. He is struggling with the inadequacy of rhetoric as it was humanistically conceived to deal with the social and political realities of his day. He still knows what prudence meant to the Quattrocento humanists but, unlike them, he does not find this faculty of judgment exemplary for civic life—not least because the conditions of civic life had themselves changed radically. Hobbes is writing in a time of civil war, a war that, as he tells us in *De cive*, is due precisely to "private men being called to councils of state, [and desiring] . . . to prostitute justice . . . to their own judgments and apprehensions" (*EW* 2.xiii). This prostitution takes the form of rhetoric, which gives individuals the power to "represent to others, that which is Good in the likeness of Evill; and Evill in the likenesse of Good; and augment, or diminish the apparent greatnesse of Good and Evill; discontenting men, and troubling their Peace" (*L* 17.226). But rhetoric is not only the cause of disorder, it may also be the effect. As Ben Jonson remarked in his *Discoveries*, "Wheresoever, manners, and fashions are corrupted, Language is. It imitates the publicke riot."[1] The problem that Hobbes faced was how to speak of the institution of the commonwealth when traditional notions of order and authority, and the traditional humanist rhetoric, had been undermined by the "publicke riot" of civil war.

In a certain sense this is the problem that Machiavelli faced as well. As J. G. A. Pocock and others have argued, the "decay of citizenship" and consequently of the ideals of civic humanism led Machiavelli to revise the traditional mirror-of-princes genre in favor of "an analytic study of innovation and its consequences."[2] Machiavelli's innovation in genre was both a response to and a program for political innovation. But while Machiavelli separated ethics from politics and thus prudence humanistically conceived from prudence as the cunning or *versutia* (*L* 8.138) the humanists were so intent on repudiating, Hobbes takes the further step of rejecting prudence altogether: political science cannot, according to Hobbes, be practical and prudential in the Aristotelian sense, since prudence is based on experience that yields only the knowledge of probable effects (*L* 3.96), while science requires universal truths, that is, the conditional knowledge of logical consequences. Hobbes thus substitutes the goal of objective, mathematical certainty for the practical certainty of the Quattrocento humanists. His aim in the *Leviathan* is accordingly to develop a language commensurate with this new scientific notion of politics, a logic of invention that would do what the humanists' prudential rhetoric had failed to do: bridge the gap

153

between intention and action, between the cause and effect of persuasion.[3]

On the one hand, like the early humanists, Hobbes had a strong sense of the realm of contingency and the impossibility of certain knowledge of the external world. One could argue that he would have sided with Salutati in the debate on the relative virtues of law and medicine, since his defense of political science, like Salutati's defense of law, presupposes that we can only know what we produce or make ourselves. The further implication for Hobbes is that knowledge is valuable only insofar as it allows us to produce the object of our knowledge, that is, insofar as it is a source of power. This definition of knowledge in terms of power is reminiscent of Bacon, but it is important to stress that Hobbes's science is not inductive like Bacon's, but deductive and hypothetical like Salutati's prudence.

On the other hand, whereas for the early humanists the possibility of arguing on both sides of a question was an occasion for the exercise of prudential judgment and the development of civic consciousness, for Hobbes this possibility of contradiction is the source of civil war. Furthermore, Hobbes does not share the humanist's conviction of a God-given standard of practical reason. In fact, it is precisely because, like Montaigne, he doubts the accessibility or legibility of such a standard that he sees the necessity for the arbitrary authority of the sovereign.[4] But if Hobbes shares with Montaigne an essentially Pyrrhonist epistemology, he differs in one crucial respect: for while Montaigne's skeptic needs to invent a new language of doubt, Hobbes wants to invent a new language of certainty, a sovereign logic that will effectively exclude all further rhetoric *in utramque partem*.

Hobbes's own education in rhetoric is pertinent. Though Hobbes registers the typical humanist complaints against the Scholastic nonsense taught in the universities, he certainly received training in both rhetoric and logic while he was at Oxford. And what he did not receive in the way of a humanist education he acquired soon after graduation. By all accounts Hobbes was an accomplished classicist. He often wrote in Latin and was proficient in Greek, as his translations of Thucydides (*The History of the Graecian War*, 1628) and Homer (*Iliads* and *Odysses*, 1675) testify. Finally, he composed a *Brief* of Aristotle's *Rhetoric* (published 1637), a work that, Leo Strauss has argued, was influential on Hobbes's account of the passions in the *Leviathan*.[5]

In Hobbes's *Brief* rhetoric is defined as "that Faculty, by which we understand what will serve our turn, concerning any Subject to win belief in the hearer."[6] The best way to win belief is to rely on artificial proofs or inferences that, according to Aristotle, rhetoric shares with dialectic. Like Aristotle, Hobbes attributes the ability to discover these proofs first of all to the logician: "All *Inferences* being *Syllogismes*, a *Logician*, if he would observe the differences between a plain *Syllogisme*, and an *Enthymeme*, (which is a *Rhetoricall Syllogisme*,) would make the best *Rhetorician*. For all *Syllogismes* and *Inferences* belong properly to *Logick*, whether they infer truth or probability." Yet, while the conception of a "brief" or abstract of a longer work suggests the influence of Ramus, Hobbes's work presents an essentially humanist view of rhetoric, one in which logic and rhetoric are counterparts of each other and make use of the same arguments.[7] In fact, the rhetoric portrayed in the *Brief* would seem to go a long way toward explaining the fusion of rhetoric and logic in the *Leviathan*, for, like Aristotle, Hobbes takes a negative view of the orator's appeal to the passions and stresses instead force of argument. At the same time, like Aristotle he recognizes that such appeal is often necessary because of the "defects of our hearers." What keeps us from simply applying the *Brief* to an interpretation of the *Leviathan* is Hobbes's attempt to distinguish, both in the *Leviathan* and in earlier texts, between a rhetoric of probability, opinion, and experience on the one hand, and a logic of universal truths on the other; between a prudential and a scientific method; or between a rhetoric *in utramque partem* and a logic of noncontradiction.[8]

For example, in the *Philosophical Rudiments concerning Government and Society*, Hobbes distinguishes the logic of science from the false reasoning of rhetoric. The first "forms a speech from true principles," the second "from opinions already received, what nature soever they are of. The art of that is logic, of this rhetoric; the end of that is truth, of this victory" (EW 2.162). In the *Elements of Philosophy* Hobbes distinguishes between the primary and universal propositions that science rests on, and "those *petitions*, or *postulata*, (as they call them) [which] though they may be principles, yet they are not principles of demonstration, but of construction only; that is, not of science, but of power; or (which is all one) not of *theorems*, which are speculations, but of *problems*, which belong to practice, or the doing of something" (*EW* 1.82).

And yet, in the same text Hobbes describes his philosophy in a way that suggests the practical postulates he excluded from science in the passage I just cited:

> For the inward glory and triumph of mind that a man may have for the mastering of some difficult and doubtful matter, or for the discovery of some hidden truth, is not worth so much pains as the study of Philosophy requires; nor need any man care much to teach another what he knows himself, if he think that will be the only benefit of his labour. The end of knowledge is power; and the use of theorems (which, among geometricians, serve for the finding out of properties) is for the construction of problems; and, lastly, the scope of all speculation is the performance of some action, or thing to be done. [*EW* 1.7]

In the age-old debate between rhetoric and philosophy, Hobbes wants to have it both ways. He wants to formulate a political science that will be grounded on the truth, but will also be persuasive.

The scientific or logical method of investigation that Hobbes then proposes to substitute for rhetoric is one he terms the resolutive-compositive, which he borrows from Galileo. This involves analyzing the commonwealth into its constituent parts and then reassembling it in its most logical—and therefore, Hobbes argues, most convincing—form.[9] The assumption is that scientific knowledge of first principles will yield the practical knowledge of production. Hobbes's political science will then be superior to classical political philosophy to the extent that it is concerned with the commonwealth in practice and not simply in theory (*L* 31.407), but it will also be superior to the humanist rhetorical notion of practice to the extent that it grounds that rhetoric in logic. Construction will itself be a form of demonstration, and power will be constrained by science.

It is precisely because Hobbes attempts in the *Leviathan* to ground rhetoric in logic—or to put it another way, because he tries to bridge the gap between logic and rhetoric, theory and praxis—that the *Leviathan* has given rise to such a variety of interpretations. Leo Strauss's argument is suggestive in this context: according to Strauss, it was Hobbes's dissatisfaction with the traditional theoretical bias of political science that led him to history and rhetoric, disciplines concerned with the prudential application of theoretical principles;[10] but it was his desire to guarantee the consistent and authoritative application of such principles to society that led him away from history and rhetoric to the scientific method of Euclid and Galileo. Strauss's argument articulates rather than solves our problem, for it is precisely this turn to science and specifically to a logic that seems to exclude rhetorical considerations that requires interpretation. Thus, for example, Strauss stresses the tension between Hobbes's scientific method of politics and his early humanistic training; Miriam Reik argues for the continuity between Hobbes's early humanist education and his later political science; and J. W. N. Watkins argues for the relevance of Hobbes's early work in science to the political philosophy of the *Leviathan*.[11] Even if, as readers of the *Leviathan*, we ignore the problem of Hobbes's intellectual development, we are forced to ask to what extent he is in control of the obvious contradictions between his thematic statements and the rhetorical practice of his text. Read in one way, the *Leviathan* presents a logical argument whose rigor is undermined by the rhetorical dimension of the text; in another, the appearance of logical argument in the *Leviathan* is revealed to be the most persuasive and canniest of Hobbes's rhetorical postures.

The majority of Hobbes's critics, at least in the twentieth century, have persisted in reading the *Leviathan* primarily as a logical argument.[12] Two points need to be made about this approach. The first is that this reading seems to correspond, at least in part, to Hobbes's stated intention in the *Leviathan*, for, as we have seen, while rhetoric and logic were not as strictly separate in Hobbes's time as in our own, it is also clear that Hobbes wants to subordinate a rhetoric of probability and passion to a logic of certainty and reason. On the other hand, such a view of the *Leviathan* cannot come to terms with—and thus inevitably ignores—Hobbes's remarks about rhetoric and religion in books 3 and 4; the rhetorical structure of his conception of sovereignty; and his use of irony, paradox, contradiction, argument *in utramque partem*. What these critics fail to see is that rhetoric can be used for the purposes of ideological closure as well as disclosure: that is, to support the claims of logic and theoretical reason as well as to undermine these claims. Moreover, it can create the fiction of these claims, and this is what Hobbes does in the *Leviathan*. Indeed, so effective is he in constructing his logical model of argument that most readers have accepted it at face value. In an important sense, these rhetorically naive readers are the ideal subjects of the Hobbesian commonwealth: having been fully persuaded by Hobbes's logical model of state, they are incapable of seeing the contribution of rhetoric to his argument. They are the ones, in short, on whom Hobbes's rhetorical strategies have had the greatest effect.

What I want to suggest against the logical reading of the text is that the *Leviathan* acts out a *rhetoric* of logical invention in two ways. First of all, it presents us with a logical argument that, Hobbes tells us, is in itself persuasive, and thus aims to be a substitute for and to foreclose all further rhetorical debate. But once rhetorical debate has been logically foreclosed, the structure and techniques of rhetorical debate are reintroduced in what Hobbes hopes to have mapped out as the realm of logic. That is to say, the *Leviathan* both locally and as a whole is structured according to a rhetoric *in utramque partem*, but Hobbes's intention is to use this rhetoric *itself in utramque partem*, in order to purge the commonwealth of its most dangerous rivals for the subject's obedience. (In so doing, however, he suggests that his own logic of invention, which is concerned with the same contingent realm of human affairs, may itself be subject to debate—a problem to which I return at the end of this chapter.)

Even before we begin to read the first chapter of the *Leviathan*, we are alerted to the rhetorical nature of Hobbes's undertaking. First, in the prefatory letter to Francis Godolphin, Hobbes tells us that he has used "certain Texts of Holy Scripture" for "other purpose than ordinarily they use to be by others." This was necessary because "they are the Outworks of the Enemy, from whence they impugne Civill Power." Hobbes thus points out both that Scripture, like all other texts, can be interpreted *in utramque partem*, and that it is necessary to engage the enemy with enemy weapons. Accordingly, Hobbes cites Scripture throughout the *Leviathan* with the intention of undermining its authority (or rather the authority of those who would interpret it to defend the civil power of the Church).[13] Scripture is adduced to prove that obedience is due to the civil sovereign (e.g., 42.592); that there is no conflict between the ethical claims of this world and the next because there is no *other* world; that spirits are corporeal and that the Trinity consists of Moses, Christ, and the Apostles (two arguments that support Hobbes's claims for the authority of the civil sovereign).

Similarly, Hobbes uses *humanist* arguments *in utramque partem*. He argues against the criterion of usage (see especially 21.267) and against argument by example ("Examples prove nothing" [42.608]), but he appeals to usage and adduces many examples in support of his own argument. He also appeals to humanist texts to support antihumanist conclusions. For example, like the humanists, Hobbes criticizes the absurdities of Scholasticism on logical and linguistic grounds (notions such as transubstantiation involve the "enjoyning of a beliefe of contradictories" [12.179, cf. 5.113, 8.146–47, 12.171]); but he turns the humanists against themselves not only by applying his critique of contradiction to metaphor and free will (5.113), but also by conflating the Scholastic's dependence on the authority of Aristotle with the humanist's appeal to the authority of classical texts. The following quotation illustrates how Hobbes associates the appeal to the authority of the ancients with civil unrest. Like Scripture, the classics threaten the commonwealth with a competing rhetoric, a conflicting claim to the subject's obedience.

> In democracy, Liberty *is to be supposed: for 'tis commonly held, that no man is* Free *in any other Government.* And as *Aristotle*; so *Cicero*, and other writers have grounded their Civill doctrine, on the opinions of the Romans, who were taught to hate Monarchy, at first, by them that having deposed their Soveraign, shared amongst them the Soveraignty of *Rome*; and afterwards by their Successors. And by reading of these Greek, and Latine Authors, men from their childhood have gotten a habit (under a false shew of Liberty,) of favouring tumults, and of licentious controlling the actions of their Soveraigns; and again of controlling those controllers, with the effusion of so much blood; as I think I may truly say, there was never any thing so deerly bought, as these Western parts have bought the learning of the Greek and Latine tongues. [21.267–68]

In this passage, as elsewhere in the *Leviathan*, Cicero and Aristotle are called into court to bear witness against themselves. Hobbes refers to the ancients only in order to undermine them.

Finally, there is the irony of Hobbes's persona (another form of rhetoric *in utramque partem*)[14] to consider. For example, in chapter 44 Hobbes compares the Papacy with the "Kingdome of Fairies," but prefaces this passage (47.711–12) with remarks that are even more applicable to the Protestants. This passage, as Samuel Mintz has pointed out, is typical of Hobbes's use of orthodox language to make the most unorthodox and offensive points.

While Hobbes argues *in utramque partem* within each book, he also structures the *Leviathan* as a whole antithetically, placing books 3

159

and 4 in a chiasmic relation to books 1 and 2. In books 1 and 2 Hobbes wants to prove the necessity of an absolute, sovereign power in the commonwealth. To this end he argues as a skeptic that private reason is not capable of arriving at the truth, nor, since it is merely private, does it have the authority to convince others that it has the truth. Subjective certainty is a source only of contradiction, not of consensus, between individuals. Language would seem to provide us with a common sense, but our use of language is affected by our passions and our private reason. Yet the problem does not only lie in the use of persuasion for personal self-interest. For while Hobbes does direct specific criticisms against the rhetorical appeal to the passions and against the figurative language this usually involves, he also tells us that all words—whether literal or figurative—are ambiguous. All texts require interpretation but, precisely because of this, no single individual is capable of arriving at the truth of a particular text (L 26.322, 326; 30.388).

Hobbes's solution to the radical contingency of human experience is, as I have suggested, to use that contingency against itself, to argue that because our judgment is in some absolute sense arbitrary, it is necessary to institute an arbitrary absolute. He appeals to the reader's private reason to give up that reason (14.189ff.). By this act of self-sacrifice, the individual helps to constitute the common sense of the sovereign and thereby preserve himself against the threat of contradiction, which is ultimately the threat of extinction.

If in books 1 and 2 Hobbes uses contingency and rhetoric against themselves with the aim of subordinating rhetoric to logic, or rebellion to authority, in books 3 and 4 he uses authority against itself, in an attempt to turn the authority of the Church and of Scripture into rhetoric and contingency. Here Hobbes argues that there can be no contradiction between Scripture and civil law, but what he means by this is not that there is a happy coincidence of two independent authorities, but rather that the logic of the sovereign determines Christian logos. To the extent that there *is* a contradiction between the two, Christianity is relegated to the realm of opinion, of contingency, of the mere subjective certainty of faith. But if the Church is effectively subordinated to the state, rhetoric then finds itself once again, as in books 1 and 2, in the employ of logic. For the proper function of the Church, according to Hobbes, is to teach about and persuade to civil obedience.

In short, contrary to his stated intention and his thematic criticisms of paradox and contradiction, Hobbes employs the humanist strategy of argument *in utramque partem* throughout this text; at the same that he proposes a logical model of political science he fights rhetoric with rhetoric and Scripture with Scripture. In fact, one could say that, like Salutati's *De nobilitate legum et medicine,* the *Leviathan* is a text in which a humanist rhetoric is in dialogue (or a fight unto death) with a rhetoric of science. But whereas Salutati invoked the very fact of contradiction as evidence for the triumph of rhetoric and law over logic and medicine, Hobbes takes the state of contradiction (i.e., the state of war before the institution of the commonwealth) as the point of departure, the condition that proves the necessity of instituting the law of noncontradiction, that is, of the commonwealth.

The double vision engendered by the *Leviathan's* logical rhetoric is thus crucial to our understanding of this text. For Hobbes aims to educate the reader both to the primary necessity of rhetoric in the construction of the commonwealth, and to the further necessity of disguising this rhetoric as logic. Finally, the rhetorical strategy of the *Leviathan* as text is designed to involve the reader in a process of reading that mirrors the process of constructing the commonwealth.

Hobbes's Exclusion of Rhetoric and Prudence from the Commonwealth

The use of rhetoric to stir up the passions is associated by Hobbes with "private reason" or prudential self-interest. It is no surprise, then, that throughout the first two books of the *Leviathan* Hobbes tries to define reason in a way that would differentiate it from considerations of prudence or, as we shall see, from rhetoric.

> Reason is not as sense, and Memory, borne with us; nor gotten by Experience onely; as Prudence is; but attayned by Industry; first in apt imposing of Names; and secondly by getting a good and orderly Method in proceeding from the Elements, which are Names, to Assertions made by Connexion of one of them to another; and so to Syllogismes, which are the Connexions of one Assertion to another, till we come to a knowledge of all the Consequences of names appertaining to the subject in hand; and that is it, men call SCIENCE. And whereas Sense and Memory are but knowledge of Fact, which is a thing past, and irrevoca-

ble; *Science* is the knowledge of Consequences, and dependence of one fact upon another. [5.115]

As the reference to names suggests, Hobbes's distinction between science and prudence depends on his account of the relation of language to thought. At the beginning of the *Leviathan* Hobbes defines a thought as the *"Representation* or *Apparence,* of some quality, or other Accident of a body without us" (1.85; cf. 3.99) and mental discourse as the *"Consequence* or TRAYNE of Thoughts," or "succession of one thought to another" (3.94). Since our natural passions involve only the desire for the knowledge of consequences of a particular event (3.96), and since, in any case, experience can give us no certain knowledge of the consequences of such events (3.94), mental discourse can only take the form of prudential conjecture (3.97). Only through language can men formulate the general or universal propositions characteristic of reason (4.103–4), "there being nothing in the world Universall but Names" (4.102), and only in language can there be such a thing as truth.[15]

Language then seems to provide the means of transcending mere private reason; it seems in short to provide us with a common sense and thus with the possibility of a consensus and a commonwealth. But, as it turns out, for Hobbes as for Montaigne language is not exempt from the skeptic's doubts about the possibility of consensus in interpretation. The following quotation begins to suggest such doubt: "For *True* and *False* are attributes of Speech, not of Things. . . . Seeing then that *truth* consisteth in the right ordering of names in our affirmations, a man that seeketh precise *truth,* had need to remember what every name he uses stands for; and to place it accordingly; or else he will find himself entangled in words, as a bird in lime-twiggs; the more he struggles, the more belimed" (4.105).

Although reason is dependent on language, it is equally clear from these last remarks that reason must also in some sense be independent of language if it is not to be contaminated by rhetoric. For "in the right Definition of Names, lyes the first use of Speech; which is the Acquisition of Science; And in wrong, or no Definitions, lyes the first abuse" (4.106). This occurs when "men register their thoughts wrong, by the inconstancy of the signification of their words; by which they register for their conceptions, that which they never conceived; and so deceive themselves" (4.102). The deception consequent upon the intentionally improper use of words is then extended to the intentional use of figurative language: the second abuse Hobbes describes occurs when men "use words metaphorically; that is, in other sense than that they are ordained for; and thereby deceive others" (4.102). This abuse is associated throughout the *Leviathan* with the use of language to communicate (and not simply register) our conceptions and passions.[16] For the passions are notoriously inconstant, and therefore of inconstant signification (4.109). First, the signs of the passions can be feigned (6.129), and can therefore deceive us as metaphor does (5.114, 7.132). Second, our feelings about those things which affect us, "that is, which please and displease us" (4.109), affect the way we refer to them. We are not to be trusted when we speak about those things we feel passionately about.

But, as the following passage illustrates, the passions also affect the rational use of language in general, by turning even those abstract concepts that do not refer to the passions into metaphors for the speaker's own disposition: "And therefore in reasoning, a man must take heed of words; which besides the signification of what we imagine of their nature, have a signification also of the nature, disposition, and interest of the speaker; such as are the names of Vertues, and Vices; For one man calleth *Wisdome*, what another calleth *feare*; and one *cruelty*, what another *justice*. . . . And therefore such names can never be true grounds of any ratiocination" (4.109–10, cf. 6.120). Hobbes's first solution, like Locke's in the *Essay on Human Understanding* (book 3), is to insist on the exact definition of our words: "To conclude, the Light of humane minds is Perspicuous Words, but by exact definitions first snuffed, and purged from ambiguity. . . . And on the contrary, Metaphors, and senseless and ambiguous words, are like *ignes fatui*; and reasoning upon them, is wandering amongst innumerable absurdities; and their end, contention, and sedition, or contempt" (5.116–17, cf. 5.114).

The suggestion, paradoxically relayed by a highly metaphorical passage (what does it mean to snuff the light of human reason if not to put it out?), is that we have only to define our terms rationally and properly in order to avoid the abuse of reason by the passions and by metaphor. (While Hobbes does not directly argue like the humanists that the abuse of language is the precondition of its right use, he does claim that the possibility of abuse need not affect its right use.) Yet, as Hobbes tells us elsewhere, the problem does not finally lie in the deceptive or seductive use of metaphor, but in the fact that all language is ambiguous, all texts require interpretation, and all interpretation is debatable. One can never be sure whether one's reasoning (or even that of the majority) is correct, because the logical or cognitive dimension of language is always threatened by the rhetorical dimension. Here Hobbes, like Montaigne, diverges from the humanists: diversity in interpretation, far from indicating the possibility of consensus about the meaning of a text, suggests only the possibility of consensus about the impossibility of consensus—a statement that is paradoxical in the same way as the skeptic's assertion that he knows nothing. But this agreement to the second degree is a crucial moment in Hobbes's argument, since it allows Hobbes to move from rhetoric, which involves an appeal to the passions, to logic, which involves reasoning about the passions. We should agree then, Hobbes finally argues, that because we cannot agree, an arbitrary representative of reason must be decided upon: "And therefore, as when there is a controversy in an account, the parties must by their own accord, set up for right Reason, the Reason of some Arbitrator, or Judge, to whose sentence they will both stand, or their controversie must either come to blowes, or be undecided, for want of a right Reason constituted by Nature; so is it also in all debates of what kind soever" (5.111).[17] Right reason is illegible in nature, so a fictional but persuasive standard of right reason must be decided upon, that is, there must be a sovereign. As the skeptical critique of language and cognition in book 1 reveals, Hobbes wants to contain the threat of rhetoric by acknowledging it, and thus the necessity of repressing it by means of the arbitrary institution of meaning. But paradoxically, this attempt to suppress the rhetorical dimension of language ends up by reintroducing it in another way, that is, by raising the question of obedience. As Hobbes is well aware, he has not solved the problem of diversity in interpretation and its relation to an authoritative standard of judgment. He has not, in short, solved the problem of authority. He has simply transferred it from the realm of cognition to the realm of persuasion. We must next address the question of how and why the fiction of right reason is persuasive, and in order to do this we must consider Hobbes's depiction of the state of nature.

The Sovereign as Representative and the Rhetoric of Representation

Hobbes's nominalist and ultimately skeptical analysis of the use and abuse of language is mirrored in and supported by his analysis of the state of nature, which also concludes with the necessity of an arbitrary sovereign. But whereas in the first case Hobbes stressed the impossibility of cognitive certainty and the inevitability of contradiction given the lack of an authoritative standard of judgment, in the second case he introduces the fear of violent death attendant upon such contradiction as the means of overcoming the state of contradiction. He is not concerned with whether such a state of nature actually existed (in fact, he doubts it did [13.187]); rather, he is interested in devising a hypothetical account that will be logically compelling: if you accept the argument that all individuals fear violent death, you will perforce accept the conclusion of the necessity of an arbitrary and absolute sovereign power.[18] Logic is not separate from the passions, as Hobbes makes clear: "The passion to be reckoned [reasoned] upon, is fear" (14.200). The difference in this case between Hobbes's logic and the rhetorical appeal to the passions that he condemns is that the former, both in the form of its argument and in its effect, aims to transcend private reason, whereas the latter does not.

If in the analysis of language Hobbes argues *in utramque partem* both formally and thematically (i.e., he uses the possibility of debate against itself, as evidence for the necessity of doing away with debate) and thereby opposes the humanist ideal of the *consensus omnium*, in his analysis of the state of nature he launches a full-scale attack on the humanist belief in the dignity of man. Here the passion of fear turns out to be the equivalent of linguistic ambiguity, but here again Hobbes uses fear against itself in his attempt to convince the reader of the necessity of a sovereign power.

Consequently, whereas in the analysis of language the sovereign was defined in terms of his ability to hand down an authoritative interpretation, here the sovereign is defined in terms of his power to enforce that interpretation in civic (if not in private) life. Authoritative interpretation, as Hobbes makes clear here and later in the *Leviathan*, is not a matter of cognition but one of power. A close look at Hobbes's analysis of the state of nature will show that his conception of the sovereign as representative of the people implies a nonmimetic, fundamentally rhetorical notion of representation.

The waywardness of logical error, of contradiction, and of metaphor finds a persuasive equivalent for Hobbes in the state of nature where all men have the right to all things (14.190) and thus, properly speaking, to nothing. By this he means that the question of property, of ownership and propriety (15.202), has not yet been decided, so that while each individual may *claim* the right to ownership, no one is recognized as actually owning any particular thing.[19] The state of nature is thus a state of war, for as long as all men have the right to all things, men will of necessity be in competition for the same things. And since there is no security in this state (14.190), they will be tempted to, and will use violence to secure their ends.

If the state of nature is thus one in which men act according to their passions (competition, diffidence, glory), it is only when they begin to reason about the passions (13.186) that they begin to emerge from this state. We can anticipate Hobbes's argument *in utramque partem* at this point—his use of the passions against the passions or of private reason against itself—by remarking that such reasoning is itself passionately self-interested, for it is the individual's overwhelming fear of violent death that leads him to contract with others to renounce his right to all things, including the use of violence. But reason is not only motivated by fear; it is also validated by fear, for the covenant is invalid unless it is supplemented by a coercive power: "For he that performeth first, has no assurance that the other will performe after; because the bonds of words are too weak to bridle men's ambition, avarice, anger, and other Passions, without the feare of some coercive Power; which in the condition of meer Nature, where all men are equall, and judges of the justnesse of their own fears cannot possibly be supposed" (14.196). Hence the necessity of the sovereign, the person to whom the individual's rights have been transferred (14.191) and who as a result can compel the obedience of every individual to a single sovereign power.[20]

The sovereign thus performs two related functions in Hobbes's analysis of political obligation. In his function as representative he gives unity to the diverse wills of the citizens, and thereby does away (at least in theory) with the possible conflict of individual wills (16.220, 17.224–25, 17.227). But he can effectively do so only to the extent that each citizen resigns his right "to use his own power"

(14.189), thereby establishing the sovereign as the common power, which gives force to the covenant. As Hobbes writes in chapter 17 of the *Leviathan*, the "reall Unitie" of men is the person of the sovereign, which is created by the covenant which grants the sovereign power: "For by this Authoritie, given him by every particular man in the Common-Wealth, he hath the use of so much Power and Strength conferred on him, that by terror thereof, he is inabled to forme the wills of them all, to Peace at home, and mutuall ayd against their enemies abroad" (17.227–28). The paradox here, of course, is that the sovereign as represenative is created by the covenant, but the coercive force of the sovereign is what validates the covenant and his own legitimacy as representative. The sovereign's power is in fact created by a complicated rhetorical maneuver, in which the effect of the covenant is necessarily presupposed as its cause. A closer look at Hobbes's idea of the sovereign as representative will begin to clarify the way in which this notion is an essentially rhetorical one—the figure that is the "origin" of the ability to make distinctions between literal and figurative, mine and thine.

Hobbes's theory of political representation is inseparable from his notion of a "person," for "a person, is he *whose words or actions are considered, either as his own, or as representing the words or actions of an other man, or of any other thing to whom they are attributed, whether Truly or by Fiction. . . .* Of Persons Artificiall, some have their words and actions *Owned* by those whom they represent. And then the Person is the *Actor*; and he that owneth his words and actions, is the AUTHOR: In which case the Actor acteth by Authority" (16.217–18). Hanna Pitkin has argued that this notion of the sovereign as authorized representative or artificial person solves a number of problems that had troubled Hobbes in *The Elements of Law* and *De cive*—namely, how to avoid dissension or contradiction by unifying the wills of the individual citizens in the single will of the sovereign (16.220: "A Multitude of men, are made *One* Person, when they are by one man, or one Person, Represented"), while exempting the sovereign from the responsibilities incumbent upon those who have participated in the contract (916ff.). But she argues further that defining representation in terms of "acting for" rather than "standing for" leads to an empty, formalistic concept of representation: "A sovereign given complete power for all perpetuity, with no obligation to consult the wishes of his subjects and no duties toward them which they can claim—surely nothing could be further from what we ordinarily think of as representation or representative government!" (917). Or, in the words of Morton Kaplan, whom Pitkin cites, "All do not authorize [the sovereign] to act as a representative in any *literal* meaning of the term" (917 n. 78; emphasis Pitkin's).[21] But this is precisely the point Hobbes wishes to stress.

The representative is not a literal representative (as though such a thing were not in itself an oxymoron), because the author cedes his right of action to the representative. Once this initial authorization has taken place, the author retains no control over the sovereign's actions. The sovereign-representative who is thus authorized is effective, that is, powerful, precisely because he is *not* bound by any contractual obligations to act as his subjects would act.[22] Hence, no doubt, Hobbes's interest in the etymology of the word "person," which seems to lend support to his insistence on the essential incommensurability of author and actor in political representation: "The word Person is latine: insteed whereof the Greeks have *prosopon*, which signifies the *Face*, as *Persona* in latine signifies the *disguise*, or *outward appearance* of a man, counterfeited on the Stage; and sometimes more particularly that part of it, which disguiseth the face, as a Mask or Visard" (16.217). This theatrical use of the term "person" (which is already a translation and effacement of its Greek etymology, and which defines the person in terms of the possibility of disguise, and representation as [the possibility of] misrepresentation) is then further "translated," Hobbes tells us, from the stage "to any Representer of speech and action, as well in Tribunalls, as Theaters" (16.217). The concept of person thus introduces the possibility of artifice within the natural (or—what is structurally similar—of the effect of logic within rhetoric) for, by Hobbes's definition, even the individual who acts or speaks on his own account is a person. He is both author or owner of his actions and actor: the natural person who yet adopts the artifice of a mask by acting or representing himself. To own and therefore represent one's actions is thus already to be capable of misrepresenting them, or being dispossessed of them, for a man may counterfeit his own intentions and actions as well as those of another. Indeed, this possibility is touched on shortly after the etymological discussion, when Hobbes writes, "Of persons Artificiall, *some* have their words and actions *Owned* by those whom they represent" (16.218; first emphasis mine). The exceptions are inanimate objects, children, fools, madmen and—swindlers (Pitkin, 332), who are artificial persons acting on their own authority, or natural persons pretending to be artificial persons.

The paradox of the natural person is essential to Hobbes's account of the generation of society from nature, for it is clear that one could never get out of the state of nature unless representation were always already a natural possibility. The contract is the first step out of this state, but insofar as everyone who acts represents himself, the formation of the contract is already an act of representation. Yet precisely because the possibility of representation is also the possibility of misrepresentation, the individual must give up his own (potentially aberrant) rights of representation to the sovereign. Here, in a civil context, what had been in nature the constant threat of diverse and aberrant wills, of representation as the noncorrespondence of act and author, and therefore of misrepresentation or deceit, is now seen as the source of the sovereign's power.[23] He is not bound to represent his subjects if representation is understood to imply correspondence to a preexisting or literal truth, or the control of the representative by the author. A nonmimetic notion of representation, based on power, is thus substituted for a mimetic conception of representation, based on cognition;[24] the vulnerability of the mimetic concept (that the sign can never fully represent the signified) is thus turned into a positive strength. If rhetoric and representation figure as potentially wayward and coercive in the state of nature, they are also, according to Hobbes, what allow us to escape from this state. Hobbes can thus once again be seen to use rhetoric against itself, in order to establish the fiction of a logically deduced artificial person who represents us only "figuratively," that is, who does not own his actions but has power precisely because of this.

But the contract that is described as the mutual transferring of rights and powers is itself only artificial (17.226), since one cannot "really" (Hobbes) transfer one's rights, one can only refuse to exercise them.[25] And, as Pitkin remarks, this still doesn't solve the problem of the source of the sovereign's power.[26] As we saw earlier, it is not the rational act of authorization or the transfer of rights that validates the covenant, but the passion of fear: "For the Lawes of Nature . . . of themselves, without the terrour of some Power, to cause them to be observed, are contrary to our naturall Passions, that carry us to Partiality, Pride, Revenge, and the like. And Covenants, without the Sword, are but Words, and of no strength to secure a man at all" (17.223, cf. 17.227, 21.262–64). But the problem of the origin of the sovereign power is the same as that of the authorization of the covenant. For just as the sovereign is necessary to validate the covenant that creates the sovereign, so fear of the sword is necessary for the effective transfer of rights and power, which creates the "publique Sword" (18.231).

Here again Hobbes's concept of representation and of power turns out to be rhetorical. The sovereign is powerful, he suggests (18.231), because his power is doubly metaphorical: that is, not only because it is not properly speaking his own but has been transferred to or "conferred upon" (17.227) him by the makers of the covenant, but also because this "transfer" is itself metaphorical. This is not to say that the sovereign's power is not real or effective, but that it is first of all rhetorically effective in persuading the individual citizen that this power both is and is not his own. The power *is* the citizen's because the commonwealth is instituted when a multitude of men *"Covenant, every one, with every one,* that to whatsoever *Man,* or *Assembly of Men,* shall be given by the major part, the *Right* to *Present* the Person of them all . . . every one, as well he that *Voted for it,* as he that *Voted against it,* shall *Authorise* all the Actions and Judgements, of that Man, or Assembly of men, in the same manner, as if they were his own" (18.228–29). In taking this "as if" for the truth, in accepting the fictional or hypothetical unity of author and actor in the artificial person, the subject gives up all claims to exercise his own power against the sovereign, for to do so would be to act against himself. Furthermore, since the sovereign's actions are not properly his own, he can never commit "Injustice, or Injury in the proper signification" (18.232), and therefore can give no proper grounds for revolt (21.265).

But the sovereign power is also *not* the subject's, as the ambiguity of the "as if" suggests, for the sovereign is powerful precisely to the extent that the individual citizen no longer recognizes his power as his own, but transfers it to the sovereign. The individual is persuaded to fear and therefore obey the sovereign because he does not recognize that what he fears is (the nonexercise of) his own power.

The sovereign's power is rhetorical in another sense as well. He controls his subjects' actions because he controls their opinions: "It belongeth therefore to him that hath the Soveraign Power, to be Judge, or constitute all Judges of Opinions and Doctrines" (18.233). And this judgment is not a logical inference of the truth, but a rhetorical and prudential consideration of the effects of certain doctrines: the truth is defined as that which "prevent[s] Discord and Civill Warre" (18.233). "For Doctrine repugnant to Peace, can no more be True, than Peace and Concord can be against the Law of Nature." And since the law of nature is subject to controversy, it is up to the sovereign to interpret this law for his subjects.[27] In a dialectic that is similar to that of the master-slave dialectic in Hegel's *Phenomenology*, the sovereign is finally seen to be the subject's fiction of the perfect orator. Thus, in a passage reminiscent of the figure of Lady Rhetoric, who binds her listeners with the golden chains of eloquence flowing from her mouth,[28] Hobbes writes: "But as men, for the atteyning of peace, and conservation of themselves thereby, have made an Artificiall Man, which we call a Common-wealth; so also have they made Artificiall Chains, called *Civill Lawes*, which they themselves, by mutuall covenants, have fastened at one end, to the lips of that Man, or Assembly, to whom they have given the Soveraigne Power; and at the other end to their own Ears" (21.263–64).

Sovereign and Church

A number of critics have argued that Hobbes's failure to provide a logically compelling ground for obedience to the sovereign in his analysis of the passion of fear obliges him to introduce the supplementary authority of Scripture in books 3 and 4 of the *Leviathan*.[29] The problem left unsolved in books 1 and 2, according to this interpretation, is that if the individual believes there is a power greater than the sovereign—especially one that promises eternal life—he will not be afraid to risk his life in this world in an act of rebellion against civil authority. But if the sovereign power is seen to be authorized by God, then there is no such greater power, and no rebellion is possible. Hence the turn to biblical history to justify—to authorize—this authorization. As I have argued, this rhetorical moment is already present in the "logical" analysis of books 1 and 2. But whether Hobbes's primary concern is to supplement his deficient logical analysis or, as I argue below, to subvert the claims of the competing rhetoric of Scripture, it is clear that the consequence of the analysis of Scripture in books 3 and 4 is to conflate the authority of Church and State, and thus do away with conflicting claims to the subject's obedience.[30] Hobbes does so by maintaining that Scripture itself instructs the reader in obedience to the civil sovereign.

Pierre Manent has argued that the attempt to shore up the sovereign's power by the appeal to an authority—Scripture—that Hobbes also desires to undermine is necessarily contradictory (106). The preceding analysis should suggest, however, that what is contradiction from a logical point of view may be devastating irony from the perspective of rhetoric. Hobbes may seem to be appealing to the authority of Scripture, but his aim is precisely to undermine that authority, to subordinate belief in Scripture to belief in the state. The following pages aim to clarify the function of the analysis of belief in books 3 and 4 in the rhetoric of the *Leviathan*.

If one of the consequences of Hobbes's theory of representation as authorization is to divorce the author from his actions, a further implication is to divorce the divine author from his scriptural text. Just as one cannot refer to divine or natural law to justify one's judgment (since one can know nothing about God [18.230]), so one cannot refer to divine intention to justify a reading. Scripture has no intrinsic authority; *pace* Luther, it provides no authoritative key to its own interpretation. This view has important consequences for Hobbes's science of the Christian commonwealth, since knowledge of divine law and of the Christian state is derived from the reading of Scripture.

In book 3 of the *Leviathan* Hobbes tells us that God declares his laws in three ways: "by the Dictates of *Naturall Reason*," by revelation, and by prophecy (31.396). Revelation is always made to the individual, and does not involve the transmission of universal laws. The precepts of natural reason, Hobbes tells us, are self-evident and inscribed on every man's heart (33.426). Prophecy has long since been replaced by Scripture, "from which, by wise and learned interpretation, and carefull ratiocination, all rules and precepts necessary to the knowledge of our duty both to God and man, without Enthusiasme, or supernaturall Inspiration, may easily be deduced" (32.414). The irony of Hobbes's insistence on the self-evidence of natural law and of Scripture is clear both from the skeptical analysis of cognition in book 1 and from the fact that in Hobbes's own time different interpretations of Scripture had led to civil turmoil and conflict between Church and State. Hobbes sets out to solve this "conflict of interpretations" by arguing, like Erasmus, that the question is not about the authority of Scripture, but about its meaning, that is, the authority of one's interpretation. Everyone agrees that God must be obeyed: "But the question is not of obedience to God, but of *when*, and *what* God hath said; which to Subjects that have no supernaturall revelation, cannot be known, but by that naturall reason, which guided them, for the obtaining of Peace and Justice, to obey the authority of their severall Common-wealths; that is to say, of their lawfull Soveraigns" (32.415). Similarly, everyone believes that Scripture is the word of God (33.425), but "it is manifest, that none can know they [Scriptures] are Gods Word . . . but those to whom God himself hath revealed it supernaturally; and therefore the question is not rightly moved, of our *Knowledge* of it. Lastly, when the question is propounded of our *Beleefe*; because some are moved to beleeve for one, and others for other reasons, there can be rendred no one generall answer for them all. The question truly stated is, *By what Authority they are made Law"* (33.425).

Hobbes then argues (illogically but rhetorically) that Scripture itself provides the solution to this interpretive dilemma in those passages which state that there can be only one supreme authority in the Christian commonwealth, and therefore only one authoritative interpreter: the sovereign. The argument runs as follows: The Bible tells us that the kingdom of God is temporal rather than eternal (35.447–48, 38.484); God first established a covenant with the Jews and Moses was the sovereign; Christ will restore this kingdom *on earth* at the second coming.[31] The consequences of this literal interpretation of God's kingdom are politically significant, for if the kingdom of God were eternal then it could oppose its claims to those of the civil commonwealth. But if it is temporal, then its claims must be *postponed* and the laws of the current commonwealth must be obeyed (42.526–27): "The Kingdome of Christ is not of this world: therefore neither can his Ministers (unlesse they be Kings,) require obedience in his name" (45.525). Since only the sovereign can require obedience, it is only by the sovereign's authority that the precepts of Scripture are made law (33.425–27). The result is that only the sovereign has the right to interpret Scripture: "For, whosoever hath a lawfull power over any Writing, to make it Law, hath the power also to approve, or disapprove the interpretation of the same" (33.427, cf. 40.501–5).[32]

As a result of Hobbes's interpretation of the kingdom of God, the three roles of Christ (as savior, teacher, and king) are also conceived of diachronically (41.514). Christ will begin to be king at the "generall resurrection," but he is not now. Thus, although he will command and coerce his subjects then (as kings do), his function now is

173

to preach, to instruct, and to persuade: "So that there are two parts of our Saviours office during his aboad upon the Earth: One to Proclaim himself the Christ; and another by Teaching, and by working of Miracles, to perswade" (41.515–16, cf. 42.525, 551, 557–58, 588, 592, 596). In other words, the function of religion in a Christian commonwealth is not to exert temporal power in the way the sovereign does, but to advise and counsel.

In defining religion in terms of persuasion rather than coercion and command, Hobbes effectively subordinates the Church to the State, but he also allows rhetoric back into the commonwealth in a supplementary and supportive role,[33] not least of all because part of what religion counsels is obedience to civil law: "For our Saviour Christ hath not given us new Laws, but Counsell to observe those wee are subject to" (43.611). It is no surprise, then, that while rhetoric was defined as seductive and coercive in the discussion of the civil commonwealth in books 1 and 2, it is law that is coercive and rhetoric that is positively persuasive in the Christian commonwealth. But this positive view of rhetoric in books 3 and 4 is itself part of Hobbes's rhetorical strategy to subvert the Church's claim to temporal power. For Hobbes has nothing against coercion per se; he simply wants to avoid two sources of it in the commonwealth. Fortunately, it is doctrinally sound as well as politically useful to argue that Christ "never accepteth forced actions, (which is all the Law produceth,) but the inward conversion of the heart; which is not the work of Laws; but of Counsell, and Doctrine" (42.592).

But the rhetorical function of religion is not simply supportive of Hobbes's political science. For Hobbes's introduction of rhetoric in the context of a nominalistic negative theology supports our argument for the rhetorical, nonmimetic dimension of the notions of science and sovereignty that he elaborates in books 1 and 2 of the *Leviathan*. We can clarify this point by turning to chapter 45 where, in a discussion of idolatry, Hobbes makes a distinction between a mimetic and a nonmimetic notion of representation. "An IMAGE," he tells us, "(in the most strict signification of the word) is the Resemblance of some thing visible" (in the external world or the mind of the maker [668]). It is evident, then, that "there can be no Image of a thing Infinite. . . . And therefore there can be no Image of God." As a result, science and theology are mutually exclusive. For "the *subject* of Philosophy . . . [is any body] capable of composition and resolution; that is to say, every body of whose generation or properties we can have knowledge" (*EW* 1.10), and we can have

174

no knowledge of God. "But in a larger use of the word Image, is contained also, any Representation of one thing by another. So an earthly Soveraign may be called the Image of God" (45.669). The sovereign is made in the image and likeness of God not because he resembles God in any visual way, but because the way in which the commonwealth is constructed resembles the performative utterance or *fiat* by which God created the world ("Introduction," 81–82). Once again, representation is conceived of in terms of a voluntaristic model of power rather than in terms of a visual model of cognition.

If we now return to the first book of the *Leviathan*, we see that Hobbes conceives of reasoning in terms of imagery "in the most strict signification":

> Whatsoever we imagine, is *Finite*. Therefore there is no Idea, or conception of anything we call *Infinite*. . . . When we say any thing is infinite, we signifie onely, that we are not able to conceive the ends, and bounds of the thing named; having no Conception of the thing, but of our own inability. And therefore the Name of *God* is used, not to make us conceive him . . . but that we may honour him. Also because whatsoever . . . we conceive, has been perceived first by sense, either all at once, or by parts; a man can have no thought, representing any thing, not subject to sense. [3.99]

It is clear, however, that the common or universal names that are necessary for reasoning are analogous to those images that do *not* correspond to any visible or imagined thing. These names are as rhetorical as the name of God, by which we do not conceive of God but of "our own inability." And this cognitive disability betrays the similarity between the political scientist and the priest or poet. For just as God's "Attributes cannot signifie what he is, but ought to signifie our desire to honour him" (46.694), so the attributes of sovereignty represent our desire to be persuaded to obedience, our desire, in short, for authority. The use of language and with it the institution of sovereignty, does not simply presuppose the possibility of abuse; it is identical with it.

Hobbes: Christ or Sovereign?

In writing of the "Kingdome of God, and Policy Ecclesiasticall," Hobbes tells us, he pretends "not to advance any Position of [his] . . . own, but only to shew what are the Consequences that seem to [him] . . . deducible from the Principles of Christian Politiques, (which are the holy Scriptures)" (43.625–26). The vocabulary of consequence and deduction suggests that Hobbes sees the interpretation of Scripture as an essential part of his political science. But if the only authoritative interpreter of Scripture is the sovereign, what is the status of Hobbes's deduction? Furthermore, if reasoning presupposes fixed definitions, but all language is (potentially) inconstant and all interpretation biased, how are we to understand Hobbes's reasoning about the passions and, in particular, his assertion that all men in the state of nature have the same fear of violent death and the same belief that peace is a good (16.216)?

In the "Conclusion" Hobbes writes that these statements are not empirical but hypothetical (727). If men had the same fear, then they would arrive at the dictates of reason that Hobbes has enumerated: "These dictates of Reason, men use to call by the name of Lawes; but improperly: for they are but Conclusions, or Theoremes concerning what conduceth to the conservation and defence of themselves, wheras Law, properly is the word of him, that by right hath command over others" (15.216–17). Furthermore, the sovereign who can bind us to these "conclusions," who can "convert this Truth of Speculation, into the Utility of Practice" (31.408), is himself a conclusion derived from the dictates of reason. And this means finally, as Hobbes himself recognized, that the existence of natural reason or natural law or the primary passion of fear is itself hypothetical or axiomatic ("Conclusion," 726), and "those that by Writing, or Publique Discourse, or by their eminent actions, have already engaged themselves to the maintaining of contrary opinions, they will not bee so easily satisfied" (726).

This problem then leads us to consider Hobbes's own rhetorical situation as a writer in a time of civil war, that is, in the absence of a sovereign. When Hobbes claims for his text the status of political science rather than of rhetoric, he is setting himself up as sovereign. But he realizes at the same time that the theorems of natural reason he is expounding are by no means as self-evident as he sometimes pretends (33.426). The very fact that he feels the need to write the *Leviathan* in the first place, the fact of civil war, suggests that "the grounds of these Rights [of the sovereign], have the rather need to be diligently and truly taught" (30.377). As he writes in the "Conclusion," "though this Law [that every man is bound to protect in war the sovereign authority that protects him in peace] may bee drawn by consequence, from some of those that are there already mentioned; yet the Times require to have it inculcated, and remembred" (719).

Elsewhere Hobbes explicitly acknowledges that since he is not the sovereign, he can make no assertions: "But because this doctrine (though proved out of places of Scripture not few, nor obscure) will appear to most men a novelty; I doe but propound it; maintaining nothing in this, or any other paradox of Religion; but attending the end of that dispute of the sword, concerning the Authority, (not yet amongst my Countrey-men decided,) by which all sorts of doctrine are to bee approved, or rejected" (38.484). Accordingly, Hobbes's role is not that of the dispassionate scientist, but of the rhetorician, teacher (31.408, "Conclusion," 726), or "prudent Counsellor" (25.310). For "COMMAND," as he tells us, "is, where a man saith, *Doe this*, or *Doe not this*, without expecting other reason than the Will of him that sayes it. . . . [But] COUNSELL, is where a man saith, *Doe*, or *Doe not this*, and deduceth his reasons from the benefit that arriveth by it to him to whom he saith it" (25.303). Like Aristotle's political orator, Hobbes realizes that "counsel can only be given on matters about which people deliberate; matters, namely, that ultimately depend on ourselves, and which we have it in our power to set going" (*Rhet.* 1359a 35). So "in this time, that men call not onely for Peace, but also for Truth," Hobbes "offer[s] such Doctrines as [he] . . . think[s] True, and that manifestly tend to Peace and Loyalty, to the consideration of those that are yet in deliberation" ("Conclusion," 726). He does not offer the truth, but what he thinks true. Yet, as with the humanist proponents of the *vita activa* who preceded him, Hobbes hopes not simply to prove a point, but to persuade his readers to prudent action (31.408). He differs from the humanists only in hoping to do so more effectively in the *person* of a political scientist. As Aristotle writes in one of my—now obviously ironic—epigraphs to this chapter, "rhetoric masquerades as political science, and the professors of it as political experts."

As we have seen, the adopting of this persona clearly does not exclude the use of rhetoric, but it does require that eloquence (appear to) be reduced to the status of "adornment" of the truth. Against those who claim that Eloquence and Reason are "contrary Faculties," Hobbes argues: "Judgment, and Fancy may have place in the same man; but by turnes; as the end which he aimeth at requireth. . . . So also Reason, and Eloquence, (though not perhaps

177

in the Natural Sciences, yet in the Morall) may stand very well together. For wheresoever there is a place for adorning and preferring of Errour, there is much more place for adorning and preferring of Truth, if they have it to adorn" ("Conclusion," 718; cf. Aristotle, *Rhet.* 1355a 20–25). The reason, of course, that one would need to adorn and prefer the Truth is that one doesn't simply have it to adorn—as though one were dressing up the sovereign in his robes of state. The naked truth has no authority of its own; in fact, it cannot be seen at all, for truth itself is an effect of the belief (the rhetorical *fides*) in authority.[34]

Hobbes goes on to tell us that "there is nothing I distrust more than my Elocution; which nevertheless I am confident (excepting the Mischances of the Presse) is not obscure," and that he has "neglected the Ornaments of quoting the ancient Poets, Orators, and Philosophers, contrary to the custome of late time" (726–27). Yet while Hobbes may not have sprinkled his text with the frequent allusions and citations typical of his humanist predecessors, he shares, as we have seen, their concern with a rhetorical, that is, persuasive, conception of the truth. And if he does not argue from authority or tradition, it is because he is even more skeptical than they were of the availability of some shared standard of practical judgment, even more conscious of the necessity of an arbitrary, fictional authority. For prudence is for Hobbes not Aristotelian practical reason, but personal self-interest. And it is this which finally unmasks the *person* of Hobbes the prudent counselor in the guise of the political scientist.[35]

But Hobbes is like the humanists in still another way. The interest of self-interest for Hobbes is that like rhetoric it contains within itself the seeds of its own destruction, and this dialectical moment makes it the ironic counterpart of practical reason. The goal is the same in both cases—the constitution and government of the commonwealth—but for the humanists positive law is a reflection of a genuine consensus and ultimately of divine law, whereas for Hobbes positive law is instituted arbitrarily by the sovereign. The further irony is that in aiming to persuade us of the necessity of this sovereign, Hobbes must presuppose a community of readers who are capable of exercising their own judgment, and this exercise is associated throughout the *Leviathan* with a prudential activity that has much in common with the humanists' conception of prudence.

The difference between sapience and prudence, Hobbes tells us in chapter 5, is not analogous to the difference between theory and practice, but between two praxes, one of which is infallible.

> As, much Experience, is *Prudence*; so, is much Science, *Sapience*. For though wee usually have one name of Wisedome for them both; yet the Latines did always distinguish between *Prudentia* and *Sapientia*; ascribing the former to Experience, the later to Science. But to make their difference appeare more cleerly, let us suppose one man endued with an excellent naturall use, and dexterity in handling his armes; and another to have added to that dexterity, an acquired Science, of where he can offend, or be offended by his adversarie, in every possible posture, or guard: The ability of the former, would be to the ability of the later, as Prudence to Sapience; both usefull; but the later infallible. But they that trusting onely to the authority of books, follow the blind blindly, are like him that trusting to the false rules of the master of Fence, ventures praesumptuously upon an adversary, that either kills, or disgraces him. . . .
> But in any businesse, whereof a man has not infallible Science to proceed by; to forsake his own natural judgement, and be guided by generall sentences read in Authors, and subject to many exceptions, is a signe of folly, and generally scorned by the name of Pedantry. And even of those men themselves, that in Councells of the Commonwealth, love to shew their reading of Politiques and History, very few do it in their domestique affaires, where their particular interest is concerned, having Prudence enough for their private affaires. [117–18]

It is a mistake simply to accept a text as authoritative; one must judge for oneself. And this means in turn that prudence is required for reading (since, as Hobbes tells us, all texts are debatable—as long as debate is permitted). So the reader of Hobbes's *Leviathan* must exercise his own judgment in the interpretation of the text. This rhetorical appeal to the reader's prudential judgment is nowhere more evident than in the "Introduction" to the *Leviathan*, where Hobbes urges the reader, "*Nosce teipsum, Read thy Self*," arguing that if he reads himself "he shall thereby read and know, what are the thoughts, and Passions of all other men, upon the like occasions." In short, the individual reader can reason by analogy to a knowledge of mankind. The conclusion, of course, is contained in the assumption of the validity of such analogy. But this assumption, as Hobbes argues in the course of the *Leviathan*, is justified by its practical effects rather than by any correspondence to theoretical truth. Hobbes's appeal to introspection is a far cry from the infallible

179

method of science he speaks of elsewhere in the text, at the same time that it is also the prerequisite of this science, for only if we accept the axiom that all individuals in the state of nature fear violent death will we accept the logic of the *Leviathan*.[36]

If we now return to one of Hobbes's early humanist projects, his translation of Thucydides, we can see that the logic of the *Leviathan* is designed to engage the reader in the same process of deliberation that Hobbes claimed for Thucydides' rhetoric, but only in order to convince the reader of the failure of humanist rhetoric, as Hobbes had become convinced of its failure subsequent to translating Thucydides. The good reader of history, according to Hobbes, is a spectator of the author's narration. This does not mean that the reader is dazzled by the spectacle, but rather that he is capable of judging it. "Good judgment and education" (*EW* 8.xi) are the precondition of the benefit we gain from reading Thucydides.[37] Whereas for the Quattrocento humanists the prudence of the author was ideally the cause of the reader's prudence, for Hobbes the prudence of the "better sort of reader" (*EW* 8.x) alone is the cause as well as the effect of right reading. This is one of the reasons Hobbes concludes that his original motive for translating Thucydides was misguided. The other is that less prudent readers will disagree in their judgments of the text.

> These virtues of my author did so take my affection, that they begat in me a desire to communicate him further: which was the first occasion that moved me to translate him. For it is an error we easily fall into, to believe that whatsoever pleaseth us, will be in like manner and degree acceptable to all: and to esteem of one another's judgment, as we agree in the liking or dislike of the same things. And in this error peradventure was I, when I thought, that as many of the more judicious as I should communicate him to, would affect him as much as I myself did. [*EW* 8.viii–ix][38]

It is just this variety of judgment or taste on the part of the average reader that Hobbes wants to combat in the *Leviathan*, for a commonwealth of the "better sort of reader" is just the sort of utopia that Hobbes scorns. In other words, it is precisely because Hobbes desires to affect the common reader the way Thucydides affects the superior reader (or, to put it another way, because Hobbes wants to create the Common-Reader) that he wants to subordinate rhetoric to logic and prudence to science. The paradox of this endeavor, however, is that to the extent that the *Leviathan* presupposes a reader capable of reasoning in his self-interest, it assumes the ideal commonwealth of readers whose existence would render the *Leviathan* superfluous.

For all these reasons, the distinction between prudence and science in the *Leviathan* finally breaks down. Earlier I said that science for Hobbes involves the necessary and universal knowledge of consequences, whereas prudence, like history, is merely conjectural and hypothetical. The problem is that once Hobbes tries to apply this science to the realm of contingency, he is obliged to reintroduce the prudential and rhetorical moment he had appeared to exclude. In subordinating rhetoric to logic, that is, in attempting to substitute logic for rhetoric, Hobbes must make his logic fulfill the persuasive function of rhetoric in the realm of contingent, particular affairs— the realm that includes, among other things, the judgment of particular readers. And, as Aristotle tells us, there can be no science of particulars. Rhetoric does not remain subordinate or external to logic in Hobbes's *Leviathan*; rather, (the reader's conviction of) logic is itself seen to be the unpredictable effect of rhetoric.[39]

As I have argued, Hobbes was clearly aware of the necessity of using rhetoric to fight rhetoric and to clear the way for logic. But, against the preceding reading, one would have to say that he seems also to have been confident of containing the threatening relativism of the rhetorical moment of his argument. For the humanists' belief in the resistance of practical certainty to Pyrrhonist skepticism, Hobbes substitutes his own notion of logical certainty. This logic might finally be described as a kind of prudence to the second degree, for science is for Hobbes prudential deliberation that takes as its object the impossibility of civic prudence, and thereby sacrifices itself to the necessary fiction of a commonwealth. With this sacrifice, Renaissance humanism comes to an end.

7 Conclusion

> Every art or applied science and every systematic investigation, and
> similarly every action and choice, seem to aim at some good; the
> good, therefore, has been well defined as that at which all things
> aim. But it is clear that there is a difference in the ends at which they
> aim: in some cases the activity is the end, in others the end is some
> product beyond the activity.
>
> —Aristotle, *Nicomachean Ethics*

The preceding pages have explored through a series of close
readings the articulations and revisions of one convention of reading in the Renaissance: the humanist assumption that reading not
only persuades us to prudential action but is itself a form of prudence. I began by arguing that a certain interpretation of Aristotle's
Ethics and of the classical rhetorical tradition in the Renaissance
contributed to the humanists' emphasis on the ethical processes or
activities of reading and writing. I then tried to clarify the different
ways in which this practice was understood—the different forms
practice took—by means of a close examination of the rhetorical
practice of a selection of Renaissance texts. As I argued in the Introduction, this methodology of "close reading" was required on both
historical and theoretical grounds: the first, because the humanists
themselves insisted on the inseparability of rhetorical and ethical
practice; the second, because we cannot understand the meaning of
a concept—in this case the concept of prudence—until we understand how such a concept is used. Roland Barthes was writing both
as a Renaissance humanist and as a contemporary theorist of literature when he claimed that "the theory of the text can coincide only
with a practice of writing."[1]

The assumption that reading persuades to prudent action was, as
we saw, reflected on the one hand in a variety of textual rhetorics *in*

utramque partem, while on the other it allowed the readers of such texts to make sense of rhetorical strategies that, from a logical point of view, are simply contradictory. This was particularly the case in the work of Salutati and Pontano. In examining the works of the Quattrocento humanists and of their northern counterparts, I further tried to show how the arguments of Academic skepticism could be used to dramatize a practical conception of the truth, and how those of Pyrrhonist skepticism could be used to undermine the alliance of rhetoric and Academic skepticism, thereby suggesting the more radical analogy of skepticism and faith. In the case of Valla and Erasmus, I concentrated on the analogy between rhetoric and faith, or the way in which faith can intervene to resolve the aporia of persuasion. In the *Essais* of Montaigne, the analogy of rhetoric and skepticism was most apparent, in the way in which Montaigne used rhetorical argumentation *in utramque partem* to develop a new skeptical mode of writing. Finally, Hobbes tried to circumvent the aporetical or skeptical moment of persuasion by instituting a political science: a politics that was founded on a rhetorical and religious *fides*.

On the basis of the readings of the preceding chapters, I argued that at least some of the work of Erasmus, Montaigne, and Hobbes reflected a questioning of Quattrocento humanist attitudes toward rhetoric. These authors were sensitive to the epistemological objection that knowledge must precede persuasion, and that the claim to a persuasion based on practical certainty is subject to the same cognitive critique. Whether they conceived of the text as the passage between *gnosis* and *praxis*, or as the place where that passage is suspended, they were concerned to reflect on the conditions of the possibility of their own reflection and activity. Rhetoric, in their texts, is the vehicle by which the prudential analogy between skepticism and action (the assumption that prudence represents "a new practical intellectualism") is itself put in question.

In their different ways, Salutati, Valla, Pontano, Erasmus, and Hobbes denied or tried to overcome the problems of epistemological skepticism by a faith in the possibility of praxis, and this involved in part the use of hypothetical arguments that do not make assertions, but aim instead at persuasion to action. Montaigne, on the other hand, was not concerned with getting beyond (or around) skepticism. In contrast, for example, to Erasmus, who wanted to defend the possibility of persuasion, predication, and action against

183

Luther's objection that we must know what we can do before we attempt to do anything, Montaigne assumed that language is always already beyond the epistemological impasse of skepticism—not because it allows us to know anything, but because it is itself a practice. But, of course, this notion of practice—the practice of language as a substitute for rather than as analogous to political action—proves to be an ironic version of the Quattrocento notion of prudence. In a different way Hobbes's political science could also be seen as an ironic version of prudence: whereas for the Quattrocento humanists contradiction was a sign of the possibility of prudential action, for Hobbes the only legitimate prudential act was the self-sacrifice of prudence to the law of noncontradiction, that is, to the commonwealth.

It will by now be obvious that to the extent that the judgment of prudence is seen to inform the concept of decorum, it impinges upon almost every major text in the Renaissance: statements about the nature and the possibility of decorum can be read as statements about prudence, and examples of decorum may also be interpreted in the same way. Prudential considerations of a different sort, therefore, have dictated the exclusion of many texts that might have been included in this anatomy of prudence and of humanist rhetoric. Castiglione and Machiavelli, in particular, come to mind.

If, as I have argued, the Quattrocento effected a rhetorical synthesis of prudence, skepticism, and faith, Castiglione and Machiavelli represent two versions of the disintegration of this synthesis: on the one hand the aesthetic, on the other the political. Numerous critics have remarked on the essentially aesthetic definition of *sprezzatura,* and on the fact that while Castiglione alludes to Cicero's *De oratore* at the beginning of *Il cortegiano,* the effect of this allusion is to emphasize the distance between Cicero's prudential conception of judgment and the aesthetic judgment of *sprezzatura.* In at least three of the four books, the courtier is fundamentally concerned with a discrete form of self-praise or self-display. While it is true that this self-praise does indirectly urge the reader to imitate the courtier, just as it urges the prince to favor him economically, both favor and imitation are described in aesthetic rather than political terms.[2] The result is that epideictic loses its wider political or civic implications both for the courtier and for Castiglione's reader. It is significant, in this context, that Federico's defense of the courtier's art of indirection is aesthetic rather than moral. To Gaspar

184

Pallavicino's charge of deceit, he replies: "Even if it [is] deceit, it is not to be censured. . . . If you have a beautiful jewel with no setting, and it passes into the hands of a good goldsmith, who with a skillful setting makes it appear far more beautiful, will you say that the goldsmith deceives the eyes of one who looks at it? Surely he deserves praise for that deceit, because with good judgment and art his masterful hand often adds grace and adornment."[3] In short, while reading *Il cortegiano* obviously involves us in an activity of judgment or discrimination, there is little suggestion in the first three books that this activity is to be conceived of as an instance of practical reasoning. And when there is such a suggestion by Ottaviano in book 4, several courtiers express the fear that the courtier has been defined out of existence. *Il cortegiano* is one text for which the intellectual historians' remark about the shrinking of rhetoric to epideictic—understood as aesthetic display—seems to be right. But this is not because all epideictic is essentially "literary" rather than rhetorical and therefore divorced from action, but because epideictic in *Il cortegiano* has become self-reflexive and paradoxical. Emilia hints at as much when she says to Federico in book 2, "If it is true, as I have heard, that a man has been known to be so clever and eloquent as not to want for material in writing a book in praise of a fly, others in praise of the quartan, another in praise of baldness, then can you not manage to talk about Courtiership for one evening?" (109–10; 122). The paradoxical encomium, rather than the encomium per se, may be the form that most lends itself to the subversion of the Quattrocento humanists' claims for the analogy between the practice of reading and practical reason. But *Il cortegiano* is a paradoxical encomium not only because it involves the paradox of self-reference[4] but because, even as it deviates from the early humanist ideal of prudence, it provides its own critique of the courtier in book 4. A return to our earlier scheme of the practical and aesthetic conceptions of reading will help to clarify this point.

We saw that *sprezzatura*, by definition, appears to be intransitive and ornamental—that the courtier appears to aim only at the aesthetic effects of wonder and surprise. Yet the courtiers themselves raise the question of the use of such ornament, as well as the objection of its possible deceitfulness. To the extent that it involves indirection, even the supposedly disinterested aesthetic attitude is subject to the charge of deceit and must, as a result, provide an ethical defense. Book 4 of *Il cortegiano* provides two: on the one hand the humanist prudential defense, on the other the Neoplatonic allegorical defense. Here it becomes clear that *Il cortegiano* offers its own anatomy of Renaissance humanist rhetoric by isolating and counterpointing as different ideologies and postures the spheres that were so precariously synthesized in the Quattrocento: the aesthetic, political, and religious. Thus in book 4 Ottaviano answers the objection to *sprezzatura* by reintroducing the humanist defense of aesthetics. He insists, in other words, on the transition from aesthetics to praxis. Virtue, he says, "often comes to nothing if it is not helped by cultivation. For if it is to pass to action [Erasmus's *transire in mores*] and to a perfect operation, nature alone does not suffice, as has been said, but the practice of art and reason is required. . . . Hence virtue can almost be called a kind of prudence." (297–98; 295: *Però la virtù si po quasi dir una prudenzia*). Bembo, on the other hand, introduces the allegorical defense of aesthetics by insisting on the Neoplatonic analogy between earthly and heavenly beauty. While Ottaviano argues for the moral and practical dimension of *sprezzatura*—for the rhetorical dimension in the humanist sense, Bembo tries to purify *sprezzatura* of practical rhetorical considerations, to provide us with sublimity as (in Kenneth Burke's words) a kind of pure persuasion. In both cases, the possibility of *sprezzatura* as it was earlier defined is put in question.

Machiavelli represents the political alternative to Castiglione's aesthetic redefinition of prudence.[5] In *Il principe*, prudence has become what its critics always feared it would: a technical skill divorced from ethical considerations. As Eugene Garver has shown, there is a politics of rhetorical invention in *Il principe*, and the examples that are introduced are presented not so the prince will imitate one or the another of them, but so that his own faculty of *virtù* will be exercised. Yet, while the reader is thus invited to engage in an activity of judgment, there is no suggestion that this activity is intrinsically moral. To the contrary chapter 25 tells us that the way to be absolutely successful in the contingent realm of human affairs is to be as flexible, as capable of change, as amoral as fortune is. And as we know from Pontano and other Quattrocento humanists, if an individual were as amoral as Fortune, he would not be happy, since happiness depends on moral virtue; he would be a sophist as Fortune is. Machiavelli's prince is the sophist as portrayed by Plato: a master of dissimulation for the purposes of self-aggrandizement.

But *Il principe* too can be seen as a paradoxical encomium within the humanist rhetorical tradition—not only because this prince has none of the virtues for which praise is the traditional reward, but because the skills for which Machiavelli does praise the prince are repeatedly illustrated by examples of failed *virtù*. Thus Garver remarks that *"The Prince* is filled with examples of princes going wrong by imitating examples. The moral Machiavelli draws is not that they are the wrong examples (as it would be if he had some new and different values to offer), but that imitation, defined as the relation of past act, value and future act, is not as simple as one might expect or like."[6] One could argue that a further implication is that *virtù* is just as much an ideal as those ideal commonwealths which Machiavelli censures early in *Il principe*.

It is significant in this regard that Machiavelli concludes *Il principe* by introducing the previously excluded figure of God: "Behold how she [Italy] prays God to send some one to redeem her from this barbarous cruelty and insolence. Behold her ready and willing to follow any standard if only there be someone to raise it. There is nothing now she can hope for but that your illustrious house may place itself at the head of this redemption, being by its power and fortune so exalted, and being favoured by God and the Church, of which it is now the ruler."[7] While this is in part ironic, the irony touches the prince as well, as though Machiavelli were admitting that the absolute flexibility the prince requires is nothing short of divine.[8]

It is important to remark at this point that while Castiglione and Machiavelli no longer subscribe to the ideology of Quattrocento humanism, they participate in it to the extent of proposing revised versions of prudential judgment: on the one hand *sprezzatura*, on the other *virtù*. Furthermore, they are influenced by that ideology insofar as they aim to educate the reader by means of a certain rhetorical practice—by dramatizing in this practice the *sprezzatura* or *virtù* that the reader is invited to imitate. The point, once again, is not that the reader should imitate any single example of the text (in *Il cortegiano* they are contradictory; in *Il principe* they are as well, insofar as they are examples of failed *virtù*), but rather that he should imitate the author's judgments of decorum. In both cases, there is a pedagogical claim; in both cases there is the conviction that it is possible, however indirectly, to educate the judgment.

In the English Renaissance humanism is shaped by indigenous social and political circumstances, and humanist rhetoric is transformed in a number of ways. One paradigm for this transformation is offered by Daniel Javitch, who argues that it is the indirection of Castiglione's courtier rather than the rhetoric of the humanist orator that provides the model of literary and social decorum for the Tudor court.[9] When we consider the literary production of such figures as Ascham, Elyot, More, Sidney, Jonson, and Spenser,[10] I think it is fairer to say that the rhetorical tradition of humanism continued alongside and entered into various relations with the interests of courtliness. While a detailed analysis of these relations is well beyond the scope of this conclusion, a few remarks about Sidney's *Apology for Poetry* may serve to illustrate my point. For, as many students of the English Renaissance have recognized, Sidney's *Apology* is a particularly good example of the simultaneous assertion and questioning of the claims of humanist rhetoric, on the part of a courtier who is dissatisfied with the forced indirection of the Elizabethan court.

The rhetorical structure of the *Apology* has long been acknowledged; familiarity with Quattrocento arguments *in utramque partem*, however, allows us to see not only that Sidney's defense is structured as a public oration, but also that the thematic contradictions and inconsistencies are part of a rhetorical strategy to engage the reader in a process of judgment that is itself instructive. According to this reading, although Sidney defends the persuasive force of poetry in terms of the examples of virtue and vice that it presents for the reader's imitation, the ironic attitude of the speaker, the logical contradictions of his argument, and finally the failure of the examples he adduces to prove the power of poetry to persuade force the reader to exercise his judgment, to engage in a process of discrimination between thematic claim and rhetorical practice, and to imitate not any single example but rather the activity of judgment that produced the defensive rhetoric of Sidney's text. Like the reader of Xenophon, who learns "why and how that maker made" the poetic Cyrus (101), the reader of Sidney's defense grows to a "judicial comprehending" (107) of Sidney's own rhetorical practice.

Furthermore, one could argue that Sidney's praise of poetry, although not at first glance a paradoxical encomium, exhibits some of the same ambivalence toward its subject as does Folly's praise of folly. Just as Folly mocks her audience and herself in referring to the foolish self-love (*Philautia*) that motivates her speech, so Sidney begins with the story of Pugliano's praise of horsemanship and his own critical response to this self-interested performance. In so doing, he distances himself ironically from the claims that follow and from the rhetorical force of his own defense. He becomes, in short, a poetic example of the critical posture he would have the reader adopt toward his text. What follows is an ideal Neoplatonic definition of poetry that presupposes a theological and hierarchical model of cause and effect in emphasizing the poet's fore-conceit as the source of the poet's rhetorical power to persuade.

Sidney, however, is all too aware that bad poems are written and that good poems often fail to persuade. While clearly sensitive to the rhetorical force of the Neoplatonic argument, he proceeds to re-define poetry in terms of an Aristotelian emphasis on right action. Yet he knows that even this claim for the power of poetry to per-suade to right action depends on the reader's praxis *as reader*, that is, his access to a standard of judgment that would enable him to make an appropriate interpretation of and response to the text. Reading would ideally be both the cause and the effect of prudence, but Sidney is skeptical about the force of this ideal. For this reason he repeatedly calls our attention to the hypothetical nature of his de-fense and to his ambivalence about poetry's ability to persuade.[11]

Whereas the early humanists argued for the analogy between prudential reading and prudential action, for Sidney the definition of poetry in terms of the act of reading seems to be a substitute for rather than a means to action. It seems, in short, to be a defensive admission that there is no guarantee that poetry will persuade us to act virtuously. It is significant in this context that Sidney moves in the course of the *Apology* from a defense of poetry in terms of its power to persuade to a defense of poetry as mere "play." Margaret Ferguson has accordingly characterized this second moment in the *Apology* as an aesthetic one, the moment at which Sidney tries to defend poetry against the charge of abuse by defining it as a harmless, powerless phenomenon. But, she argues, Sidney is not trying to do away with this power. Rather, the suspension of poet-ry's claim to power is only one moment in the ambivalent rhetoric of the defense.[12]

Precisely because it is defensive, Sidney's retreat to the "aesthet-ic" position is instructive with regard to our own twentieth-century notions of poetry, our bias against the persuasive power of liter-ature. For while Sidney's emphasis on the activity of reading can be understood in formal terms (that is, without reference to the specific content of the examples, claims, or practices one is judging) to anticipate the Kantian notion of the noncognitive aesthetic judgment that informs so much of our own nonrhetorical conception of poetry, it finally uncovers the rhetorical and practical moment that the Kantian notion of aesthetics seeks to suppress: the fact that even arguments for the aesthetic effect of poetry are governed by rhetorical considerations, that the aesthetic experience has a claim on us only because it engages the mind in an activity that is ultimately conducive to ethical action. Thus even Kant writes in the *Kritik der Urteilskraft* (par. 29; see also par. 59) that aesthetic judgment is "purposive in reference to moral feeling."

The question of aesthetics returns us to Hobbes, for Hobbes's subordination of the prudential moment of judgment to a scientific logic of objective certainty signals both the end of the Renaissance and the beginning of the Englightenment, when aesthetics as a formal discipline comes into its own. Familiarity with the humanists' prudential conception of judgment should now allow us to see more clearly why the articulation of the concept of the aesthetic coincides with the attempt to define politics in terms of the science of mathematics rather than in terms of civic prudence. When the model of political science is objective certainty, then a realm of subjective aesthetic experience can be isolated as well. In fact, the invention of a political science *depends* on the exclusion of the humanist notion of rhetoric and the consequent redefinition of aesthetic experience as the most apolitical (i.e., disinterested) of experiences.[13] Thus, while this process culminates in Kant, it could be said to begin with Hobbes, who like the humanists sees the analogies between prudence, poetry, and religious faith, but who unlike the humanists wants precisely for this reason to subordinate these unpredictable and potentially disruptive aspects of human experience to the arbitrary authority of the sovereign.

The conflict between philosophy and rhetoric continues in the twentieth century. As I argued in the Introduction many of the issues I have dealt with might be reformulated in terms of contemporary debate between logicians and pragmatists, or between, in Richard Rorty's words, idealists and textualists.[14] It is no doubt in part because this is the case that we can read the Renaissance humanists with a strong sense of recognition. But if, for example, the modern problematic of deconstruction allows us to read humanist texts for what they have to say about rhetorical versus logical notions of representation, the humanists' concern with praxis in turn allows us to see how much the deconstructive view of rhetoric is determined by theoretical and epistemological concerns.

The deconstructive critic tends to view rhetoric in terms of the epistemological consequences of figurative language. Action, accordingly, is a subset of cognition, performative language is subject to the same epistemological critique as constative language. The early humanists, however, tended to be unconcerned with the epistemological problems of figurative language—partly because they were aware that such language is useful precisely because it allows us to conceive of or assume what we can never know. They were not unaware of the arguments of skepticism; indeed, they embraced them. But undecidability for them was an ethical rather than an ontological issue: the potential reversibility of every figure was seen as the occasion for change. While the deconstructive notion of undecidability has similarities with the formalist critic's skeptical approach to meaning, that is, with the traditional analogy between epistemological skepticism and the hypothetical structure of fictional discourse,[15] for the humanist, as we have seen, the skeptical or hypothetical dimension of the text exemplifies the condition of the possibility of action. In this sense the humanists are more like Dewey than Derrida. Indeed, William James's remark that his first free act would be to assume the existence of free will is one with which, as we have seen, the humanists would have sympathized.

In conclusion, I would like to underscore two of the more general claims of the readings in this book. The first is implicit in the choice of texts. The humanist conception of rhetoric is a capacious one: as a theory of discourse it embraces a wide range of genres. But the move from the Quattrocento treatise and dialogue to the paradoxical encomium, essay, and treatise on political science functions not only as an heuristic typology of genres within the humanist tradition, but also as an allegory of the tensions within the humanist conception of rhetoric—tensions that eventually result in, to borrow Paolo Valesio's phrase, a rhetoric of antirhetoric, a turning of humanist rhetoric against itself.[16] This antirhetoric takes the form of "literature" or of political science, the assumption being that literature (whether conceived of on the model of eighteenth-century aesthetics or twentieth-century literariness) appears at the same time that politics becomes a science. From our modern perspective, the more paradoxical and ironic texts of the sixteenth and seventeenth centuries seem to reflect a greater degree of literary sophistication, but I would like to suggest that this is true only if we privilege a posthumanist definition of the "literary." Self-reflexivity is not missing from the earlier works, but it is in the service of a—broadly speaking—political education.

The second point, which is allied to the first, is that for the Renaissance humanist hermeneutics, conceived of as the theory of interpretation, is not divorced from poetics, conceived of as the metalinguistic study of the formal conventions governing a text.[17] Rather, the gap between the formal and the semantic is bridged by a *rhetoric* that both exemplifies and encourages a *practice* of reading. The implications of this alliance of hermeneutics and poetics are not confined to the study of the Quattrocento. Of particular interest for scholars of later periods, as well as for modern criticism, is the realization that many of those writers who contested the early humanists' faith in the alliance of rhetoric and prudence—their faith in a rhetorical poetics—nevertheless dramatized in their own practice an already well-established belief in the reader's active role in the production of meaning. In taking this conviction as a methodological axiom, I hope to have shown that the investigation into the conventions of interpretation in a given period is inseparable from close rhetorical analysis.

Any conclusion to such analysis is bound to seem anticlimactic, for if there is a general or theoretical lesson to be learned from the humanist practices of reading and writing, it is that poetics, hermeneutics, and rhetoric are not concepts that we can define once and for all. And this is not only true because the meaning of these terms changes from one historical period to another; since the same must be said of the spectrum of meanings of prudence or practice within the Renaissance as well. What these Renaissance texts finally teach us is that meaning is not, in Aristotle's terms, a *product*. Rather, it is inseparable from the historically situated *activity* of reading. Accordingly, the arguments I have presented must now be considered as topics for the reader's own invention, or as a truth of this author's speculation (that is, a hypothetical truth) which the reader must put into practice, for "when I shall have set down my own reading orderly, and perspicuously, the pains left another, will be onely to consider, if he also find not the same in himself. For this kind of Doctrine, admitteth no other Demonstration" (L 83).

Notes

Preface

1. In the following pages, I mean the term "humanist" to include both the Quattrocento humanists and the humanists of the Northern Renaissance, and to designate those writers who were concerned with the recovery and imitation of classical texts and classical notions of rhetoric, the criticism of Scholasticism, and the development of an ethic and rhetoric of decorum which, at least in Italy, would be responsive to a newly developing civic consciousness.

2. See Petrarch, *De sui ipsius et multorum ignorantia,* in Francesco Petrarca, *Prose,* ed. G. Martellotti et al. (Milan, Naples, 1955), 748; English translation by Hans Nachod, "On His Own Ignorance," in *The Renaissance Philosophy of Man,* ed. Ernst Cassirer, Paul Oskar Kristeller, and John Herman Randall, Jr. (Chicago, 1969), 105: "The object of the will, as it pleases the wise, is the good; that of the intellect is truth. It is better to will the good than to know the truth." See also Coluccio Salutati, *De nobilitate legum et medicine,* ed. Eugenio Garin (Florence, 1947), 32: "Is not the good a nobler principle of being than the true? Not the good by which we are good, but the good by which we become and are good"; and 254: "You should study moral philosophy not for the sake of knowledge, but in order to become good." All subsequent references to the *De nobilitate* will be to this edition. Leonardo Bruni, Salutati's student, makes a similar remark in "Praefatio in libros Oeconomicorum [Pseudo-] Aristotelis" (1420), in *Humanistisch-philosophische Schriften,* ed. Hans Baron (Leipzig, Berlin, 1928), 121, when he speaks of "the precepts of the active life, the knowledge of which is worth nothing unless you are led to act upon them."

The enormous critical literature on the pedagogical and persuasive force of examples in the Renaissance cannot be exhaustively examined here. See the following for an introduction: Ernst Robert Curtius, *European Literature and the Latin Middle Ages,* trans. Willard R. Trask (Princeton, 1953, 1973), 57–

62; Eckhard Kessler, *Das Problem des frühen Humanismus: Seine philosophische Bedeutung bei Coluccio Salutati* (Munich, 1968), chap. 8; Marion Trousdale, "A Possible Renaissance View of Form," *ELH* 40 (1973): 179–204; John M. Wallace, "Examples Are Best Precepts: Readers and Meanings in Seventeenth-Century Poetry," *Critical Inquiry* 1 (1974): 273–90; Karlheinz Stierle, "L'histoire comme exemple, l'exemple comme histoire," *Poétique* 10 (1972): 176–98.

3. See O. B. Hardison, *The Enduring Monument* (Chapel Hill, N.C., 1962), 22; and Bernard Weinberg, *A History of Literary Criticism in the Italian Renaissance*, 2 vols. (Chicago, 1961), vol. 1, chap. 1. Weinberg's chapter is full of quotations from Renaissance texts to the effect that poetry is a part or instrument of practical philosophy. The following passage from Piccolomini's *Annotationi nel libro della Poetica d'Aristotile* (1575) is typical: Poetry will seek as its end usefulness to human life "since poetry also is a habit of the practical intellect relevant to things that can be made, and since it may consequently be called an art, and since it is most honored among all the other habits of this kind and in nobility very close to civil prudence, which is that art to which all others are subordinate." Weinberg remarks: "The notion that civil prudence (a paraphrase for politics) is the 'architectonic' science will gain currency later in the century, and poetry will with increasing frequency be subsumed under it" (10–11). This view is characteristic of the Quattrocento humanists as well.

4. My account of the relation of the humanist rhetorical tradition to Aristotelian practical reasoning is indebted to the remarks of Hans-Georg Gadamer in *Truth and Method* (New York, 1982), 5–39, 274–89. Charles Trinkaus (*In Our Image and Likeness*, 2 vols. [London, 1970]) and Nancy Struever (*The Language of History in the Renaissance* [Princeton, 1970]) have considered the intellectual history of rhetoric in the Italian Renaissance, but neither stresses the analogy between rhetoric and prudence. Nor do they touch on the interpretation of this tradition in the later Northern Renaissance. Two important literary critics who have dealt with rhetoric but have ignored the humanists' arguments for the alliance between rhetoric and prudence are Stanley Fish, in *Self-Consuming Artifacts* (Berkeley, 1972), and Richard A. Lanham, *The Motives of Eloquence* (New Haven, London, 1976). Lanham also proposes a division between a serious and a rhetorical world view, which the humanists would not accept. John Webster, in "The Methode of a Poet," *English Literary Renaissance* 11 (1981): 22–43, has criticized Fish's identification of certain rhetorical strategies in English texts with a particular religious, otherworldly ideology, and has specifically discussed the subordination of these strategies to a Ramistic prudential rhetoric. Paul Alpers makes some very suggestive remarks about Spenser's and Sidney's practical and persuasive conceptions of reading in *The Poetry of "The Faerie Queene"* (Princeton, 1967), 20–22, 280–84. See 283: "It is worth inquiring whether moral action is a model for what occurs within the reader of a didactic poem." And on the same page: "Even when Sidney seems to speak

of poetry as knowledge, virtuous action is his model for knowing." Another work that takes account of the active nature of reading in the Renaissance is Joel B. Altman's *The Tudor Play of Mind* (Berkeley, 1978). Altman argues that Tudor plays were constructed according to the rhetorical *quaestio* and debate *in utramque partem* with the specific aim of exercising the understanding. "But true to the highest humanist ideal, the fruits of this play of mind were intended to be realized in action, through the intellectual and spiritual enrichment of the citizens of the polity" (6). In his conclusion, however, Altman explicitly rejects the analogy between rhetoric and prudence that I am arguing for here, claiming that poetry and rhetoric are seen as amoral or "morally neutral" arts in the Renaissance (389). See also Terence Cave, *The Cornucopian Text: Problems of Writing in the French Renaissance* (Oxford, 1979), which offers a series of readings of sixteenth-century texts in the context of rhetorical notions of *copia*. I am aware of no work, however, that argues for connection between prudence and reading in the way I do here.

5. Nancy S. Struever, "Topics in History," *History and Theory*, Beiheft 19 (1980): 74, on Quintilian and Cicero. I have softened the sharp dichotomy between cognition and argument in Struever's sentence.

6. See Jonathan Culler, *Structuralist Poetics* (Ithaca, 1975), 113–30; and "Prolegomena to a Theory of Reading," in *The Reader in the Text*, ed. Susan R. Suleiman and Inge Crosman (Princeton, 1980), 46–66; and Hans Robert Jauss, "Literary History as Challenge," in *Toward an Aesthetic of Reception*, trans. Timothy Bahti (Minneapolis, 1982).

1. Introduction

1. Rosemond Tuve, *Elizabethan and Metaphysical Imagery* (Chicago, 1947), 180 and passim; Hans Robert Jauss, "Literary History as Challenge," in *Toward an Aesthetic of Reception*, trans. Timothy Bahti (Minneapolis, 1982), 21.

2. The phrase is taken from Eugenio Garin's discussion of Coluccio Salutati in *L'umanesimo italiano* (Rome, Bari, 1947, 1978), 39. See also Salutati, *De nobilitate legum et medicine*, ed. Eugenio Garin (Florence, 1947), 136; see also 244 and 266, and the section on Salutati in chap. 3.

3. The critical work on literature as a self-reflexive act or as a speech act is too vast to be taken account of here. For an excellent review and critique of the work of John Austin and Emile Benveniste in this regard, see Rodolphe Gasché, "*Setzung* and *Übersetzung*: Notes on Paul de Man," *Diacritics* 11 (1981): 36–57. On the concept of literature or "literariness" as the most self-consciously rhetorical and therefore privileged instance of language, see Paul de Man, "The Resistance to Theory," in *The Pedagogical Imperative: Teaching as a Literary Genre*, ed. Barbara Johnson, Yale French Studies 63 (1982), 3–20; and *Allegories of Reading* (New Haven, London, 1979), 10, 19, 105, and 109. See also Michel Foucault, *The Order of Things* (New York, 1973), 299–300, 303–4,

on the "appearance of literature," i.e., radically intransitive (300) or non-representational discourse, at the end of the eighteenth century (304). A good account of the historical development of this conception of literature can be found in Raymond Williams, *Marxism and Literature* (Oxford, 1977), 45–55.

4. See Richard H. Popkin, *The History of Scepticism from Erasmus to Spinoza* (Berkeley, Los Angeles, London, 1979), 1, 4, passim.

5. Jonathan Culler, "Prolegomena to a Theory of Reading," in *The Reader in the Text*, ed. Susan R. Suleiman and Inge Crosman (Princeton, 1980), 65: "If we want to understand the nature of literature and of our adventures in language we will have to recognize that the 'openness' and 'ambiguity' of literary works result not from vagueness nor from each reader's desire to project himself into the work, but from the potential reversibility of every figure." The following sentence, "Any figure can be read referentially or rhetorically," seems to me to express too sharp a dichotomy.

6. Fredric R. Jameson, "The Symbolic Inference, or, Kenneth Burke and Ideological Analysis," in *Representing Kenneth Burke, Selected Papers from the English Institute*, n.s. 6, ed. Hayden White and Margaret Brose (Baltimore, 1982), 88–89.

7. Franco Moretti, *Signs Taken for Wonders*, trans. Susan Fischer, David Forgacs, and David Miller (London, 1983), 2.

8. When conventions are defined, as they are by Moretti and by Terry Eagleton, as forms of "ideological agreement" (Moretti, *Signs Taken for Wonders*, 14), rhetoric can become an instrument of Marxist criticism. Thus Eagleton has suggested that classical rhetoric, rather than Marxism, is our first example of a political literary criticism, of a theory of discourse devoted to analyzing all signifying practices, including the "discursive practices of the juridical, political and religious apparatuses of the state" (*Walter Benjamin, or Towards a Revolutionary Criticism* [London, 1981], 101; see the whole section entitled "A Small History of Rhetoric," 101–13).

9. See Rodolphe Gasché, "Deconstruction as Criticism," *Glyph* 6 (1979): 177–215, for a cogent discussion of the differences between French and American deconstruction. The following remarks are indebted to this article.

10. Richard Rorty, *Consequences of Pragmatism* (Minneapolis, 1982), xl. Further references will be given in the text.

11. In this, as in so many other ways, the humanists are harking back to Aristotle. Jürgen Habermas discusses the normative conception of politics in chap. 1 of *Theory and Practice*, trans. John Viertel (Boston, 1973).

12. Gasché, "*Setzung* and *Übersetzung*," 45. Another way of distinguishing between deconstruction and the humanists' pragmatic skepticism is in terms of the status of contradiction in each case. Whereas for deconstruction, contradiction is constitutive of philosophic discourse, for pragmatic skepticism it is a possibility contained within discourse. According to Gasché, this second notion of contradiction is closer to ambivalence or ambiguity which, Derrida says, "requires the logic of presence even when it begins

to disobey that logic." Contradiction exists here between "two articulate presents, two points or instants of presence, and . . . thus remains a linear concept" ("Deconstruction as Criticism," 215 n. 112).

13. See de Man, *Allegories of Reading*, esp. 103–31.

14. Lorenzo Valla, *In quartum librum elegantiarum praefatio*, in *PLQ*, 622.

2. Humanist Rhetoric

1. On civic humanism, see the following: Hans Baron, "Das Erwachen des historischen Denkens im Humanismus des Quattrocento," *Historische Zeitschrift* 147 (1933): 5–20; "The Historical Background of the Florentine Renaissance," *History* 22 (1937–38): 315–27; "Cicero and the Roman Civic Spirit in the Middle Ages," *Bulletin of the John Rylands Library* 22 (1938): 72–97; "Secularization of Wisdom and Political Humanism in the Renaissance," *Journal of the History of Ideas* 21 (1966): 131–50; *The Crisis of the Early Italian Renaissance*, rev. 1-vol. ed. (Princeton, 1966). Jerrold Seigel contested Baron's interpretation of Quattrocento humanism in "'Civic Humanism' or Ciceronian Rhetoric?" *Past and Present* 34 (1966): 3–48. Baron responded with "Leonardo Bruni: 'Professional Rhetorician' or Civic Humanist?" *Past and Present* 36 (1967): 21–37. In *The Machiavellian Moment* (Princeton, 1975), 58ff., J. G. A. Pocock argues aginst Baron's identification of civic humanism with republican sentiment, though he agrees with Baron that an ideology of civic humanism did exist.

2. The assertion of the interconnection of rhetoric and prudence in the Renaissance is intimately tied to the political function of rhetoric. See Weinberg, *A History of Literary Criticism in the Italian Renaissance*, 2 vols. (Chicago, 1961), chap. 1. Delio Cantimori, "Rhetoric and Politics in Italian Humanism," *Journal of the Warburg and Courtauld Institutes* 1 (1937): 83–102; August Buck, "Humanismus und Politik," in *Die humanistische Tradition in der Romania* (Berlin, Zurich, 1968), 253–99; Eugenio Garin, *Medioevo e rinascimento* (Bari, 1954), 124–49; *L'umanesimo italiano*, esp. chap. 8 (193–211); and "Note su alcuni aspetti delle Retoriche rinascimentale e sulla 'Retorica' del Patrizi," in *Testi umanistici su la retorica*, ed. Eugenio Garin, Paolo Rossi, and Cesare Vasoli (Rome, Milan, 1953). The other essays in this collection are pertinent as well. See especially Paolo Rossi, "Il *De principiis* di Mario Nizolio" (59–93); Nizolio's defense of rhetoric has much in common with Salutati's, Bruni's, and Valla's.

It is not my intention to present an overview of all the relevant discussions of prudence and eloquence, or the related issues of decorum and the *vita activa* in the Renaissance. The following critical works do provide such an overview, as well as further bibliographical information: Eugene F. Rice, *The Renaissance Idea of Wisdom* (Cambridge, Mass., 1958), esp. 30–57; Pocock, *The Machiavellian Moment*, 3–83; Eckhard Kessler, *Das Problem des frühen*

Humanismus: Seine philosophische Bedeutung bei Coluccio Salutati (Munich, 1968), passim, esp. chaps. 3–4, 7–8; Mario Santoro, *Fortuna, ragione e prudenza nella civiltà letteraria del Cinquecento* (Naples, 1967). For a wide-ranging and important discussion of the *vita activa*, see also Hannah Arendt, *The Human Condition* (Chicago, 1958). For a discussion of prudence as artistic decorum, see Charles Dempsey, *Annibale Carracci and the Beginnings of Baroque Style* (Glückstadt, 1977), 56–60; as well as Robert Klein, "Giudizio et Gusto dans la théorie de l'art au Cinquecento," in *La forme et l'intelligible* (Paris, 1970), 341–53, where Klein discusses Renaissance notions of artistic judgment in general. Early Quattrocento works that discuss the alliance of rhetoric and prudence will be examined in the pages that follow; for a late treatise that provides a clear statement of the humanists' belief in the inseparability of the two, see A. M. De' Conti, *De eloquentia dialogus*, in *Trattati di poetica e retorica del Cinquecento*, 4 vols., ed. Bernard Weinberg (Bari, 1970), 2: 141–62, esp. 159–60.

3. R. R. Bolgar, *The Classical Heritage and Its Beneficiaries* (New York, 1964), 277, writes that Aristotle "found more translators [into Latin] during the fifteenth century than any other pagan author, in spite of the fact that the medieval versions were still used in the universities. Bruni, Manetti, Theodore of Gaza, George of Trebizond, Agyropoulos, Gregorio Tifernas, Bessarion and Andronicus Callistus, all tried their hand at one or more of his major works." For a discussion of the availability and the influence of the *Nicomachean Ethics* on Quattrocento humanists, and for further bibliography, see Eugenio Garin, "La fortuna dell'Etica Aristotelica nel Quattrocento," in *La cultura filosofica del rinascimento italiano* (2d ed., Florence, 1979), 60–71. See also Lorenzo Minio-Paluello, "Attività filosofico-editoriale Aristotelico dell'Umanesimo," in *Umanesimo europeo e umanesimo veneziano*, ed. Vittore Branca (Venice, 1960), 245–62; *Platon et Aristote à la Renaissance*, XVIᵉ Colloque International de Tours (Paris, 1967); Hanna-Barbara Gerl, *Philosophie und Philologie, Leonardo Brunis Übertragung der Nikomachischen Ethik in ihrer philosophischen Prämissen* (Munich, 1981); and Charles B. Schmitt, *Aristotle in the Renaissance* (Cambridge, Mass., London, 1983). A number of the Italian humanists' lectures on and prefaces to Aristotle's works, in particular the *Nicomachean Ethics*, are collected in Karl Müllner's *Reden und Briefe italienischer Humanisten* (Vienna, 1899; Munich, 1970).

4. Paul Oskar Kristeller ("Humanism and Scholasticism in the Italian Renaissance," in *Renaissance Thought* [New York, 1961], 92–120), argues that the humanists were professional rhetoricians. Hanna H. Gray criticizes Kristeller's definition as excessively narrow and reminds us that while the humanists most frequently called themselves orators, "by this they meant not that they made a living by the teaching or practice of oratory, but that they wished to be known as men of eloquence. An 'orator' could have made his career in government, in the Church, in leisured study and collecting, in teaching or writing or scholarship. He might have written poetry or history or commentaries on classical texts; he might have composed treatises on

moral or political philosophy; he might have devoted himself to translation or editing. Usually, of course, his work included a variety of these activities" ("Renaissance Humanism: The Pursuit of Eloquence," *Journal of the History of Ideas* 24 [1963]: 500).

5. See Jerrold Seigel, *Rhetoric and Philosophy in Renaissance Humanism* (Princeton, 1968), 21–28, for the influence of Peripatetic ethics on Cicero.

6. I do not mean to suggest that Cicero knew the particular Aristotelian texts discussed in the following pages, nor that the Ciceronian notion of prudence is in all respects identical with Aristotle's. See Pierre Aubenque, *La prudence chez Aristote* (Paris, 1963), 33ff. Aubenque points to the passage from *De officiis* cited below (see p. 35) as being more Aristotelian than many other passages in Cicero's work. Dietrich Harth, in *Philologie und praktische Philosophie, Untersuchungen zum Sprach- und Traditionsverständnis des Erasmus von Rotterdam* (Munich, 1970), 13, also touches on the difference between the Aristotelian and Ciceronian views of prudence. He argues, as I do in this chapter, that Ciceronian prudence *requires* eloquence, whereas *phronesis* does not.

In drawing these parallels between the *Nicomachean Ethics* and the *Rhetoric*, I do not mean to suggest that the Quattrocento humanists were directly influenced by the *Rhetoric*. I mean rather to elucidate Aristotle's direct comparison between rhetoric and practical reason in the *Ethics*, and to shed light on why the humanists found this text so suggestive for their own rhetorical ethic of prudence. Aristotle's *Rhetoric* did, however, have an indirect influence on the humanists through Cicero's rhetorical works and his *Topica*. On the availability of Aristotle's *Rhetoric* in Greek and in Latin translation in the Middle Ages and early Renaissance, see Marvin T. Herrick, "Aristotle's *Rhetoric* in England," *Philological Quarterly* 5 (1926): 242–57: "In 1481 a Latin translation of the *Rhetoric* was published at Venice. In 1495–8 Aldus published his magnificent *Opera omnia* of Aristotle but apparently he could not lay his hand on the texts of the *Rhetoric* and *Poetics*, for these were not included. In 1508–9 he included both in his edition of the *Rhetores Graeci*, the *editio princeps* of Aristotle's *Rhetoric* and *Poetics*" (246). See also *Aristotle's "Rhetoric": Five Centuries of Philological Research*, ed. Keith V. Erickson (Metuchen, N.J., 1975).

7. Gray, "Renaissance Humanism," 505. See also 506: "The terms '*decorum*' and '*imitatio*,' for example, are central in both rhetoric and moral philosophy, and the humanists often appear to fuse their meanings whatever the context. Thus, the imitation of stylistic and of ethical models are spoken of in identical terms; or the idea of always speaking appropriately, of suiting style and manner to subject, aim, and audience is treated as the exact analogue of behaving with *decorum*, of choosing the actions and responses which are best in harmony with and most appropriate to individual character and principles on one hand, the nature of circumstances on the other."

8. See also *NE* 6.1140b 27; 6.1141aff. For further discussion of classical

analogies between decorum and prudence, see Heinrich Lausberg, *Handbuch der literarischen Rhetorik*, 2 vols. (Munich, 1960), 1: 1055–62. For rhetoric as an appeal to deliberative judgment see *Rhet.* 1354a, 1354b, 1362a 18. For the similarities between rhetoric and prudence, see *NE* 1.1094b 11–27; 3.1112a 17–1112b 15. Lois S. Self, "Rhetoric and *Phronesis*: The Aristotelian Ideal," *Rhetoric and Philosophy* 12 (1979): 130–45, provides a good summary of the analogy between rhetoric and prudence.

9. Aubenque, *Prudence chez Aristote*, 34.

10. A. E. Taylor, *Aristotle* (New York, 1955), 98. The vocabulary of determinant and reflective judgments is borrowed from Immanuel Kant, *Kritik der Urteilskraft*, pars. 4, 19–20. See Hans-Georg Gadamer's discussion of the judgment of prudence as a reflective judgment in *Truth and Method* (New York, 1982), 286–88. Gadamer writes that *phronesis* differs from *techne* in requiring a moment of self-reflection: "Certainly technical knowledge, if it were available, would render superfluous any consultation with oneself concerning that of which it was the knowledge. Where there is *techne*, one simply has to learn it, and then one knows how to find the appropriate means. On the other hand, we see that moral knowledge always, and unavoidably, requires such consultation with oneself. . . . Moral knowledge can never be knowable in advance in the manner of knowledge that can be taught. The relation of ends and means is not such that the knowledge of the correct means can be had in advance, because the knowledge of the right end is just as little the object of mere knowledge" (286–87; here and below the translation has been slightly modified). See also Thomas Aquinas, *Summa theologica*, Q. 47, Art. 3, Reply Obj. 3.

11. Gadamer, *Truth and Method*, 281. For further discussion of the differences see 281–89, and *NE* 1140b 20–25.

12. See *NE* 63–64 n. 15, and Aubenque, *Prudence chez Aristote*, 44–51.

13. The following paragraph relies on Klaus Oehler's analysis of Aristotle's views in "Der Consensus omnium als Kriterium der Wahrheit in der antiken Philosophie und der Patristik," *Antike und Abendland* 10 (1961): 103–10.

14. It is beyond the scope of this chapter to analyze the similarities between Aristotelian and Sophistic epistemology. For arguments that the two are closer than has often been recognized, see Pierre Aubenque, *Le problème de l'être chez Aristote* (Paris, 1962), esp. 94–305, and W. K. C. Guthrie, *The Sophists* (Cambridge, Eng., 1971), 51–54. See also Eric Havelock's remarks on Aristotle in *The Liberal Temper in Greek Politics* (New Haven, 1957). Havelock argues that Aristotle "returned to the pragmatic point of view of Sophistic which he endeavours not very completely to rationalize" (194). Paolo Valesio also discusses the similarities between Aristotle and the Sophists, in *Novantiqua, Rhetorics as a Contemporary Theory* (Bloomington, Ind., 1980), 75ff. For more recent discussions of the Sophistic epistemology underlying the views of many Renaissance humanists, see Nancy Struever, *The Language of History in the Renaissance* (Princeton, 1970), 5–39 and passim;

and Charles Trinkaus, *The Poet as Philosopher: Petrarch and the Formation of Renaissance Consciousness* (New Haven, London, 1979), 5–7; also "Protagoras in the Renaissance: An Exploration," *Philosophy and Humanism: Renaissance Essays in Honor of Paul Oskar Kristeller*, ed. E. P. Mahoney (Leiden, 1976), 190–213.

15. *Rhet.* 1354a–1358a; *Topics* 1.1 and 1.12; *Prior Analytics* 2.27.

16. For examples of Aristotle's own arguments from the *consensus omnium*, see *NE* 10.1172b–1173a, and *Metaphysics* 999a30–b19. For further discussion of the role of *endoxa* in dialectical syllogisms, see J. D. G. Evans, *Aristotle's Concept of Dialectic* (Cambridge, Eng., 1977), 7–53.

17. Oehler, "Consensus omnium," 110; *Tusculan Disputations*, trans. J. E. King, Loeb Classical Library (Cambridge, Mass., 1971), 3.1.2. The quotation below from *De officiis* is from the translation by Walter Miller, Loeb Classical Library (Cambridge, Mass., London, 1968).

18. Cicero, *Orator*, trans. H. M. Hubbell, Loeb Classical Library (Cambridge, Mass., London, 1942), 21.70–72.

By *sapientia* here Cicero seems to mean prudence or practical wisdom, since it is the latter that is governed by considerations of decorum. See n. 19, below.

19. It may seem that *sapientia* and *prudentia* are being confused in this account of Cicero's position, but in fact they are confused in Cicero's own arguments as well. When Cicero makes a distinction between philosophy and rhetoric, he seems to understand philosophy as theoretical wisdom or speculation, one discipline—if the most exalted—among many that contribute to the orator's storehouse of arguments (*Orator* 4.14; 33.118). But when he argues for the inseparability of wisdom and decorum, wisdom and eloquence, he seems to understand *sapientia* as *prudentia* or practical wisdom. Thus in the passage from *De officiis* he begins by distinquishing the two, and ends up by identifying them: wisdom within the social and political sphere *is* prudence. Accordingly, while Cicero borrows from Aristotle, he is philosophically less rigorous, and occasionally at variance with Aristotle. See the note on this point in the Loeb edition (156–57). Seigel argues in *Rhetoric and Philosophy*, 20, that Cicero's reading of the Middle Stoics contributed to his identification of *sapientia* with decorum. See the discussion below for further differences between the positions of Cicero and Aristotle with respect to rhetoric and prudence.

20. See *De inv.* 1.1, 1.5.6; *De orat.* 3.16.59–61, 3.31.122, 3.35.142. For other passages in Cicero on the inseparability of eloquence and prudence, or for the use of the word *prudence* to mean the judgment of rhetorical decorum, see: *De fin.* 4.27.76; *Ad Her.* 3.2.3ff.; *De orat.* 1.2.5, 1.13.60, 1.20.90, 1.48.209, 2.1.1., 2.3.11, 2.30.132, 2.35.149, 2.38.160, 3.14.55–56, 3.16.60, 3.24.95, 3.55.212; *De off.* 1.31.114, 1.40.142–43; *Tusc.* 1.4.7. For discussions of prudence itself, see *De inv.* 2.53.160; *Tusc.* 5.25.72; *De fin.* 3.9.31, 5.6.16–19, 5.13.36, 5.19.43, 5.21.58, 5.23.67; *De off.* 1.23.81, 1.34.122, 3.9.24; *De orat.* 1.44.197. See also Wesley Trimpi, "The Quality of Fiction: The Rhetorical

Transmission of Literary Theory," *Traditio* 30 (1974): 100 n. 117, on the connection between arguments *in utramque partem*, deliberative rhetoric and prudence in Aristotle.

21. See Paolo Valesio, *Novantiqua*, 81ff. on Aristotle's dialectical conception of rhetoric, and on rhetorical argument pro and contra (*Rhet.* 1.1355a 29–38). On the similarities of or alliance between the orator and the Academic skeptic, see Cicero, *Acad.* 1.12.46; *De nat. deorum* 2.1.1, 2.57.168; *Tusc.* 2.2.5, 2.3.9; *De orat.* 3.19.71; *De fin.* 5.4.10. In *Tusc.* 2.3.9 and *De orat.* 3.27.107, Cicero tells us that the Academic skeptics and the Peripatetics invented the method of arguing *in utramque partem* independently. See also Seigel, *Rhetoric and Philosophy*, 17–18. For a recent discussion of the influence of Academic skepticism on the Quattrocento dialogue, see David Marsh, *The Quattrocento Dialogue* (Cambridge, Mass., 1980). For a discussion of the influence of Cicero's *Academica* in the Renaissance, see Charles B. Schmitt, *Cicero Scepticus: A Study of the Influence of the "Academica" in the Renaissance* (The Hague, 1972); as well as "The Recovery and Assimilation of Ancient Scepticism in the Renaissance," *Rivista critica di storia della filosofia* 27 (1972): 363–84, and the revised version of this article, "The Rediscovery of Ancient Skepticism in Modern Times," in *The Skeptical Tradition*, ed. Myles Burnyeat (Berkeley, Los Angeles, London, 1983), 225–52.

22. Seigel, *Rhetoric and Philosophy*, p. 17.

23. See ibid., 109ff. for a discussion of this frequent remark of Bruni's (e.g., in his *Ad Petrum Paulum Histrum Dialogus* and the *Praemissio quaedam ad evidentiam novae translationis Politicorum Aristotelis* [Leonardo Bruni, *Humanistisch-philosophische Schriften*, ed. Hans Baron (Leipzig, Berlin, 1928), 74]). See also *Ep.* 4.19–20: "Cicero used to say of Aristotle that [his speech] was a river of flowing gold"; and Cicero, *Acad.* 2.38.119: "Aristotle, pouring forth a golden stream of eloquence." Cicero discusses Aristotle as a teacher of oratory in the following passages: *Tusc.* 1.4.7; *De orat.* 1.10.43, 1.11.49, 3.19.71. See also 2.36.152 and 3.21.80.

24. See Seigel, *Rhetoric and Philosophy*, 15.

25. Leonardo Bruni, *Isagogicon moralis disciplinae*, in *Schriften*, 39.

26. The medieval defense of allegory as involving the exercise of the mind also defines reading as a practice, but this practice is not seen as analogous to action in a social and political context. See Phillips Salman, "Instruction and Delight in Medieval and Renaissance Criticism," *Renaissance Quarterly* 3 (1979): 303–32, especially 308ff. Salman argues that in medieval defenses of allegory the exercise of the mind is subordinate to the contemplative goal of arriving at the transcendent truth. See also *De doctrina* 2.6.7, on the pleasure we take in the difficulty of figurative, i.e., allegorical, language. For a lengthy discussion of the theory of allegory in the Middle Ages, see D. W. Robertson, *Preface to Chaucer* (Princeton, 1962).

27. Cited in *Ep.* 4.247. All subsequent references will be given in the text.

28. This argument appears most commonly in connection with the literature of the Northern Renaissance. See Daniel Javitch, *Poetry and Courtliness*

in Renaissance England (Princeton, 1978), 1–17. Javitch relies on Eugenio Garin's *L'educazione in Europa 1400–1600* (Bari, 1966). On the rhetorical view of literature in the Renaissance see, among others, Charles Sears Baldwin, *Renaissance Literary Theory and Practice* (Gloucester, Mass., 1959), 15ff.; William G. Crane, *Wit and Rhetoric in the Renaissance* (New York, 1937), 57ff.; and Weinberg, *History of Literary Criticism*; for the same in antiquity see Roland Barthes, "L'ancienne rhétorique," *Communications* 16 (Paris, 1970): 178–79. See also Wesley Trimpi, "The Ancient Hypothesis of Fiction," *Traditio* 27 (1971): 63–64, on the conservative, i.e., rhetorical and didactic, interpretation of Aristotle's concept of mimesis during the Hellenistic period. On the fusion of Aristotelian and Horatian poetics in the Renaissance, see Marvin T. Herrick, *The Fusion of Horatian and Aristotelian Criticism, 1531–55,* Illinois Studies in Language and Literature (Urbana, 1946).

29. For some suggestive remarks about the conflation of the essentially oral tradition of classical rhetoric with the written tradition of poetics in the Renaissance, see Hans-Georg Gadamer, "Rhetorik, Hermeneutik und Ideologiekritik," in *Hermeneutik und Ideologiekritik*, ed. Jürgen Habermas, Dieter Heinrich, and Jacob Taubes (Frankfurt am Main, 1971), 62–63.

30. See Gadamer, *Truth and Method*, 274–89.

31. See *Ep.* 2.295: "Let others engage in speculation and prove those things with torturous and intricate reasons, if those things are provable which can neither be grasped by the intellect nor maintained against the force of a subtler mind; [such] things, after they are known, neither make men more moral nor more prudent in human affairs. With you and others eager to learn of these things, I will study the past, not only in order to know about it, but to use it in meditating, consulting, writing." See also Lionardo Salviati (1584) in Weinberg, *History of Literary Criticism*, 1: 15, on the prudence that is achieved by the pleasure inherent in reading.

32. See Pontano, *De prudentia (Florence, 1520)*, 88, 91, and *PLQ*, 1026, 1046–50, 1062; also the following pages in the *Dialoghi*, ed. C. Previtera (Florence, 1943), where prudence is described in terms of artfulness or decorum, or vice versa: *Antonius*, 68, 71, 77, 83; *Actius*, 161, 167,174, 178, 185, 188. Pontano describes the educative force of reading in the *Actius*, 218, 225, and 227: history teaches historians not simply what happened, but how to write history. For a translation of this discussion of history, see the Ph.D. dissertation of Hanna Holborn Gray, "History and Rhetoric in Quattrocento Humanism" (Radcliffe College, 1956), 265–326. See also the passage from Fracastoro's *Naugerius* cited in n. 42 below.

33. Aristotle suggests this in *Rhet.* 1414a. See Kenneth Burke's discussion of this passage in *A Rhetoric of Motives* (Berkeley, 1950), 70–72.

34. Cited by Harth, *Philologie und praktische Philosophie*, 93. The phrase is from Erasmus's *Ratio seu methodus compendio perveniendi ad veram theologiam*.

35. See A. Leigh Deneef, "Rereading Sidney's *Apology*," *The Journal of Medieval and Renaissance Studies* 10 (1980): 155–91. Commenting on this passage, Deneef declares: "Sidney implies that it is not the artistic product that

is significant, but the process, the art by which that product is made, be it a concrete ethical action, a man, or a poem" (163). Given this argument, it is hard to see how Deneef could then distinguish between the "central issues" of Sidney's logical argument and the "ancillary . . . strategies of performance" (157).

36. See *EW* 7. 184: "The science of every subject is derived from a precognition of the causes, generation, and construction of the same; consequently where the causes are known, there is place for demonstration. . . . Figures from which we reason are drawn and described by ourselves; and civil philosophy is demonstrable, *because we make the commonwealth ourselves*" (my italics). See also *EW* 1.10–11.

37. Pontano, *De sermone*, ed. S. Lupi and A. Risicato (Lugano, 1954), 20. Further references will be given in the text.

38. The agreement of skepticism and faith (i.e., the preparation for faith by skepticism) was widely acknowledged in the Renaissance. See in particular Henri Estienne's Preface to the 1562 edition of Sextus Empiricus, reprinted in *Oeuvres choisies de Sextus Empiricus*, trans. Jean Grenier and Geneviève Goron (Paris, 1948), 22–23. See also Gianfrancesco Pico della Mirandola's *Examen vanitatis* (1520); Agrippa's *De incertitudine*; (1531); Hiram Haydn, *The Counter Renaissance* (New York, 1950), 101–2 on the fideistic tendencies of the 1542–47 Council of Trent; Richard H. Popkin, "Skepticism and the Counter-Reformation in France," *Archiv für Reformationsgeschichte* 51 (1960): 58–86; and Charles B. Schmitt, *Gianfrancesco Pico della Mirandola (1469–1533) and his Critique of Aristotle* (The Hague, 1967).

39. See Struever, *The Language of History*, 60: "Erik Erikson has suggested that the Renaissance represents the regaining of the executive power of the will; similarly, Renaissance rhetoric illustrates the regaining of the executive power of language." See also *Ep.* 3.377. In a discussion of rhetoric Salutati writes: "What deceives more effectively than the composed and ornate sweetness of praise? What is more pleasing than speech reflecting a polished style in every part? What draws, moves and bends the human mind more than speech based on profound thoughts? What delights more than sweet and artful narration? This dominates the mind most, since it pleases, moves and recalls the will."

40. See, for example, Northrop Frye's remarks on satire in *The Anatomy of Criticism* (Princeton, 1957), 231; see also 74, 271.

41. My account of the aesthetic conception of art derives from Kant's *Kritik der Urteilskraft*. See par. 5 on the effect of contemplation.

42. This is true even for those Renaissance authors who are usually described as anticipating a properly aesthetic conception of the work of art, e.g., Pontano in the *Actius*, and Fracastoro, who relies directly on Pontano. See *Naugerius sive de poetica dialogus*, where Fracastoro discusses the way in which the formal properties of poetry educate the judgment: "It is evident how useful the poet's style is. . . . For in itself it means knowledge of all the excellencies, all the beauties in every form of speech. Moreover, since

whoever knows the good and the beautiful will know at the same time the evil and the ugly, he will necessarily be able to judge wherein all the other styles differ from the best. Therefore, if speech is something great and desirable, which sets man off from the other animals and one man from another man, certainly he attains great usefulness who knows the excellencies, and refinements, and beauties of speech." Fracastoro goes on to say, with respect to subject matter, that the poet can imitate things that pertain to the will and the intellect; in the first case, these things will produce "prudentiam ac virtutes alias" (prudence and the other virtues); poetic examples make the reader "multo prudentiores, & longe practicos magis" (much more prudent and experienced). I have modified slightly the translation by Ruth Kelso, Illinois Studies in Language and Literature 9 (1924): 67–68. In fact, one could say that when pleasure is given a role independent of ethics in the experience of reading, humanism has come to an end. See Giancarlo Mazzacurati, La crisi della retorica umanistica del Cinquecento (Naples, 1961).

43. On the moment of self-reflection common to practical and aesthetic judgments, see Gadamer, Truth and Method, 5–39 and n. 7 above. See also the excellent discussion of Gadamer by David Couzens Hoy, The Critical Circle: Literature, History, and Philosophical Hermeneutics (Berkeley, Los Angeles, London, 1978).

44. Kant, Kritik der Urteilskraft, pars. 18–22.

45. Ibid., par. 41.

46. See, for example, O. B. Hardison's condemnation of the Renaissance humanists for "confusing" rhetoric with poetics, in "The Orator and the Poet: The Dilemma of Humanist Literature," Journal of Medieval and Renaissance Studies 1 (1971): 33–44. According to Hardison, Kant solves the problem in which the Renaissance humanists were unwittingly entangled. For a critique of aesthetic readings of Renaissance texts similar to the one I am making here, see Margaret W. Ferguson, Trials of Desire (New Haven, London, 1982), 1–17.

47. Kenneth Burke, A Rhetoric of Motives (New York, 1950), 267ff.

48. Indeed, this ever-threatening alliance of rhetoric and skepticism was one of the chief reasons for Plato's attack on the Sophists. See Guthrie, The Sophists, 47, 50, chap. 8; Mario Untersteiner, The Sophists, trans. Kathleen Freeman (Oxford, 1954); and Jean-Paul Dumont, Le scepticisme et le phénomène: essai sur la signification et les origines du pyrrhonisme (Paris, 1972). Classical scholars disagree as to similarities and differences between Sophistic and skeptical epistemology (not least of all because of the variety of positions subsumed under each of these labels). For a discussion of the different positions within the Sophist camp, see Untersteiner, The Sophists. For the differences between Academic and Pyrrhonist skepticism, see Dumont, Scepticisme et le phénomène.

49. See Schmitt, "Recovery and Assimilation of Ancient Scepticism in the Renaissance," 370–71.

50. I take the following characterization of the differences between the two schools of skepticism from *Outlines of Pyrrhonism*, in *Sextus Empiricus*, trans. R. G. Bury, Loeb Classical Library, 3 vols. (London and New York, 1933), vol. 1, bk. 1, chap. 33, esp. 226–35. The Academic skeptic asserts that nothing is knowable, while the Pyrrhonist refuses to assert even this. Yet while the Academic might seem to be more radical in his assertion of the impossibility of knowledge, he does believe in the possibility of cognitive and moral judgments based on the criterion of probability, and in the possibility of acting according to this criterion. The Pyrrhonist, on the other hand, refuses to claim probability for his opinions; his goal is to suspend his judgment and to conform to the "law and customs, and natural affections" (1:231). This position is epistemologically more radical than that of the Academic skeptic, for while the Pyrrhonist refuses to assert the impossibility of knowledge, he also refuses to affirm the standard of probability. In so doing, he attacks one of the fundamental convictions of the Quattrocento humanists.

51. See Richard H. Popkin, *The History of Scepticism from Erasmus to Spinoza*, xvi ff. and chap. 1, "The Intellectual Crisis of the Reformation," esp. 4, 19; Schmitt, "Recovery and Assimilation of Ancient Scepticism," 368. See also 365–66: "Of the three major ancient writings on scepticism still extant—Sextus Empiricus' *Opera*, Diogenes Laertius' *Life of Pyrrho*, and Cicero's *Academica*—the first and the third were known to a very few in the West during the Middle Ages, while the second was apparently wholly unknown. The writings of Sextus Empiricus, by far the most important and most detailed of the three, exerted no visible influence during the Middle Ages, although we know of two early 14th century manuscripts of a complete Latin translation of the *Outlines of Pyrrhonism*. Yet, no evidence has thus far appeared to indicate that anyone other than the translator actually read the work." See 365, 367ff. on protoskeptical trends and texts in the Middle Ages (fideism, anti-intellectualism, the *Imitatio Christi* of Thomas à Kempis, a text, I would add, that was extremely influential on the Brothers of the Common Life, who educated Erasmus).

52. This is Popkin's view as well. See *History of Scepticism*, chap. 1.

53. For a similar analysis, with reference to the development of the city-state of Florence, see Marvin Becker, *Florence in Transition*, 2 vols. (Baltimore, 1968), 2: 7ff.

54. On the humanists' rhetorical theology, see Trinkaus, "*Theologia Poetica* and *Theologia Rhetorica* in Petrarch's *Invectives*," in *The Poet as Philosopher*, 90–114; and Salvatore I. Camporeale, *Lorenzo Valla, Umanesimo e teologia* (Florence, 1972); as well as the section on Valla in chap. 1.

55. See George P. Klubertanz, S. J., *St. Thomas Aquinas on Analogy* (Chicago, 1960), 14. The three kinds of theological analogy, which are all based on the likeness of effect to cause, are "(a) an analogy of attribution in which a concept is drawn from God and used to designate creation extrinsically; (b) an analogy in which the image is designated from its archetype, because

of an analogous perfection which exists perfectly in God, imperfectly in creatures; and (c) an analogy in which the first Cause is designated from its effects, the perfections of which exist in a higher way in their cause." Further references will be given in the text.

56. George Puttenham, *The Arte of English Poesie* (Kent, Ohio, 1970), (268–69. The square brackets appear in the original.

57. Annabel Patterson, *Hermogenes in the Renaissance* (Princeton, 1970), 213. See also Barthes, "L'ancienne rhétorique," 200, for the connection between the rhetorical *exemplum* and reasoning by analogy.

58. For a similar analysis of the lessening of confidence in an objective standard of artistic decorum in the later Renaissance, see Erwin Panofsky, *Idea, A Concept in Art Theory*, trans. Joseph J. S. Peake (New York, 1968). Panofsky charts a development in the conception of artistic imitation from the medieval imitation of a metaphysically substantial Idea to the Renaissance conviction that the Idea exists both in the artist as subject and in nature as object (36), and finally to an understanding of the Idea as created by the artist in generalizing from experience (32). This last step raises the problem of the legitimation of the Idea, and gradually leads in the seventeenth century to the consideration, not of how to imitate but (in anticipation of eighteenth-century aesthetics) of the conditions of the possibility of artistic representation in general. In the seventeenth century there is also a temporary return to Neoplatonic doctrine (Ideas are in the mind of God and in man by participation) in an attempt to legitimate artistic creation once again. For a discussion of Panofsky's argument, see Ernst Cassirer, *The Individual and the Cosmos in Renaissance Philosophy*, trans. Mario Domandi (Philadelphia, 1963), 163, 164 n. 62.

59. See Giovanni Pontano's dialogue *Aegidius*, in *Dialoghi*, 275, 279, for a discussion of the way the will operates *in utramque partem*. See also the section on Pontano in chap. 1.

60. William J. Bouwsma, "The Two Faces of Humanism: Stoicism and Augustinianism in Renaissance Thought," in *Itinerarium Italicum*, ed. H. A. Oberman with T. A. Brady, Jr. (Leiden, 1975), 37.

61. See Struever, *The Language of History*, 44, 59 and passim. See also Trinkaus, *In Our Image and Likeness*, 2 vols. (London, 1970), passim, but esp. pt. 1, chap. 1. On nominalism, see Heiko A. Oberman, "Some Notes on the Theology of Nominalism, with attention to its relation to the Renaissance," *Harvard Theological Review* 53 (1960): 47–76, as well as the articles in *The Pursuit of Holiness in Late Medieval and Renaissance Religion*, ed. Charles Trinkaus and Heiko A. Oberman (Leiden, 1974): William J. Courtenay, "Nominalism in Late Medieval Religion" (26–59), and Steven Ozment, "Mysticism, Nominalism and Dissent" (67–92). In this collection, see also the more general article by Charles Trinkaus, "The Religious Thought of the Italian Humanists and the Reformers: Anticipation or Autonomy?" 339–66.

62. The phrase is taken from Trinkaus, *In Our Image and Likeness*, 1: 47.

63. Kant, *Kritik der reinen Vernunft*, A 172.

64. J.-J. Rousseau, *Emile, Oeuvres complètes de Jean-Jacques Rousseau*, Bibliothèque de la Pléiade, 4 vols. (Paris, 1969), 4: 571.

65. See Alain Michel, *Les rapports de la rhétorique et de la philosophie dans l'oeuvre de Cicéron* (Paris, 1960), 40–46 for a discussion of the debate about whether eloquence is to be defined as speaking well (in conformity with the good) or speaking persuasively. Also see Quintilian, *Institutio oratoria*, 2.14.5–2.15.38, 2.17.23.

66. See, for example, Erasmus's early *Antibarbari*, cited in Paul Mestwerdt, *Die Anfänge des Erasmus* (Leipzig, 1917), 266: "How much more religious Augustine was than we, who with rude spirits, do not proceed slowly to the mysteries of divinity, but burst upon them, do not ascend, but fly, and like giants, who have piled up great arsenals in heaven, strive to seize the citadel of Jove. Because Augustine proceeded gradually he was received [into the citadel], while we are repelled, dislodged, thrown down."

67. For a discussion of this tendency in Italian humanism, see Struever, *The Language of History*, e.g., 39: The humanist creation of a public role for the orator "militates against philosophical or religious withdrawal and helps make possible a methodic 'saving of phenomena' and thus a saving of history."

68. See Cassirer, *The Individual and the Cosmos*, 22–24.

69. For the historical background of this interpretation of Christ, see Eugenio Garin, "La 'Dignitas Hominis' e la letteratura patristica," *La Renascita* 1 (1938): 102–46. For the influence of Ficino on Colet, and the similarities of Colet's humanism and that of the Brothers of the Common Life, who educated Erasmus, see Ernst Cassirer, *The Platonic Renaissance in England*, trans. James P. Pettegrove (New York, 1953), esp. 16ff. See also Fredric Seebohm, *The Oxford Reformers of 1498* (London, 1867).

70. See De' Conti, *De eloquentia dialogus*, in Weinberg, *Trattati*, 2:151: "You cannot condemn eloquence without eloquence."

3. The Quattrocento

1. All references to the *De nobilitate legum et medicine* are to the edition of Eugenio Garin (Florence, 1947). On Salutati's life, see B. L. Ullman, *The Humanism of Coluccio Salutati* (Padua, 1963). See also Ronald G. Witt, *Hercules at the Crossroads: The Life, Works, and Thought of Coluccio Salutati* (Durham, N.C., 1983). This magisterial work appeared when the present chapter had been completed. I have, however, been able to indicate in the notes some of the pages that are relevant to my discussion of the *De nobilitate*. On Salutati's political rhetoric, see the following in particular: Hans Baron, *The Crisis of the Early Italian Renaissance*, rev. 1-vol. ed. (Princeton, 1966), esp. 104–21, 146–67; Daniela De Rosa, *Coluccio Salutati: il cancelliere e il pensatore politico* (Florence, 1980), esp. 135–68; Peter Herde, "Politik und Rhetorik im

Florenz am Vorabend der Renaissance," *Archiv für Kulturgeschichte* 47 (1965): 141–220; Ronald G. Witt, "Coluccio Salutati, Chancellor and Citizen of Lucca (1370–72)," *Traditio* 25 (1969): 191–216, and *Coluccio Salutati and the Public Letters* (Geneva, 1976). On the active and contemplative lives, see Eugenio Garin, *L'umanesimo italiano* (1947; Rome, Bari, 1978), 193–212; Robert A. Bonnell, "An Early Humanist's View of the Active and Contemplative Life," *Italica* 43 (1966): 225–39; Fritz Schalk, "Il tema della 'vita activa' e della 'vita contemplativa' nell'Umanesimo italiano," in *Umanesimo e scienza politica*, ed. E. Castelli (Rome, Florence, 1949, Milan 1951), and "Aspetti della vita contemplativa nel rinascimento italiano," in *Classical Influences on European Culture A.D. 1500–1900*, ed. R. R. Bolgar (Cambridge, Eng., 1971).

2. It is unclear how familiar the second generation of humanists was with the *De nobilitate*, though we know that the work was the only one of Salutati's writings that saw publication in the Renaissance (Venice, 1542). I am not arguing for the direct influence of this treatise on the Quattrocento humanists, but for its usefulness in determining Salutati's conception of prudence, which clearly was influential.

3. Exceptions are Charles Trinkaus, *In Our Image and Likeness*, 2 vols. (London, 1970), 1: 51–102, 2: 553–70; De Rosa; and Jan Lindhardt, *Rhetor, Poeta, Historicus: Studien über rhetorische Erkenntnis und Lebensanschauung im italienischen Renaissance-humanismus.* (Leiden, 1974).

4. See Lynn Thorndike, *Science and Thought in the Fifteenth Century* (New York, 1963), 29–30, who writes that there is some question whether the genre was well established (in the appendix to this work Thorndike discusses other examples of this genre in the fifteenth century). See also the discussion by Eugenio Garin in the preface to *La disputa delle arte nel Quattrocento* (Florence, 1947).

5. See Eugenio Garin, ed., *De nobilitate legum et medicine* (Florence, 1947), xxiv.

6. For further remarks on the active and contemplative lives, see *Ep.* 2.308, 319–20, 368, 372, 453–54, 3.50–51, 301–8, 531.

7. Ullman, "Coluccio's Influence," chap. 8, *Humanism of Coluccio Salutati*, 117–26, records some of the other Quattrocento humanists' remarks about Salutati: Pier Paolo Vergerio called himself a "discipulus" of Salutati, and he and Poggio described Salutati as "communis omnium magister" (the common teacher of us all). Ullman quotes from the minutes of the 1388 meeting at which Coluccio was reelected chancellor of Florence; Salutati is referred to as "the pupil of the fountain head of eloquence, that most dazzling of all orators, Cicero, and [as] the only mirror of all natural and moral philosophy, through whose outstanding qualities the city of Florence is conspicuous throughout the world, since she has been wonderfully honored by his letters, composed in a dignified and discriminating style" (14, cf. 112). This sentence is also quoted in *Ep.* 4.465.

8. See *Ep.* 3.131: "You know my habits. You know that I am not able to be still, you know how it always pleases [me] to teach what I have learned and

how urgently I seek things I do not know, and how much pleasure it gives me *even to dispute of things not known.*" Cited by Neal Gilbert, "The Early Humanists and Disputation," in *Renaissance Studies in Honor of Hans Baron,* ed. Anthony Molho and John A. Tedeschi (DeKalb, Ill., 1971), 217.

9. Lorenzo Valla, "In Bartolomaeum Facium Ligurem invectiva," *OO* 1: 504.

10. It is significant that Salutati defines the good as an activity rather than an essence. See the section on Valla, below.

11. In the *De prudentia* (Florence, 1520), 60, Pontano also draws on the Aristotelian distinction between *agere* and *facere* and argues that prudence governs action.

12. Ullman, *Humanism of Coluccio Salutati,* 216, 228, tells us that Salutati owned the *NE* in a medieval Latin translation, as well as Eustratius's commentary on the text. The MS contains many marginal notes by Salutati. Cf. also *Ep.* 3.391–92, 4.37–39, on Salutati's reading of commentaries on the *NE,* and Witt, *Hercules,* 299, 358. Witt argues (299) that "there is no solid proof that [Salutati] . . . read the . . . [*Nicomachean Ethics*] before 1390" but that after this date references to the *Ethics* abound in Salutati's work.

13. Cf. *Ep.* 1.247 for a description of the effects of charity that suggests Cicero's civic rhetoric: "This alone nourishes the family, makes cities prosperous, guards the state, and preserves by its virtue the work of the whole world, composed of contrary qualities." In a paper entitled "Lorenzo Valla: Contemplation Is Action," given at a conference on the *vita activa* and the *vita contemplativa* (Eidgenössische Technische Hochschule, Zurich, June 17–19, 1981), Letizia A. Panizza pointed out that Valla also identifies action and contemplation in many of his works. See, for example, his criticism of Aristotle on the gods in *Dialecticae disputationes, OO* 1: 660: "Although he denies them action, nevertheless he attributes contemplation to them, as though to contemplate were not to act and contemplation [not] action." For a more detailed analysis of Salutati's argument in chaps. 22 and 23, see my "Coluccio Salutati on the Active and Contemplative Lives," forthcoming in *Vita Activa/Vita Contemplativa,* edited by Brian Vickers.

14. As he writes in the very beginning, he will proceed "without form or rules of disputation"—a remark that, Garin tells us (*De nobilitate,* 340), alludes to Isidore of Seville's distinction between dialectic and rhetoric: "Dialectic is the science or rule of disputation, which sharpens the intellect and enables us to distinguish true from false. Rhetoric is the science of speaking, the knowledge of law, which orators follow."

15. For other appeals to the *consensus omnium* (which gets tied up in Cicero and Salutati with the notion of natural law), see 4, 10, 16 (with quotes from Cicero's *De legibus*), 18, 44, 52, 58 (describes the nature of the *consensus omnium*), 102, 130 (*communes . . . rationes*), 136, 252 (*gentium consensus*).

16. See Lisa Jardine, "Lorenzo Valla and the Origins of Humanist Dialectic," *Journal of the History of Philosophy* 15 (1977), 158; and Nancy Struever,

"Fables of Power," *Representations* 4 (1983): 108–27. For a different interpretation from the one that follows, see Witt, *Hercules*, 209–15, 236–37, on the medieval character of Salutati's interest in etymology.

17. See Cicero, *Topics*, 35: "cum ex vi nominis argumentum elicitur" (from the force of names, arguments are elicited); and Isidore of Seville, *Etymologiarum liber*, 1.29: "vis verbi vel nominis per interpretationem colligitur" (the force of the verb or the noun should be inferred from its [original] meaning). Cited in Ernst Robert Curtius, *European Literature and the Latin Middle Ages*, trans. W. R. Trask (New York, 1963), 497. Cf. Cicero, *Acad.* 1.8.30–33; *Topica* 2.8.35; Quintilian, *Institutio oratoria*, 1.6.1; 1.6.28ff.

18. Nancy Struever, "Fables of Power," 111.

19. Cited in Struever, "Fables of Power," p. 112; see P. Guiraud, "Etymologie et ethymologia; (motivation et rétromotivation)," *Poétique* 4 (1972): 405–13.

20. Salutati's argument here is analogous to Lorenzo Valla's reduction of such concepts as the good (*bonum*) to a good thing (*bona res*). See the section on Valla, below.

21. For discussions of the linguistic criterion of usage, see *De nobilitate*, 252, and *Ep.* 3.606 (where Salutati cites Cicero [*De orat.* 1.3.12]: "vitium vel maximum sit a vulgari genere orationis atque [a] consuetudine communis sensus abhorrere" [it is the greatest vice to reject the common manner of speaking and the custom of common sense]); 3.610; 4: 142. See also n. 54 below.

22. See Garin, *De nobilitate*, 364, for Salutati's emphasis on the will. On the productive and self-constituting nature of human activity in the *De nobilitate*, see in particular Matteo Iannizzotto, *Saggio sulla filosofia di Coluccio Salutati* (Padua, 1959), esp. 61ff.

23. Cf. on free will *Ep.* 2.228ff. (esp. 235–36, where Salutati refers to the notion of free will as a "cornutus paralogismus"), 2.320ff. Here and in his *De fato, fortuna et casu*, Salutati insists on the paradoxical coexistence of divine foreknowledge and human free will, a paradox that cannot be understood, but can only be worked out *in practice*. See the chapter on Erasmus, below, for a different treatment of the relationship of contradiction to paradox in the figure of wise folly. On the dialogic structure of *De fato*, see W. Rüegg, "Entstehung, Quellen und Ziel von Salutatis *De fato et fortuna*," *Rinascimento* 5 (1954): 143–90, esp. 184–89; and on the dialogic and rhetorical nature of Salutati's thought in general, see Jan Lindhardt, *Rhetor, Poeta, Historicus*, 76ff., 127. See also Eugenio Garin, "A Proposito di Coluccio Salutati," *Rivista critica di storia della filosofia* 15 (1960): 73–82 who speaks of Salutati's "rhetorical transformation of argument by pro and contra, *sic et non*" (77). On Salutati's practical solution to the problem of free will, see Trinkaus, *In Our Image and Likeness*, 1: 96; Garin, *L'umanesimo italiano*, 39; and Giuseppe Sciacca, "Il valore della storia nel pensiero di Coluccio Salutati," *Palermo* 3 (1950): 360.

24. The following relies on Ronald G. Witt, "Coluccio Salutati and the Conception of the *Poeta theologus* in the Fourteenth Century," *Renaissance Quarterly* 30 (1977): 538–63. See also Witt, *Hercules*, 181–226, 422.

25. The important letters that set forth Salutati's views on poetry are *Ep.* 1.298–307, esp. 300 (1378), 1.321–29 (1379); 3.318–22 (1398), 3.539–43 (1401, to Giovanni da Samminiato); 4.170–205 (1405–6?, to the same), 4.205–240 (1406, to Giovanni Dominici). These letters are translated in Ephraim Emerton, *Humanism and Tyranny, Studies in the Italian Trecento* (Cambridge, Mass., 1925), 287–377. See also *De laboribus Herculis*, ed. B. L. Ullman, 2 vols. (Zurich, 1951), esp. bk. 1. For the similarities between rhetoric and poetry, see *Ep.* 3.493; 4.196–97, 202, 230–31; as well as the rhetorical definition of poetry in *De laboribus* (10, borrowed from Averroes' paraphrase of Aristotle's *Poetics*): "All poetry is a speech of blame or praise; the orator praises and attacks, but orally, while the poet accomplishes this in a poem." Witt, *Hercules*, 222, comments on Salutati's occasional reticence about affirming the existence of divine truth in all pagan poetry. After a discussion of *De laboribus*, Witt warns that "any attempt to be precise about Salutati's conception of the origin of truth contained in poetry would falsify what was a very confused and fragmented attitude" (226). He also reminds us of Salutati's criticism of pagan literature later in life (403, 413, 428).

26. What is clear from this letter is that while Salutati's allegorical conception of reading presupposes the priority of truth, that is, of God, this is a truth that is never literally accessible, only figuratively. It is not available to logic or cognition but only to the will, that is, to poetry and rhetoric. On Salutati's letter to Giovanni da Samminiato, see Emerton, *Humanism and Tyranny*, 314, and Trinkaus, *In Our Image and Likeness*, 1: 62ff.; as well as 2: 563–70, 697–704.

27. There are suggestions of such a view of reading, that is, of reading as a formal activity that is in itself morally educative, in a letter to Juan Fernandez de Heredia (*Ep.* 2.289–302), where Salutati argues that reading history trains the judgment and makes us more prudent: "This knowledge of history is useful wherever you turn; it moderates favorable events, consoles you in adverse ones, strengthens friendship, makes your conversation copious and ornate. It is both doctrine and guide to advice; the rule for fleeing dangers and the certain lesson of how to conduct your affairs well" (2.292). "With you and with others eager to learn of these things, I study the past, not only that I might know about it, but also that I might use it in meditating, consulting, and writing" (2.295). It is not clear in the first quotation whether Salutati is stressing that we learn rules of judging from history or whether our reading itself exercises that judgment; whether reading is judging, or right judgment is an effect of reading. For further remarks on the value of studying history, see 2.31; 3.171, 605. Letters in which Salutati stresses the active nature, the *exercitio*, of writing are: 3.307, 411, 602, 605, 614. See also 2.430: "Examples of virtue lie hidden in literature; so does moral knowledge; and all things which it is not enough to know but must be

put into practice"; and 1.122, where Salutati equates virtue with the study of literature: "virtuti vel studio litterarum" ([virtue or the study of letters], cited in Ullman, *Humanism of Coluccio Salutati*, 74).

28. The edition of the *De prudentia* and the *De fortuna* cited throughout is *Ioannis Ioviani Pontani opera soluta oratione composita in sex partes divisa* (Florence, 1520). The pagination is sequential from one treatise to the other. The particular treatise will be indicated where important. References to the *Dialoghi (Charon, Antonius, Actius, Asinus, Aegidius)* are to the edition by Carmelo Previtera (Florence, 1943). References to the *De sermone* are to the edition of S. Lupi and A. Risicato (Lugano, 1954). For Pontano's criticism of his contemporaries' confusion of *sapientia* and *prudentia*, see *De prudentia*, 65–67. See n. 32, below, for twentieth-century critics' negative views of Pontano as a philosopher.

29. See Pontano, *Charon, Dialoghi*, 42.

30. See Petrus Summontius's prefatory letter to the *De prudentia*, 2, and the dialogue *Aegidius*, 259, 280.

31. See Pontano, *Aegidius*, 284; *Charon*, 15; *De prudentia*, 55. See also the tie between the *vita activa, vitae consilia*, and the *loquendi usus* in the *De prudentia*, 27. This point will be discussed at greater length below. For a discussion of Bruni's analogous position, see Hanna-Barbara Gerl, *Philosophie und Philologie, Leonardo Brunis Übertragung der Nikomachischen Ethik in ihrer philosophischen Prämissen* (Munich, 1980), chap. 1, "Die Relation von Philosophie und Philologie bei Leonardo Bruni."

32. See the remarks by Giuseppe Toffanin in *Giovanni Pontano fra l'uomo e la natura* (Bologna, 1937), 73, 75. For Umberta Renda's disparaging remarks about Pontano as a philosopher see *Giovanni Pontano* (Turin, 1939), 83, 111: "Pontano is not a philosopher, nor a thinker, nor a scientist," because he doesn't transcend "the sphere of practical life." Francesco Tateo, in *Umanesimo etico di Giovanni Pontano* (Lecce, 1972), tends to be more sympathetic to Pontano's conflation of *retorica* and *sapienza*. See Tateo's *Astrologia e moralità in Giovanni Pontano* (Bari, 1960) for a discussion of the *De fortuna* and *De prudentia*. Tateo sees Aristotle's *Nicomachean Ethics* as the primary source of Pontano's two treatises. Tateo provides a useful summary of Pontano's argument in the *De fortuna* in particular, but he does not examine the rhetorical organization of the work. See also Mario Santoro, *Fortuna, ragione e prudenza nella civiltà letteraria del Cinquecento* (Naples, 1967). Santoro sees the *De prudentia* as a modification of the views of Aristotle and Aquinas on prudence. He argues that Pontano has a more active, dramatic, or "agonistic" sense of prudence as choice, and a richer, more realistic analysis of the different parts of prudence (51–52). For a lengthy paraphrase of the *De prudentia*, see Santoro, "Il Pontano e l'ideale rinascimentale del 'prudente,'" *Giornale italiano di filologia* (1964), 29–54. Finally, in "Il 'De prudentia' di Giovanni Pontano e la morale indipendente," *Sophia* (1942), 82–99, Ermenegildo Bertola argues that Pontano's views anticipate Kant's notion of the categorical imperative (95). This is a defense of Pontano as a philoso-

pher, but it depends on the identification of philosophy with theoretical rather than practical reason.

33. See *De fortuna*, 129: "Sometimes it brings prosperity, other times calamity, nor are these things foreseen, nor even, as I have said, expected, and often little merited, not rarely iniquitous and unjust; and fortune herself may rightly be accused on both sides [*in utramque partem*], whether on account of success or adversity."

34. W. B. Gallie, "Essentially Contested Concepts," in *The Importance of Language*, ed. Max Black (Englewood Cliffs, N.J., 1962), 123. I am indebted to Eugene Garver, who equates essentially contested arguments with rhetorical arguments: "Since arguments [in rhetoric] are about what can be otherwise, the arguments themselves can 'be otherwise.' . . . Rhetorical arguments are therefore essentially contested arguments because they are by their nature open to opposed argument. . . . It is the arguments, not something extraneous, that are contested" ("Rhetoric and Essentially Contested Arguments," *Philosophy and Rhetoric* 11 (1978): 157–58).

35. On the dating of these two treatises, see Umberto Renda, *Giovanni Pontano*, 56, who argues for the 1498–99 composition of the *De prudentia*, and Vittorio Rossi, *Il Quattrocento* (Milan, 1953), 486, who argues for 1496. For the date of publication of these works, see Previtera, *Dialoghi*. Caraciolus and Pudericus appear as interlocutors in the *Actius*, and *Aegidius*.

36. See *Rhet.* 1355b 20: "What makes a man a 'sophist' is not his faculty, but his moral purpose. In rhetoric, however, the term 'rhetorician' may describe either the speaker's knowledge of his art, or his moral purpose." The version of the Sophist position I am presenting here is the one adopted by Plato and Aristotle, not the one reconstructed from fragments of Sophist works by such scholars as Eric Havelock and Werner Jaeger.

37. The Renaissance reader might have been predisposed to such a reading, given the classical and medieval tendency to view Fortuna as a goddess. See Howard Rollin Patch, *The Tradition of the Goddess Fortuna*, Smith College Studies in Modern Languages 3 (1922), 131–35.

38. Cicero uses the phrase *in utramque partem* to mean arguing on both sides of a question in the following works (I have not listed the occurrences of the phrase *in contrarias partes* which, however, has the same meaning): *De orat.* 1.62.264; 3.21.80 (*in utramque sententiam*), 27.107; *Acad.* 1.12.46; 2.39.124; *De nat. deorum* 2.57.168; *De fin.* 5.4.10; *De off.* 1.23.81 (where *prudentia* is defined as being able to see "quid accidere possit in utramque partem"), 2.2.8 ("ex utraque parte"). For a discussion of arguing *in utramque partem* in Cicero's works, see Alain Michel, *Les rapports de la rhétorique et de la philosophie dans l'oeuvre de Cicéron* (Paris, 1960), 158–73. Pontano uses the phrase in the *De fortuna* on the following pages: 129, 134, 138, 158, 191 (where it refers to the individual's capability of responding *in utramque partem* to fortune), 194. Pontano refers to Cicero's description of fortune in *De fortuna*, 132, 138.

39. See *Charon*, 22–23, where Mercury argues that humans cannot have

foreknowledge but that we do have free will; cognitive ignorance is compatible with action. For further remarks on free will, see *Aegidius*, 273ff.

40. This is the same argument that Salutati makes in the *De fato*. See n. 23, above. See also *Aegidius*, 278: "Not only do things themselves and [our] actions testify that the will is free, but also the very fact [name] of deliberation, that is, because judgment is free in the act of discerning"; and *De prudentia*, 62 on deliberation and free will.

41. For a similar argument, see Erasmus, *De libero arbitrio, diatribe seu collatio, LB*, passim, but especially 1247 D–1248 A. This text is discussed below, in the chapter on Erasmus and Luther.

42. I have reversed the order in which these two passages appear in Pontano's text.

43. Kenneth Burke, *A Rhetoric of Motives* (New York, 1950), 50.

44. See the discussion of Aristotle's defense of arguments from usage in chap. 2.

45. See *De prudentia*, 47: "From choice, as from a source, flow the rivers of opprobrium and commendation, in undertaking actions and in the habit of preparing for them *in utramque partem*"; see also 55. The connection between prudence as knowledge *in utramque partem* of what to seek and what to avoid (*De prudentia*, 47, 59, 62, 65, 77) and epideictic rhetoric of praise and blame (*in utramque partem*) is apparent everywhere in the two treatises. See 12, 15, 18, 25, 30, 47, 142, 193. For Aristotle's remarks in the *Rhetoric* on the relation of epideictic rhetoric to urging a course of action, see 1367b 30–35. For rhetoric as involving arguments about what to seek and what to avoid, see 1360b, 1394a 25, 1399b 30.

46. See Preface, n. 2. For Aristotle on the connection between deliberative rhetoric and examples, see *Rhet.* 1368a 29. For a recent article which gives references to arguments for the prudential value of examples, see J. H. M. Salmon, "Cicero and Tacitus in the Sixteenth Century," *The American Historical Review* (1980): 307–31.

47. See *De prudentia*, 26, on *energeia* as "actio secundum virtutem." Contrary to subsequent interpretations of *energeia* in terms of visual brilliance (an interpretation which Pontano endorses on occasion), Pontano here emphasizes *energeia* as action, thereby suggesting that textual *energeia* engages us in activity, rather than impressing us as passive observers. See also Rosemond Tuve's helpful remarks on *energeia* in *Elizabethan and Metaphysical Imagery* (Chicago, 1947), 29 n. 4.

48. See *Charon*, 3; *Antonius*, 50. See also the praise of the active life in *De prudentia*, 13, 27.

49. See Mario Santoro, *Fortuna, ragione e prudenza*, 11–29 on the importance of the 1494 French invasion for Pontano's writings on prudence and fortune.

50. Pontano's remarks on the death of his wife, Adriana, are also an example of the transformation of fortune into prudence in the text. See 3, 32, 56. Death becomes an occasion for an encomium of her prudence: "I

seem to enjoy her face, sight, speech, and to entrust to her my domestic affairs, to take counsel with her about personal matters, and to find peace in her assistance and prudent advice" (56). See also the remarks following this on Adriana's teaching us to nurture that virtue "quae prudentia dicitur" (56). For the use of autobiography in philosophical argument, see Eckhard Kessler, "Autobiographie als philosophisches Argument," in *Studia humanitatis, Ernesto Grassi zum 70. Geburtstag*, ed. Eginhard Hora and Eckhard Kessler (Munich, 1973), 171–87.

51. See Nancy S. Struever, "Lorenzo Valla: Humanist Rhetoric and the Critique of the Classical Languages of Morality," in *Renaissance Eloquence*, ed. James J. Murphy (Berkeley, Los Angeles, 1982), 191–206. See also *Dialecticae disputationes, OO* 1.644, for Valla's criticism of Aristotle for not engaging in civic affairs.

52. Salvatore I. Camporeale, "Lorenzo Valla tra medioevo e rinascimanto, *Encomion S. Thomae*—1457," *Memorie domenicane*, n.s. 7 (1976): 63ff., referring to the work of J. Isaac.

53. Throughout this section quotations from *De libero arbitrio* are from the translation by Charles Trinkaus, in *The Renaissance Philosophy of Man*, ed. Ernst Cassirer, Paul Oskar Kristeller, and John Herman Randall, Jr. (Chicago, London, 1948). All other translations are my own. The Latin texts of Valla's *De libero arbitrio* and of the prefaces to the *Elegantiae* are from *PLQ*. In the text, references to the English translation will be followed by references to the Latin. "Lorenzo" refers to the fictional Lorenzo of the dialogue. References to *De vero falsoque bono* are to the edition of Maristella de Panizza Lorch (Bari, 1970). See n. 73 on the dating of *De libero arbitrio*. See Valla's *In Pogium antidotum IV* (*OO* 1: 344) for his response to Poggio's remarks about Valla's hubris in *De libero arbitrio*. On this exchange, see Salvatore Camporeale *Lorenzo Valla, umanesimo e teologia* (Florence, 1972), 341–44.

Even Valla's admirers remarked on his slanderous way of speaking on occasion. Pontano praises Valla's eloquence in *De prudentia* (66), but includes him as an example of a "contentiosus" in chap. 18 (29) of the *De sermone*. See also Erasmus's remarks on Valla's "mordacitas" in letter no. 182 (to Christopher Fischer, March 1505) in *Opus epistolarum*, ed. P. S. Allen, 12 vols. (Oxford, 1906–58). See letter no. 26 for an earlier defense of Valla.

54. On the criterion of usage, see *In eundem Pogium libellus secundus*, (*OO* 1.385), "consuetudo verò certissima loquendi magistra" (custom is the most certain mistress of speaking); as well as Valla's response to Poggio's misinterpretation of Quintilian (1.6) on usage in Valla's *Apologus* of 1452–53, discussed by Marsh in the article cited below. See also Camporeale 1972, esp. 149–71; Cesare Vasoli, *La dialettica e la retorica dell 'umanesimo,' 'invenzione' e 'metodo' nella cultura del XV e XVI secolo* (Milan, 1968), chap. 2, esp. 43–44, 66, 73; Sarah Stever Gravelle, "Humanist Attitudes towards Convention and Innovation in the Fifteenth Century," *Journal of Medieval and Renaissance Studies* 11 (1981); 193–212; and David Marsh, "Grammar, Method and Polemic in Lorenzo Valla's *Elegantiae*," *Rinascimento* 19 (1979): 91–116.

Marsh argues that "together with the philological principle of usage, Quattrocento humanists developed a relativistic notion of semantics and ethics; earth, not heaven, provides the key to the problems of language and logic" (106). Usage may be associated with relativism on one level for Valla, but the right use of usage is ultimately grounded in faith.

55. See, for example, the preface to the first book of the *Dialecticae disputationes*, and the opening of *De vero falsoque bono*, where Valla and Vegio respectively say that they will speak as orators. The first passage is discussed by Lisa Jardine, "Lorenzo Valla and the Intellectual Origins of Humanist Dialectic," 154ff. See also her substantially revised version of this article, "Lorenzo Valla: Academic Skepticism and the New Humanist Dialectic," in *The Skeptical Tradition*, ed. Myles Burnyeat (Berkeley, Los Angeles, London, 1983), 253–86. The second passage is discussed by Jardine, "Intellectual Origins," 157, and by Letizia A. Panizza, "Valla, Lactantius and Oratorical Scepticism," *Journal of the Warburg and Courtauld Institutes* 41 (1979): 89ff.

56. See *Elegantiae*, preface 4 (*PLQ*, 622), where Valla describes eloquence as "regina rerum . . . et perfecta sapientia" (queen of all things and perfect wisdom). For a wide-ranging discussion of Valla's rhetorical theology, see Salvatore I. Camporeale, "Lorenzo Valla tra medioevo e rinascimento," esp. 110–48 (pt. 3: "La rhetorica come *modus theologandi*").

57. On *facere fidem*, see Cicero, *Part. or*. 9.31; *Brutus* 50.187; *De off*. 2.9.33; Quintilian, 5.7.47. On the tie between rhetoric, dialectic, and belief (the fact that all three are concerned with practical or affective rather than logical certainty), see Eugenio Garin, "Note su alcuni aspetti delle Retoriche rinascimentale e sulla 'Retorica' del Patrizi," in *Testi umanistici su la retorica*, ed. Eugenio Garin, Paolo Rossi, and Cesare Vasoli (Rome, Milan, 1953), 31ff.

58. See the discussions by Camporeale, *Lorenzo Valla, umanesimo e teologia*, 231–33; and Myron Gilmore, "*Fides et Eruditio*: Erasmus and the Study of History," in *Humanists and Jurists* (Cambridge, Mass., 1963), esp. 112–13.

59. For another discussion of Valla's critique of prudence, see Charles Trinkaus, *In Our Image and Likeness*, 1: 157.

60. Valla argues for the reduction of the ten predicaments to *actio*, *qualitas*, and *substantia* in the *Dialecticae disputationes* 1.6, 13–14, 16 (*OO* 1: 656, 673–81). On this "reduction," see Camporeale, *Lorenzo Valla, umanesimo e teologia*, 354; Struever, "Valla," 193; and Vasoli, *La dialettica e la retorica*, 57–62. As Struever and Vasoli point out, although Valla includes the category of *substantia* in his final reduction, he does not often make use of it.

61. See Struever, "Valla," on Valla's insistence on defining the virtues through the practice of virtue. See also *Dialecticae disputationes* 3, Preface (*OO* 1: 731) for Valla's criticism of the "pseudo-dialectici": "qui nova quaedam vocabula ad perniciem adversariorum confixerunt, relicta veterum

consuetudine loquendi" [who abandon the old customary way of speaking and attack their adversaries with a new vocabulary]. This is not to deny that dialectic is a part of rhetoric for Valla (see the preface to Book 2 of the *Dialecticae disputationes* [*OO* 1: 693–94] as well as 2.19 (*OO* 1.718); but in being included in rhetoric (as a part of invention) dialectical procedure is subjected to the rhetorical consideration of decorum in argumentation. The inadequacy of dialectic's claim to provide a context-less absolute or necessary truth is newly evident. See Quintilian, *Institutio oratoria*, bk. 5. On the breakdown of the logic/rhetoric barrier in Valla's work see Camporeale, *Lorenzo Valla, umanesimo e teologia*, passim; Vasoli, *La dialettica e la retorica*, 43–44, 73; and Giovanni di Napoli, *Lorenzo Valla: filosofia e religione nell' umanesimo italiano* (Rome, 1971), chap. 2.

62. Mentioned by Camporeale, *Lorenzo Valla, umanesimo e teologia*, 345, with reference to *De libero arbitrio*. See also *De vero falsoque bono*, bk. 3, chap. 12, for Antonio da Rho's criticism of Boethius's grammatical-theological mistake in identifying the *bonum* of the virtuous man with the *summum bonum* of Christian *felicitas*. According to da Rho, Boethius is deceived by the ambiguity of the word *bonum* and therefore identifies the goodness of virtue (which involves action) with the good of happiness (which is a quality). Ignorance of linguistic ambiguity leads to theological error. Camporeale discusses this passage in "Lorenzo Valla tra medioevo e rinascimento," 101–9.

63. On the rhetorical practice of the Quattrocento dialogue, see Francesco Tateo, *Tradizione e realtà nell'umanesimo italiano* (Bari, 1967), and David Marsh, *The Quattrocento Dialogue* (Cambridge, Mass., 1980).

64. Marsh, *The Quattrocento Dialogue*, 6, suggests the influence of Plato, not Cicero or Augustine, on *De libero arbitrio*. While this points to the inadequacy of his own Ciceronian and Augustinian models with respect to Valla's text, Marsh does not elaborate on this suggestion.

65. Panizza, "Valla," 85.

66. Citations from Lactantius, cited in Panizza, "Valla," 57, 86.

67. See *Elegantiae*, preface 1 (*PLQ*, 594), for the analogy between Roman imperialism and the Latin language.

68. See *OO* 2.285, where Latin is identified with religion: "Holy religion and true literature have always seemed to me to be very compatible, and where the one is not, the other cannot be either, and [it has even seemed] that because our religion will be eternal, Latin literature will also be." See also *Elegantiae*, preface 1 (*PLQ*, 596): "Magnum ergo latini sermonis sacramentum est, magnum profecto numen" (Latin is a great sacrament, indeed a great [and] divine power).

69. See *The Consolation of Philosophy*, in *Boethius, The Theological Tractates*, trans. H. F. Steward and E. K. Rand, Loeb Classical Library (Cambridge, Mass., and London, 1962), 404: "But the present instant of men may well be compared to that of God in this: that as you see the same things in your temporal instant, so He beholdeth all things in His actual present. Where-

fore this divine foreknowledge doth not change the nature and propriety of things." See also 388 on the eye of the understanding ("intelligentiae . . . oculus").

70. See the discussion of this passage in Trinkaus, *In Our Image and Likeness*, 1: 143–45. The English translation and Latin text are from ibid., 145.

71. See *Elegantiae*, preface 4 (*PLQ*, 622) for a similar passage on the usefulness of rhetoric to strengthen faith: "Some decorate their own houses—those who study civil or canon law, medicine or philosophy, contributing nothing to divinity: let us rhetoricians decorate the house of God, so that those entering it may be moved to religion, not to contempt, by the majesty of the place."

72. See *LB*, col. 1218; *WA* 640; and the chapter on Erasmus below. See also *Tischreden*, *WA* 1.259; 2.1470; 3.5729 (references to *Tischreden* from Trinkaus's translation of Valla's dialogue, 153).

73. See Trinkaus, *In Our Image and Likeness*, 1: 115, 140, on Valla's knowledge of *De doctrina* when he wrote the *Disputationes* and *De libero arbitrio*, which Trinkaus dates between 1435 and 1443, Hanna-Barbara Gerl (*Rhetorik als Philosophie, Lorenzo Valla* [Munich, 1974]) between 1438 and 1442.

74. See *De doctrina* 1.37.41–1.38.42 on the difference between charity and cognition.

75. This identification of charity and freedom is also made by Valla at the end of *De vero falsoque bono*, 3.10 ?: "Thus nothing is done rightly without pleasure nor is there any merit to him who patiently but not freely serves in the army of God" (cited by Panizza, in a different context, 106). See *De doctrina* 4.25.56, on how the listener should hear willingly—*libenter*. See also Antonio's remark (161; 532) on freely (*libenter*) promising not to ask more of Lorenzo if Lorenzo agrees to discuss the question of foreknowledge and free will.

76. For a discussion of the connection between this Augustinian distinction and idolatry, see John Freccero, "The Fig Tree and the Laurel: Petrarch's Poetics," *Diacritics* 5 (1975): 34–40.

77. See *PLQ*, 616–18: "And if divine truth receives much that is useful or ornamental from those who sing, paint, or sculpt well and from other arts, so that they almost seem to exist for this purpose, this is even more true of those who are eloquent. For this reason, Jerome was not accused of being a Ciceronian but of not being a Christian, which he falsely claimed to be since he despised sacred scripture. It is not the study of eloquence, but the excessive study of this or any other art, so that it ends up taking the place of its betters, that is reprehensible."

78. See Montaigne's comparison of the Pyrrhonist skeptic's language to the purgative effect of rhubarb in the "Apologie," and the discussion of this passage in the chapter on Montaigne below.

79. Compare the passage from Erasmus's *Antibarbari*, quoted in the Introduction, n. 66.

80. See Trinkaus, *In Our Image and Likeness*, 1: 143–44, on Valla's use of

light/dark imagery. See also Barbara Gerl, "Die Bedingheit des Ich: Zur Frage des Autobiographischen bei Lorenzo Valla," in *Studia humanitatis, Ernesto Grassi zum 70. Geburtstag,* 189–205.

4. Erasmus: Prudence and Faith

1. This is what the Louvain theologian Dorp accuses Erasmus of. See Erasmus's reply, printed in *The Praise of Folly,* trans. and ed. Clarence H. Miller (New Haven, London, 1979), 158. All subsequent references to the *Praise* will be to this edition, and pagination will be indicated in the text where possible. *De libero arbitrio, Diatribe seu collatio* was published in 1524, thirteen years after the *Encomium.*

2. The epigraph is from *LE* 180; *WA* 670. In his *Erasmus* (New York, 1923; rpt. 1962), 127, Preserved Smith tells us that Luther wrote in his own 1532 copy of the *Encomium:* "When Erasmus wrote his *Folly,* he begot a daughter like himself. He turns, twists, and bites like an awl, but he, as a fool, has written true folly." Smith interprets this as a criticism of the *Encomium,* but the meaning of Luther's remarks is just as difficult to pin down as is the meaning of the *Encomium.*

3. Rosalie L. Colie, "Problems of Paradoxes," in *Twentieth-Century Interpretations of "The Praise of Folly,"* ed. Kathleen Williams (Englewood Cliffs, N. J., 1969), 95–96.

4. Among the Quattrocento humanists, Valla is generally acknowledged to have been particularly influential on Erasmus. See Erasmus's preface to his *Paraphrasis in Elegantias Laur. Vallae,* in *Opera omnia Desiderii Erasmi Roterodami,* ed. C. L. Heesakkers and J. H. Waszink (Amsterdam, 1973), ser. 4, vol. 1, as well as the editors' introduction. See also Jacques Chomarat, *Grammaire et rhétorique chez Erasme,* 2 vols. (Paris, 1981), 1: 64ff., 226–66; and Salvatore Camporeale, "Lorenzo Valla tra medioevo e rinascimento, *Encomion s. Thomae—1457,*" in *Memorie domenicane,* n.s. 7 (1976), 143–48, for a discussion of Valla's influence (in particular, of the fourth preface to the *Elegantiae*) on Erasmus, and for further bibliography on this subject.

5. The following passages from the *Adages* are taken from *Erasmus on His Times, A Shortened Version of the Adages,* trans. Margaret Mann Phillips (Cambridge, Eng. 1967). In "Festina lente," Erasmus writes of the rhetorical effect of the proverb's epigrammatic form: "The interest of the idea and the wit of the allusion are enhanced by such complete neatness and brevity, necessary in my mind to proverbs, which should be as clear-cut as gems; it adds immensely to their charm. If you consider the force and significance which are contained in these words [*festina lente*], how fertile, how serious, how wholesome they are and how applicable to every situation in life, you will soon agree there is no other in the whole range of proverbs so worthy of use" (3, *LB* 2.397 DE).

6. See "Herculei labores," in *Adages*, 22, 23 where Erasmus writes of his own labor in composing the *Adages*: "There is so little agreement between these authorities [on the meaning of a particular adage] that they very often write things which cancel each other out, and the additional burden is laid on one of consulting different commentators on the same things, and—over and over again—of examining, comparing, pondering and judging" (*LB* 2.711 CD; see 710 E).

7. "Herculei labores," 25–26. To the critic who claims that Erasmus "might have treated some parts more fully and copiously" (*LB* 2.712 E), he responds: "And supposing I were to get everything together which could be applied to the amplification of this adage, every maxim, everything elegantly said or memorably done, every fable or story, every wisecrack either in favour or against? Isn't it obvious that if I had tried to do this every adage could have been made into a volume?" (25; *LB* 2.713 A). Erasmus's intention was rather to mention certain interpretations "so that an opportunity might be given to others with more leisure, better library facilities or better memories, or richer in learning, to investigate further" (*LB* 2.713 D). On the form of the *Adages*, see Margaret Mann Phillips's longer study in *The "Adages" of Erasmus: A Study with Translations* (Cambridge, Eng., 1964); as well as Thomas M. Greene, "Erasmus' 'Festina lente': Vulnerabilities of the Humanist Text," in *Mimesis, From Mirror to Method*, ed. John D. Lyons and Stephen G. Nichols, Jr. (Hanover, N.H., 1982), 132–48, and Chomorat, *Grammaire*, 2: 761–81.

8. *The Enchiridion*, trans. Raymond Himelick (Bloomington, Ind., 1963), canon 5, 113 (my emphasis); *LB* 5.32 CD.

9. "Paraclesis," in *Christian Humanism and the Reformation, Selected Writings of Erasmus*, ed. John C. Olin (New York, 1975), 105; *LB* 6. See also "Paraclesis," 100: "In this kind of philosophy, located as it is more truly in the disposition of the mind than in syllogisms, life means more than debate, inspiration is preferable to erudition, transformation is a more important matter than intellectual comprehension. Only a very few can be learned, but all can be Christian, all can be devout, and—I shall boldly add—all can be theologians. Indeed, this philosophy easily penetrates into the minds of all, an action in especial accord with human nature. Moreover, what else is the philosophy of Christ, which He himself calls a rebirth [*renascentia*], than the restoration of human nature originally well formed?" (*LB* 6). For a contrasting interpretation of Erasmus's view of Scripture in the "Paraclesis," see Marjorie O'Rourke Boyle, *Erasmus on Language and Method in Theology* (Toronto, Buffalo, 1977). Quoting the passage in the "Paraclesis" where Erasmus claims that Scripture renders the image of Christ present before the reader's eyes ("Paraclesis," 102), Boyle remarks: "The humanist persuasion that an eloquent text orates reality expands in Erasmus to a lively faith in the real presence of Christ as text" (83). This "perceptual" view of reading neglects the activity of interpretation that is constitutive of the "presence" of meaning in the text. It also neglects the difficulty of that activity and the

failure of Scripture to persuade the recalcitrant—or inactive—reader. Elsewhere, however, Boyle does take account of the reader's act of interpretation, e.g., 91. See Terence Cave, *The Cornucopian Text: Problems of Writing in the French Renaissance* (Oxford, 1979), 123ff., on the paradoxes of textual presence in Erasmus's work. See also Cave's "*Enargeia:* Erasmus and the Rhetoric of Presence," *Esprit créateur* 16 (1976): 5–19.

10. Erasmus uses the phrase "theologia practica" in the "Paraclesis" and in the *Ratio seu methodus compendio perveniendi ad veram theologiam.* For a discussion of the differences between Erasmus's *theologia practica* and classical notions of prudence, see Dietrich Harth, *Philologie und praktische Philosophie: Untersuchungen zum Sprach- und Traditionsverständnis des Erasmus von Rotterdam* (Munich, 1970), 34–35: "Aristotelian phronesis designated the capacity, in the continually changing situation of public life, to choose from among all the available means of directing one's life, the correct ones, that is to say, to conduct oneself in a politically correct fashion. The humanist, however, proceeds from the assumption of an *ordo societatis,* which is not constituted by the public *lexis* and *praxis* of free citizens, but rather which is given in a structured social hierarchy, in which the well-being of the whole must be brought about from the top."

11. See Alfons Auer, *Die vollkommene Frömmigkeit des Christen, nach dem "Enchiridion militis Christiani" des Erasmus von Rotterdam* (Dusseldorf, 1954), 83.

12. *WA* 7.97.23. See *LE* 110 (*WA* 606ff.).

13. See Charles Norris Cochrane, *Christianity and Classical Culture* (Oxford, 1940), 367, 400, 412–13, 436; and Augustine, *Confessions,* trans. William Watts, Loeb Classical Library, 2 vols. (London, New York, 1912), 1: 5 (1.2.2): "I should therefore not be, O God, yea I should have no being at all, unless thou wert in me."

14. Cited in A. Meyer, *Etude critique sur les relations d'Erasme et Luther* (Paris, 1909), 115 n. 4.

15. See *LE* 125, where Luther calls Erasmus's thoughts about God "all too human." See also 135, 184.

16. Martin Luther, *Von der Freiheit eines Christenmenschen* (1520; Stuttgart, 1962), 129.

17. See *Opus epistolarum Des. Erasmi Roterodami,* ed. P. S. Allen, 12 vols. (Oxford, 1906–58), epistles 1901, 35–50 (1527); 2175, 5–11 (1529). See also epistle 1119, 34ff. (July 6, 1520), to Spalatin: "I would prefer Luther to refrain from these contentions for a little while, and to expound the gospel simply, without admixture of personal feelings: perhaps his undertaking would succeed better. Now he is exposing even *bonae litterae* to an ill will which is ruinous to us and unprofitable to himself." Cited in John William Aldridge, *The Hermeneutics of Erasmus,* Basel Studies of Theology 2 (Richmond, Va., 1966), 25.

18. *Luther, An Introduction to His Thought,* trans. R. A. Wilson (Tübingen, 1964; London, 1970), 221.

19. See Marjorie O'Rourke Boyle, *Rhetoric and Reform, Erasmus' Civil Dispute with Luther* (Cambridge, Mass.; London, 1983). Boyle argues brilliantly that the debate between Erasmus and Luther is concerned less with the theological question of free will than it is with the rhetorical problem of how to discuss this question. For Erasmus, free will is a disputed question, which therefore requires deliberative rhetoric. For Luther the non-existence of free will is not in question, and thus allows only for judicial rhetoric. Boyle's analysis of Erasmus's position lends support to my contention that humanist rhetoric is essentially deliberative. While it is unfortunate that her work was published only when the present book was in press, I am happy to see that our studies are complementary.

20. See Erasmus, *Ratio seu methodus*, in *Ausgewählte Schriften*, vol. 3, ed. Gerhard B. Winkler (Darmstadt, 1967), 316, 320 for figurative interpretations of violent passages in the Bible. See also *Querela pacis*, in *Ausgewählte Schriften*, vol. 5, ed. Werner Welzig (Darmstadt, 1975), 372.

21. *Adages*, 143; *LB* 2.460 D: "Denique non perpendunt [Erasmus's critics] id, quod in dialogis est potissimum, personae decorum. Erasmum imaginantur loqui, non Moriam." [Finally, they do not consider what is most important in dialogues, the decorum of the character. They imagine Erasmus is speaking, not Moria.]

22. *Stultitiae laus*, in *LB* 4, 427 C. Further references will be given in the text, following references to the English translation.

23. Clarence H. Miller rightly remarks in his introduction to the new Latin edition of the *Encomium* (*Opera omnia Desiderii Erasmi Roterodami*, ser. 4, vol. 3 [Amsterdam, Oxford, 1979]), 19: Folly "uses Plato's image of the Sileni to prove an essentially sceptical or Pyrrhonist viewpoint."

24. Just as Folly's earlier definition of prudence as experience parodies the traditional humanist emphasis on the active life, so here, one could argue, she mocks the humanist concern with the world of appearances or the realm of possibility.

25. For other references of Erasmus to Christ as a moral example, see H. Humbertclaude, *Erasme et Luther: leur polémique sur le libre arbitre* (Paris, 1909), 9 n. 2.

26. *Under Pretext of Praise: Satiric Mode in Erasmus' Fiction* (Toronto, 1973), 62. See also Richard Sylvester, "The Problem of Unity in *The Praise of Folly*," *English Literary Renaissance* 6 (1976): 138.

27. *PMLA* 89 (1974): 463–76.

28. Rebhorn is persuasive when he discusses the way in which Folly as satirist shows the limitations of her initial praise of natural and social folly. But he fails to note that this same strategy of flattering the reader's illusions about the possibility of social harmony and then undeceiving him is recapitulated in the final third of the work. Furthermore, as we have seen, it is not the case that in praising Christian folly, Folly "no longer claims man's worship," since the example of Christianity is introduced in the first place precisely in order to substantiate that claim.

29. "Erasmus' Learned Joking: The Ironic Use of Classical Wisdom in *The Praise of Folly*," *Texas Studies in Literature and Language* 19 (1977): 246–67.

30. See *LE* 43, *LB* 9.1219 B: "But the authority of Scripture is not here in dispute. The same Scriptures are acknowledged and venerated by either side. Our battle is about the meaning of Scripture."

31. See Miller's introduction, *Opera omnia Desiderii Erasmi Roterodami*, 20 n. 33 for different interpretations of this third section.

32. See Joël Lefebvre, *Les fols et la folie* (Paris, 1968), 246, 247, n. 131, on the antinomies of Erasmus's thought. Although Lefebvre discusses the similarities between the first and third parts of the *Encomium*, he also remarks, "The distance between the first and third parts of the *Praise* could just as well serve to emphasize that mythology is incompatible with the Gospel," and that immanence is incompatible with transcendence (246). I am in basic agreement with Lefebvre's interpretation of the *Encomium*.

33. Erasmus, *Praise of Folly*, ed. A. H. T. Levi (Harmondsworth, Eng., 1971), 15.

34. See Quintilian, *Institutio oratoria*, 2.17.30–36.

35. This passage is taken from the 1668 translation of the *Praise of Folly* by John Wilson (Ann Arbor, 1958), 10–11.

36. *Essais* 3.9, in Montaigne, *Oeuvres complètes*, ed. Albert Thibaudet and Maurice Rat, Bibliothèque de la Pléiade (Paris, 1962), 974.

37. This is Dorp's objection to the *Encomium*. See *Praise*, 163.

38. See Paul Mestwerdt, *Die Anfänge des Erasmus* (Leipzig, 1917), 265: "In a certain sense Erasmus resolves this dilemma [of reconciling piety and erudition]. The final goal of spiritual life and the true nature of piety is the contempt (*contemptus*) of all earthly things and thus also of worldly education. But this final goal can only really be achieved on the assumption that you yourself first possess what you have contempt for. Education is the necessary means which enables man to have a correct and complete contempt for the world."

39. Wendelin Schmidt-Dengler, in his introduction to the *Encomium*, in Erasmus von Rotterdam, *Ausgewählte Schriften*, vol. 2, ed. Werner Welzig (Darmstadt, 1975), xxii, writes, "If one compares the beginning with the end, the former seems to discredit the latter. Indeed, the suspicion of blasphemy is not so farfetched."

40. See the discussion by Walter Kaiser in *Praisers of Folly: Erasmus, Rabelais, and Shakespeare* (Cambridge, Mass., 1963), 36ff.

41. In the Vulgate, "Iustitia enim Dei in eo revelatur ex fide in fidem: sicut scriptum est: Iustus autem ex fide vivit." In the King James Version, "For therein is the righteousness of God revealed from faith to faith: as it is written: The just shall live by faith."

42. Eugene Rice has written that the Reformation idea of wisdom was inseparable from revelation: "No trace of metaphysics disfigures it, no philosophy profanes it. As a knowledge of the essential points of Christian doctrine it is revealed, and, with the aid of grace, firmly believed. If one

could overthrow the poverty of words, one would see that it is not even a form of knowledge. It is certain, but cannot be demonstrated; it is true but cannot be known" (*The Renaissance Idea of Wisdom* [Cambridge, Mass., 1958], 147).

43. The capital of the Greek upsilon, which was also a symbol of the choice between good and evil. See Erwin Panofsky, "Hercules am Scheideweg," *Studien der Bibliothek Warburg* 18 (Leipzig, Berlin, 1930).

5. Montaigne: A Rhetoric of Skepticism

1. Montaigne, *Oeuvres complètes*, Bibliothèque de la Pléiade, ed. Albert Thibaudet and Maurice Rat (Paris, 1962). References are to book, essay, and page number in that order. English translations are taken from *The Complete Essays of Montaigne*, trans. Donald M. Frame (Stanford, Calif., 1965). In the text references to the English translation will be followed by references to the Pléiade edition. I have occasionally modified the Frame translation very slightly to make it more literal. Where there is only a single page reference it refers to the French edition, and the accompanying translation is my own.

2. See *Essais*, 2.12.544, for Montaigne's criticism of the Academic notions of probability and verisimilitude.

3. For a complementary view of this passage see Neil Saccamano's remarks in his unpublished essay, "Some Remarks on Language, Self-portraiture and Skepticism in Montaigne's *Essais*," 7: "Moreover, the skeptic could justify his recourse to this figure and to irony, the purpose of which is to caution his opponent to be wary of the rhetorical effects of an affirmative proposition, by arguing that the interpretation of 'j'ignore' as 'je sçais' already places logic in the employ of rhetoric. In order to combat the denial of knowledge, the adversaries of skepticism must dissociate grammar from meaning and, in so doing, must entertain the possibility that the logic of form does not govern meaning absolutely."

4. The following relies on Sextus Empiricus's *Outlines of Pyrrhonism*, Loeb Classical Library, trans. R. G. Bury (London, New York, 1933), 1.164–79. All citations are from this edition. The corpus of Montaigne criticism is obviously enormous and cannot be examined here in any depth. I have found the following works, however, particularly useful for considering questions of rhetoric and/or skepticism in the *Essais*: Philip P. Hallie, *The Scar of Montaigne* (Middletown, Conn., 1966); Terence Cave, *The Cornucopian Text: Problems of Writing in the French Renaissance* (Oxford, 1979), 271–321; Karlheinz Stierle, "L'histoire comme exemple, l'exemple comme histoire," *Poétique* 10 (1972): 176–98; Hugo Friedrich, *Montaigne*, trans. Robert Rovini (Paris, 1968), passim; Edwin M. Duval, "Rhetorical Composition and 'Open Form' in Montaigne's Early *Essais*," *Bibliothèque d'Humanisme et Renaissance* 43 (1981): 269–87; Antoine Compagnon, *La seconde main, ou le travail de la citation* (Paris, 1979), esp. 235ff. Paolo Valesio has some interesting remarks

about Montaigne in *Novantiqua, Rhetorics as a Contemporary Theory* (Bloomington, Ind., 1982), 99–103. See also his section entitled "The Rhetoric of Anti-rhetoric," 41ff. Unfortunately, the work of Christine Brousseau-Beuermann came to my attention only after I had completed this chapter. See her dissertation, "La copie de Montaigne," Harvard University, 1985. As will already be clear from the preceding chapters, I cannot agree with Cathleen M. Bauschatz, who argues that in encouraging the active participation of the reader, Montaigne's *Essais* represent a decisive break with earlier Renaissance literature ("Montaigne's Conception of Reading in the Context of Renaissance Poetics and Modern Criticism," in *The Reader in the Text*, ed. Susan R. Suleiman and Inge Crosman [Princeton, 1980]: 264–92).

5. See Sextus, *Outlines*, 2.101ff: "An 'indicative' sign, they say, is that which is not clearly associated with the thing signified, but signifies that whereof it is a sign by its own particular nature and constitution, just as, for instance, the bodily motions are signs of the soul. Hence, too, they define this sign as follows: 'An indicative sign is an antecedent judgment, in a sound hypothetical syllogism, which serves to reveal the consequent.'"

6. Charlotte L. Stough, *Greek Skepticism: A Study in Epistemology* (Berkeley, Los Angeles, 1969), 98.

7. Seneca, "On Tranquility of Mind," *Moral Essays*, trans. John W. Basore, Loeb Classical Library, 3 vols. (London, Cambridge, Mass., 1970), 2: 257. Montaigne borrows the anecdote about Canius Julius in the preceding passage of his essay from this text.

8. See Diogenes Laertius, "Zeno," in *Lives of the Philosophers*, trans. R. D. Hicks, Loeb Classical Library, 2 vols. (London, Cambridge, Mass., 1965), 2: 199, on the practicing of virtue and making "moral progress." See also *De off.* 1.4.4 for the connection between perceiving the relationship of cause and effect, and learning how to act appropriately.

9. Montaigne's playing with the different meanings of *discours, accident*, and *effect* (see below), as well as on the literal and figurative meanings of *tomber*, dramatizes the skeptic's dubious state on the semantic level. That this semantic polyvalence is not something either the author or the reader can control becomes apparent by the end of the essay.

10. For *exercitatio* as imitation of "the most accomplished writers and orators," see *De orat.* 3.31.125.

11. Frame translates *effect* in this passage as experience (271), elsewhere as action (261, 274), effects (272), and deeds (274), and "effect de la toux" is rendered simply as "cough." It seems to me that Montaigne's skeptical practice is bound up with the repetition of such polysemous words, the effect of which is often lost in translation. Randall Cotgrave defines *effect* as "an effect, or worke; the issue, or successe of a thing; a working, bringing to passe, making to be" (*A Dictionarie of the French and English Tongues* [London, 1611; rpr. Columbia, S.C., 1950]). I would argue that the definition of *effect* as effect is always one of the suggested meanings.

12. See Sextus, *Outlines*, 1.21–24.

13. Cicero himself makes an appearance at the end of the essay: "He who forbids me to speak about it [living] according to my sense, experience, and practice, let him order the architect to speak of buildings not according to himself but according to his neighbor; according to another man's knowledge, not according to his own. If it is vainglory for a man himself to publish his own merits, why doesn't Cicero proclaim the eloquence of Hortensius, Hortensius that of Cicero?" (274; 359). It is a tribute to Montaigne's "forme d'escrire douteuse" that it is impossible to say whether these remarks are to be taken seriously or ironically: whether he is using Cicero against Cicero and so offering only a mock defense of speaking of oneself, or whether Montaigne is himself the object of irony, or both.

14. Charlton T. Lewis and Charles Short, *A Latin Dictionary* (Oxford, 1879), s.v. *exagium*; Maximilien Paul Emile Littré, *Dictionnaire de la langue française* (Paris, 1873), s.v. *essai, essayer*.

15. Seneca, *Epistulae morales*, trans. R. M. Grummere, Loeb Classical Library, 3 vols. (Cambridge, Mass., 1962), 2: 281. All further references will indicate the volume, followed by the page number. I realize that the interpretation of this passage is debatable, especially since Seneca writes earlier in this letter that it is uncertain whether bees only gather honey or whether they transform it in some active way (which would support my reading of digestion as judgment). I would point to the emphasis early in the letter (276) on the exercise of judgment in reading: "Letters are necessary so that after I have learned what others have found out by their studies, I will be able to pass judgment on their discoveries and reflect upon discoveries that remain to be made." I have altered Grummere's translation slightly.

16. For a discussion of Renaissance theories of imitation and further bibliography, see G. W. Pigman, "Versions of Imitation in the Renaissance," *Renaissance Quarterly* 1 (1980): 1–32, and "Imitation and the Renaissance Sense of the Past: the Reception of Erasmus's *Ciceronianus*," *The Journal of Medieval and Renaissance Studies* 9 (1979): 155–78; as well as Thomas M. Greene, *The Light in Troy, Imitation and Discovery in Renaissance Poetry* (New Haven, London, 1982). In "La copie de Montaigne" Christine Brousseau-Beuermann argues convincingly that Montaigne is not primarily concerned with the imitation of specific authors, but with the pragmatic and often deliberately decontextualized use of quotations or commonplaces.

17. Søren Kierkegaard, *The Concept of Irony*, trans. Lee M. Capel (Bloomington and London, 1971), 285–86. Further references will be given in the text.

18. Pierre Aubenque, *La prudence chez Aristote* (Paris, 1963), 166. See "De la vanité" (3.9.766, 979) for another view of the Delphic command.

19. Eugene Rice, *The Renaissance Idea of Wisdom* (Cambridge, Mass., 1958), 141.

20. Aubenque, *Prudence chez Aristote*, 161.

21. *The Institutio Oratoria of Quintilian*, trans. H. E. Butler, Loeb Classical Library, 4 vols. (Cambridge, Mass., London, 1968), 4: 99–101.

22. Hegel, *Phenomenology of Mind*, trans. J. B. Baillie (New York, 1949), 119, 120.

23. Fredric Jameson, *Marxism and Form* (Princeton, 1971), 341. This is one phrase Jameson uses to describe dialectical thinking.

24. Montaigne, *Essays*, trans. John Florio, Everyman's Library, 3 vols. (London, 1965), 2: 201.

25. The phrase is taken from Philippe de Mornay's *A Woorke concerning the trewness of the Christian Religion*, in Sir Philip Sidney, *The Defence of Poesie, Political Discourses, Correspondence, Translations*, ed. Albert Feuillerat (Cambridge, Eng., 1923), 258.

6. Hobbes: A Rhetoric of Logic

1. *Ben Jonson*, 11 vols., ed. C. H. Herford and Percy and Evelyn Simpson (Oxford, 1925–52), 8: 593.

2. J. G. A. Pocock, *The Machiavellian Moment* (Princeton, 1970), 159. See Leo Strauss on Machiavelli as a precursor of Hobbes, in *The Political Philosophy of Hobbes*, trans. Elsa M. Sinclair (Oxford, 1936; Chicago, 1952), xv–xvi; as well as in *Natural Right and History* (Chicago, 1953), esp. 177–80. Jürgen Habermas, "The Classical Doctrine of Politics in Relation to Social Philosophy," in *Theory and Practice*, trans. John Viertel (Boston, 1973), 41–81, discusses the break with the classical notion of prudence in the work of Machiavelli, More, and Hobbes. This essay came to my attention after the completion of this chapter. Finally, in *The Revolution of the Saints* (Cambridge, Mass., 1965), Michael Walzer discusses the breakdown of traditional notions of social and political authority in seventeenth-century England, and argues that "for both Hobbes and the Calvinists, the antidote to wickedness and disorder was arbitrary power. . . . Order became a matter of power and power a matter of will, force, and calculation" (159–60).

3. See Ernst Cassirer, *The Philosophy of the Enlightenment*, trans. Fritz C. A. Koelln and James P. Pettegrove (Boston, 1955), 253ff., on Hobbes's concern with a "logic of invention."

4. Strauss, *Hobbes*, 163, argues that this skepticism or nominalism leads Hobbes to reject classical political philosophy, which "orientates itself by speech." Hobbes's rejection, according to Strauss, "arises originally from insight into the problematic nature of ordinary speech, that is, of popular valuations, which one may with a certain justification call natural valuations." For an argument against this view of Hobbes's rejection of (the power of) speech, see Gary Shapiro, "Reading and Writing in the Text of Hobbes' *Leviathan*," *Journal of the History of Philosophy* 18 (1980): 157 (the whole issue is devoted to Hobbes). Shapiro argues that the *Leviathan* is intended to provide the reader with "a new kind of rhetorical education"

(149), and that the text needs to be read with careful attention to its rhetorical structure. He does not, however, provide us with a rhetorical analysis of the text. For further discussion of Hobbes's skepticism, see Leo Strauss, *Natural Right and History*, 166–201; and Michael Oakeshott, *Hobbes on Civil Association* (Berkeley, Los Angeles, 1975), chap. 1. Oakeshott makes frequent comparisons between Hobbes and Montaigne in this regard. See also the excellent discussion in Pierre Manent, *Naissances de la politique moderne: Machiavel, Hobbes, Rousseau* (Paris, 1977), 84–91. A full consideration of Hobbes's transcendence of skepticism through science would have to take into account his affinities with the work of Descartes as well as with Marin Mersenne, *La verité des sciences contre les sceptiques ou pyrrhoniens* (1625), and with Pierre Gassendi, *Syntagma philosophicum*, a work that Popkin has described as a "*via media* between dogmatism and scepticism."

5. See Strauss, *Hobbes*, 130ff. The Brief was possibly composed in 1633. See James P. Zappen, "Rhetoric in Thomas Hobbes's *Leviathan*: Pathos versus Ethos and Logos," *Rhetorica* 1 (1983): 65–92. On the continuity of Hobbes's early humanist education and his later work in political science, see Miriam Reik, *The Golden Lands of Thomas Hobbes* (Detroit, 1977), passim, especially chap. 3. My own discussion is greatly indebted to this excellent book.

6. The text of the *Brief* is included in *Aristotle's Treatise on Rhetoric, also The Poetics of Aristotle*, ed. Theodore Buckley (London, 1857). All quotations are from this edition, 275–76 (chaps. 1, 2).

7. For a discussion of the possible influence of Ramus on Hobbes, see Walter J. Ong, "Hobbes and Talon's Ramist Rhetoric in England," *Transactions of the Cambridge Bibliographical Society* (1949–52): 260–69; James P. Zappen, "Science and Rhetoric from Bacon to Hobbes: Responses to the Problem of Rhetoric," in *Rhetoric 78: Proceedings of Theory of Rhetoric: An Interdisciplinary Conference*, ed. Robert L. Brown, Jr., and Martin Steinmann, Jr. (Minnesota, 1979): 399–419; and the article cited above.

8. See EW 1.82, 2.161–62. For Hobbes's criticisms of contradiction in the *Leviathan*, see 12.171, 12.179–82, 26.316–17, 30.393, 32.410, 43.625, 46.685–86 (with reference to Academic disputation), "A Review and Conclusion," 717ff., 727, and the discussion below. Also see the remarks of Rosalie Colie, *Paradoxia epidemica* (Princeton, 1966), 509–12, on Hobbes's rejection of contradiction and paradox.

9. On the resolutive-compositive method, see EW 1.10–11, and J. W. N. Watkins, *Hobbes' System of Ideas* (London, 1965), chap. 3.

10. Strauss, *Hobbes*, 34, 79.

11. For further discussion of the different schools of Hobbes criticism, and of the different conflicts they see within Hobbes's political theory, see W. H. Greenleaf, "Hobbes: The Problem of Interpretation," in *Hobbes and Rousseau: A Collection of Critical Essays*, ed. Maurice Cranston and Richard S. Peters (New York, 1972), 5–36.

12. Some exceptions are J. G. A. Pocock (who, however, sees no irony in

Hobbes's "authoritative" interpretation of Scripture), "Time, History and Eschatology in the Thought of Thomas Hobbes," in *Politics, Language and Time* (New York, 1973), 148–201; Samuel I. Mintz, *The Hunting of Leviathan* (Cambridge, Eng., 1962), who is particularly good on Hobbes's use of irony; Sheldon S. Wolin, *Hobbes and the Epic Tradition of Political Theory* (Los Angeles, 1970), who reads the *Leviathan* in terms of Hobbes's lifelong interest in epic poetry; C. B. Macpherson, *The Political Theory of Possessive Individualism, Hobbes to Locke* (Oxford, 1962), who argues that Hobbes's model of society is based on the political and economic conditions prevailing in England at that time; and Eldon J. Eisenach, *Two Worlds of Liberalism: Religion and Politics in Hobbes, Locke, and Mill* (Chicago, 1981). Although Eisenach does not specifically discuss the role of rhetoric in the *Leviathan*, he argues, as I do, that Hobbes reintroduces in books 3 and 4 the elements of persuasion and religion that he had excluded from the commonwealth in books 1 and 2. According to Eisenach, persuasion and instruction are necessary if theory is to be put into practice: Hobbes needs to provide a ground for the citizen's obligation to obey the sovereign. We differ in our analyses insofar as Eisenach thinks Hobbes presents a coherent logical argument, uncontaminated by rhetoric, in the first two books of the *Leviathan*. See also Shapiro, "Reading and Writing in the Text of Hobbes' *Leviathan*."

13. Hobbes interprets Scripture literally or figuratively as his argument requires. See the discussion below on Hobbes's literal interpretation of the "kingdom of heaven," but see L 44.635 for Hobbes's figurative interpretation of the doctrine of transubstantiation. See also Hobbes's analysis of 2 Thess. 3:14, which seems to enjoin obedience to St. Paul, in terms of the equivocality of the word "obey." We can obey counsel as well as law, and the word of Paul is only counsel (44.592).

14. See Letizia A. Panizza, "Valla, Lactantius, and Oratorical Scepticism," *Journal of the Warburg and the Courtauld Institutes* 41 (1979): 80.

15. See L 4.104: "[By this imposition of Names] . . . the consequence found in one particular, comes to be registred and remembred, as an Universall rule; and discharges our mentall reckoning, of time and place; and delivers us from all labour of the mind, saving the first and makes that which was found true *here*, and *now*, to be true in *all times* and *places*." That is, language, according to Hobbes, allows us to move from considerations of prudence and decorum (time and place, here and now) to universal rules. For an excellent discussion of the relation of language to thought in Hobbes, see T. A. Heinrichs, "Language and Mind in Hobbes," *Yale French Studies* 49 (1973): 56–70.

16. See L 4.102 on the uses of speech other than for simply registering our thoughts: speech is used "to shew to others that knowledge which we have attained; which is, to Counsell, and Teach one another. Thirdly, to make known to others our wills, and purposes, that we may have the mutuall help of one another. Fourthly, to please and delight our selves, and others, by playing with our words, for pleasure or ornament, innocently." See also

8.137 and 25.307–9, for the way in which metaphor stirs up the passions, and for the connection between metaphor and deceit.

Hobbes is inconsistent with regard to the relation of metaphor to deceit. He sometimes argues that metaphors are not deceptive precisely because "they profess the transferring of names from one thing to another" (*EW* 1.62–63). And in the *Leviathan* he argues that "Metaphors, and Tropes . . .are less dangerous" than the names of virtues and vices, "because they profess their inconstancy; which the others do not" (4.110). But further on (8.137), the fact that metaphor declares its deviance from literal language does not make it any less threatening to rational discourse, for the declaration of the impropriety of words is no guarantee of the possibility of reducing them to their proper meaning: "For seeing they openly professe deceipt; to admit them into Councell, or Reasoning, were manifest folly."

17. See the preface to *De cive* (*EW* 2.xiii–xiv): Since the present civil disorder is due in part to debate about opinions, it is necessary to "demonstrate that there are no authentical doctrines concerning right and wrong, good and evil, besides the constituted laws in each realm and government; and that the question whether any future action will prove just or unjust, good or ill, is to be demanded of none but those to whom the supreme hath committed the interpretation of his laws."

18. It is significant that Hobbes's most famous narrative exemplum occurs at the moment in his argument when the question of obedience—of motivation to accept the contract—enters in. The motive of Hobbes's eloquent logic is fear. See his discussion of the use of exempla and narrative in the prefatory remarks to his translation of Thucydides, "To the Readers," and "Of the Life and History of Thucydides," *EW* 8.vii–xxxii. On the logical function of Hobbes's hypothetical state of nature, see Macpherson, *Possessive Individualism*, 19–29.

19. See *L* 13.188: In the state of nature there is "no Propriety, no Dominion, no *Mine* and *Thine* distinct; but onely that [is] . . . every mans that he can get; and for so long, as he can keep it."

20. I am concerned here only with the concept of sovereignty as it is presented in the *Leviathan*. For analyses of the way in which Hobbes's theory of sovereignty develops from the earliest works up through the *Leviathan*, see David P. Gauthier, *The Logic of Leviathan* (Oxford, 1969), 99–177, and Hanna Pitkin, "Hobbes' Concept of Representation," pts. 1 and 2, *American Political Science Review* 58 (1964): 328–40, 902–18.

21. One would have to say that the authorization is not *metaphorical* either, insofar as metaphor presupposes a literal language. See *L* 38.488: "For of all Metaphors there is some reall ground that may be expressed in proper words." But there is no such language (because there is no "reall ground") before the institution of sovereignty.

22. The sovereign is bound by natural law (22.276), but not because he is bound by the covenant, since he is not a party to the covenant. See Pitkin, "Hobbes' Concept of Representation," 915.

231

23. If we return to the discussion of the "person" in chap. 16, we see that the rhetorical dimension of Hobbes's notion of truth or (mis)representation is suggested by the example he borrows from Cicero's *De oratore*. Antonius is speaking of the way in which he prepares to argue a case. After the client who has presented his point of view has left, he tells us, "in my own person and with perfect impartiality I play [Hobbes: 'beare'] three characters [*personas*], myself, my opponent and the arbitrator. Whatever consideration is likely to prove more helpful than embarrassing I decide to discuss; wherever I find more harm than good I entirely reject and discard the topic concerned" (2.102; reference from Pitkin, 217). Antonius's purpose in acting these three roles is not to represent the truth, but to discover those arguments or considerations which will prove most useful, most persuasive in court. In a later passage (17.227), which echoes Hobbes's translation of the passage from Cicero, the sovereign is said to "beare [the] Person" of the multitude who have covenanted to appoint him their representative.

24. See "Introduction," L 81–82: "The *Pacts* and *Covenants*, by which the parts of this Body Politique were at first made, set together and united, resemble that *Fiat*, or *Let us make man*, pronounced by God in the Creation." The resemblance, in other words, is in terms of the power of the imperative. Similarly, in chap. 45, the king represents God because representation is conceived of in terms of power rather than in terms of mimetic representation.

25. Pitkin, "Hobbes' Concept of Representation," 910, cites EW 4.123: "And because it is impossible for any man really to transfer his own strength to another, or for that other to receive it; it is to be understood, that to transfer a man's power and strength, is no more but to lay by, or relinquish his own right of resisting him to whom he so transferreth it."

26. See Pitkin, "Hobbes' Concept of Representation," 910, and Gauthier, *The Logic of Leviathan*, 124–27.

27. Pitkin, "Hobbes' Concept of Representation," argues that if Hobbes had seen representation in terms of "standing for" as well as "acting for," "he might have seen some of the ways in which representing means conforming to an external standard" (338). But the problem for Hobbes is that all external standards (God, natural law, the intention of the author) are, properly speaking, illegible.

28. See the illustration of Lady Rhetorica in, e.g., Cristoforo Giarda's *Icones Symbolicae* (Milan, 1628), which serves as a frontispiece to Erasmus's *De copia*, in *Collected Works of Erasmus* (Toronto, Buffalo, London, 1978). See also sonnet 58 in Sidney's *Astrophil and Stella*, and the preface to Thomas Wilson's *Arte of Rhetorique* (1553).

29. See n. 12, above, and Manent, *Naissances de la politique moderne*, 105–32.

30. This suggests that whereas the function of books 1 and 2 of the *Leviathan* is to analyze and tame the linguistic ambiguity that reflects the conflicting interests of individual citizens, the function of books 3 and 4 is to analyze conflict at the institutional level, that is, between Church and State.

31. Hobbes adds his own ironic proof of the temporal, earthly nature of this kingdom: "If the Kingdome of God . . . were not a Kingdome which God by his Lieutenants, or Vicars . . . did exercise on Earth; there would not have been so much contention, and warre, about who it is, by whom God speaketh to us; neither would many Priests have troubled themselves with Spirituall Jurisdiction, nor any King have denied it them" (35.448). Hobbes's interpretation of Scripture repeats the paradox of origin we saw in his account of language and of sovereignty. He appeals to the revelation of God's word in Scripture to prove his interpretation of the rights of the sovereign. But he tells us that Scripture can only be read as in conformity with the sovereign's interpretation (see 32.409–10). Similarly, Scripture agrees with natural law, but natural law can be interpreted in different ways (26.322), so it is necessary to obey the sovereign and accept his interpretation, which we do in accordance with natural law (33.415).

32. See *L* 26.321–22: "For it is not the Letter, but the Intendment, or Meaning; that is to say, the authentique Interpretation of the Law (which is the sense of the Legislator,) in which the nature of the Law consisteth; And therefore the Interpretation of all Lawes dependeth on the Authority Soveraign. . . . For else, by the craft of an Interpreter, the Law may be made to beare a sense, contrary to that of the Soveraign; by which means the Interpreter becomes the Legislator."

33. See William Davenant's preface (dedicated to Hobbes) to his poem "Gondibert," in *Critical Essays of the Seventeenth Century*, vol. 2, 1650–1685, ed. J. E. Spingarn (Oxford, 1908). Davenant accords an analogous rhetorical role to poetry (33, 44). See also *L* 42.526, where Hobbes redefines religion (like prudence) partly in terms of probability: "But Faith has no relation to, nor dependence at all upon Compulsion, or Commandement; but onely upon certainty, or probability of Arguments drawn from Reason, or from something men beleeve already." For the relation of faith to opinion, see bk. 1, chap. 7, and for the similarities between prudential reasoning and religion, see bk. 1, chap. 12. This chapter also discusses the usefulness to the commonwealth of the religious fictions of poetry. See Ben Jonson, *Discoveries*, in *Ben Jonson*, 8:595: "I could never thinke the study of *Wisdome* confin'd only to the Philosopher: or of *Piety* to the *Divine*: or of *State* to the *Politicke*. But that he which can faine a *Common-wealth* (which is the *Poet*) can governe it with *Counsels*, strengthen it with *Lawes*, correct it with *Judgements*, informe it with *Religion*, and *Morals*; is all these. Wee doe not require in him meere *Elocution*; or an excellent faculty in verse; but the exact knowledge of all vertues, and their Contraries; with the ability to render the one lov'd, the other hated, by his proper embattaling them."

34. On rhetorical *fides*, see Cicero, *Part. or.* 9.31; *Brutus* 50.187; *De off.* 2.9.33; Quintilian, 5.8.1; as well as chapter 3 on Valla. See also *L* 43.625: "Kings may erre in deducing a Consequence, but who shall Judge?" Philosophy, conceived of as theoretical reason or conformity to some absolute standard of truth, is finally irreconcilable with politics.

35. Gauthier, *The Logic of Leviathan,* argues, "An obligation undertaken for prudential reasons is no less a moral obligation than one undertaken for moral reasons. . . . It is not, then, Hobbes's prudential account of the grounds on which we undertake obligations which prevents us from classifying the obligations in his system as moral" (93). But the question remains whether Hobbes says we only *fulfill* obligations for prudential reasons. If this is so (as Gauthier finally argues and as I have been suggesting in this chapter), then "Hobbes's system has no place for moral obligation," since "in no system of rational prudence, in which all reasons for acting must reduce to considerations of what, in each situation, is most advantageous for the agent, can moral obligation be introduced" (97). On the historical context of Hobbes's political conception of obligation, see Quentin Skinner, "The Context of Hobbes's Theory of Political Obligation," in *Hobbes and Rousseau, A Collection of Critical Essays,* 109–42. For an argument that identifies Hobbesian prudence with morality, see Macpherson, *Possessive Individualism,* 72–78.

36. See, among others, Strauss, *Natural Right and History,* 166–201, on the conflict between Hobbes's conception of science and his appeal to the reader's experience.

37. Hobbes's discussion of the reader of history is analogous in many ways to Pontano's in the *Actius,* and Salutati's in his letter to Heredia. See *EW* 8.viii, xxii.

38. Like Thucydides, Hobbes wants to instruct the reader in the causes of war (for Thucydides, the Peloponnesian War; for Hobbes, the state of nature and the English civil war [*EW* 8.xxi, xxv]) so that he will conduct himself more prudently in the future. He shares Thucydides' dislike of democracy, his association of this form of government with contention, rhetoric, and flattery. And like Thucydides, he aims not at pleasing the reader but at writing the truth as plainly ("perspicuously") as possible. Finally, the rhetoric of the *Leviathan* as I have been describing it sounds remarkably like Hobbes's description of Thucydides: "Agreeable to his nobility, was his institution in the study of eloquence and philosophy. For in philosophy, he was the scholar (as also was Pericles and Socrates) of Anaxagoras; whose opinions, being of a strain above the apprehension of the vulgar, procured him the estimation of an atheist: which name they bestowed upon all men that thought not as they did of their ridiculous religion" (*EW* 8.xiv–xv). He then goes on to describe more precisely Thucydides' arguing *in utramque partem:* "In some places of his history he noteth the equivocation of the oracles; and yet he confirmeth an assertion of his own, touching the time this war lasted, by the oracle's prediction. He taxeth Nicias for being too punctual in the observation of the ceremonies of their religion, when he overthrew himself and his army, and indeed the whole dominion and liberty of his country, by it. Yet he commendeth him in another place for his worshipping of the gods, and saith in that respect, he least of all men deserved to come to so great a degree of calamity as he did.

So that in his writings our author appeareth to be, on the one side not superstitious, on the other side not an atheist" (*EW* 8.xv).

39. On the ultimately prudential nature of Hobbes's political science, see Watkins, *Hobbes' System of Ideas* (70–85), Gauthier, *The Logic of Leviathan,* and Macpherson, *Possessive Individualism.*

7. Conclusion

1. Roland Barthes, "From Work to Text," in *Image, Music, Text,* trans. Stephen Heath (New York, 1977), 164.

2. On the economic connotations of the term *grazia* as favor, see Eduardo Saccone, "*Grazia, Sprezzatura* and *Affettazione* in Castiglione's *Book of the Courtier,*" *Glyph* 5 (1979): 34–54.

3. Baldesar Castiglione, *The Book of the Courtier,* trans. Charles S. Singleton (New York, 1959), 138–39; all further references will be given in the text, followed by references to the Italian edition of Ettore Bonora (Milan, 1972), here 148.

4. See the remarks of Rosalie Colie in *Paradoxia Epidemica* (Princeton, 1966), 33–34, 361. An interesting article that discusses the paradoxical encomium in the Renaissance is Arthur F. Kinney's "Rhetoric as Poetic: Humanist Fiction in the Renaissance," *ELH* 43 (1976): 413–43.

5. I am grateful to Nancy Struever for sharing with me her unpublished paper, "Machiavelli and the Critique of the Available Languages of Morality in the Sixteenth Century." See also Eugene Garver, "Machiavelli's *The Prince*: A Neglected Rhetorical Classic," *Philosophy and Rhetoric* 13 (1980): 99–120, and "Machiavelli and the Politics of Rhetorical Invention," paper given at the third biennial conference of the International Society for the History of Rhetoric, Madison, Wisc. (April 1981).

6. Garver, "Machiavelli and the Politics of Rhetorical Invention."

7. Niccolò Machiavelli, *The Prince,* in *The Prince and The Discourses,* ed. Max Lerner (New York, 1950), 95; *Il principe e discorsi,* ed. Sergio Bertelli (Milan, 1977), 102.

8. On the religious language of Machiavelli's concluding chapter, see the remarks by Gennaro Sasso, *Niccolò Machiavelli, storia del suo pensiero politico* (Naples, 1958), 278–80.

9. See Daniel Javitch, *Poetry and Courtliness in Renaissance England* (Princeton, 1978). A few remarks about my disagreement with Javitch's elegant and provocative argument are in order here. First of all, many of the attitudes and rhetorical strategies that he finds characteristic of courtiers (e.g., the "distaste for 'bare' moral discourse" [98] and the use of epideictic for the purposes of flattery [116] are found equally often in early humanist texts. In addition, the conflation of the role of the poet and the orator is not new with the English Renaissance, as even a cursory examination of the works of the Quattrocento humanists will show. See Niccoli's praise of Dante, Petrarch,

and Boccaccio in book 2 of Bruni's *Dialogus*. Finally, when we turn from the question of Tudor poetry to the more general question of the status of rhetoric in this period, it is clear that the antithesis between humanism and courtliness is inadequate. While Puttenham's work may reflect the interests of courtiers, other logic and rhetoric handbooks are addressed to the middle class, as well as to lawyers, bureaucrats, and diplomats, for whom the techniques of rhetoric had an immediate practical value. This is particularly true, for example, of MacIlmaine's translation (1574) of Ramus's *Dialectica*, of the Ramist logic and rhetoric of Abraham Fraunce, and of the various "formularly" rhetorics of the later sixteenth century. The appearance of rhetoric handbooks treating only "Schemes and Tropes" (e.g., Sherry and Peacham) is not simply owing to the courtier-poet's interest in the indirection of figurative language, but is one consequence of the appropriation of rhetorical invention and disposition by Ramist logic. Ramus's goal, like that of the rhetoricians who followed him, was to methodize instruction in both rhetoric and logic, thereby making these skills accessible not to courtiers, but to "the common people" (see *The Logike of the Moste Excellent Philosopher P. Ramus Martyr*, trans. by Roland MacIlmaine, 1574, ed. Catherine M. Dunn [Northridge, Calif., 1969], 9). Ramus is, in short, one of the first rhetoricians to learn from the humanists' emphasis on practice and pedagogy only then to turn against humanism itself. In his general critique of the inefficacy of humanism, and in his subordination of rhetoric to logic, if not in the details of that logic, Ramus prefigures the work of Bacon and Hobbes. A history of the reception of the humanist rhetorical tradition in England would thus have to consider the way in which the assumptions of this tradition prove to be incompatible with the needs not only of courtiers, but also of a great number of those who shared the humanist concern with social and political reform.

10. Any account of humanist rhetoric in Spenser would have to take account of the work of Paul Alpers, who has discussed the rhetorical nature of Spenser's allegorical narrative, and has explicitly called attention to the similarities between Spenser's and Sidney's poetics. See the preface, above, n. 4. One can add further that while Spenser is writing allegory, and to that extent seems to subscribe to the hierarchical, analogical universe that informs the Greek and Neoplatonic conceptions of allegory, he is in fact concerned to question and rewrite this notion of allegory. *The Faerie Queene* takes as its subject the relation of cognition to moral action, and dramatizes over and over again the problems implicit in the attempt to reconcile the impossibility of theoretical knowledge of the truth with the necessity for prudential action. My thoughts on Spenser are indebted to an unpublished paper by Neil Saccamano on book 1 of *The Faerie Queene*.

11. The reader will no doubt have noticed that Sidney's text itself functions *in utramque partem* in the argument of this book. Invoked in the preface for its lapidary *thematic* statement of the humanist ideal of praxis, it now is seen to question in its rhetorical structure the possibility of this ideal. Works

that take account of the paradoxical nature of Sidney's praise of poetry include Catherine Barnes, "The Hidden Persuader: The Complex Speaking Voice of Sidney's *Defence of Poetry*," *PMLA* 86 (1971): 422–27; Ronald Levao, "Sidney's Feigned *Apology*," *PMLA* 94 (1979): 223–33; and the chapter on Sidney in Margaret W. Ferguson, *Trials of Desire* (New Haven, London, 1982). See also the remarks of Colie in *Paradoxia Epidemica*, 516.

12. Ferguson, *Trials of Desire*, 151.

13. See Leo Strauss's suggestive remarks in *The Political Philosophy of Hobbes*, trans. Elsa M. Sinclair (Oxford, 1936; Chicago, 1952), 161, n.2. Commenting on the way in which the anti-rationalism of Hobbes, and later Rousseau, necessitated a sovereign power defined in terms of will rather than reason, he writes, "It is thus not a matter of chance, that *la volonté générale* and aesthetics were launched at approximately the same time."

14. See Richard Rorty, *Consequences of Pragmatism* (Minneapolis, 1982), chap. 8: "Nineteenth-Century Idealism and Twentieth-Century Textualism" (139–159).

15. See Rorty, *Consequences of Pragmatism*, 155; and Terry Eagleton, *Literary Theory, An Introduction* (Minneapolis, 1983), 143–47, on the analogies between formalism, skepticism, and Anglo-American deconstruction.

16. See Paolo Valesio, *Novantiqua, Rhetorics as a Contemporary Theory* (Bloomington, Ind., 1980), 41ff. I use the word *allegory* here in part to warn against the identification of a given genre or rhetorical strategy with a single ideological or philosophical position. For example, while the paradoxical encomium seems particularly suited to the self-questioning rhetoric of the later authors examined in these pages, I do not want to suggest that the genre always, in all times, functions in this skeptical fashion.

17. I insist on this alliance because so many contemporary critics have questioned it in general terms. For an argument against the easy compatibility of hermeneutics and poetics, see Paul de Man's introduction to Hans Robert Jauss, *Toward an Aesthetic of Reception*, trans. Timothy Bahti (Minneapolis, 1982), vii–xxv. My quarrel, through the humanists, with this argument is that it presupposes an ahistorical definition of poetics and of rhetoric. In a different vein, Jonathan Culler has criticized the literary academy's concern with the interpretation of individual texts and has repeatedly called for a redefinition of the object of literary studies as the analysis of the conventions of interpretation (see preface, above, n. 6). I am in sympathy with this desideratum, but would insist, with the humanists, that our only access to such conventions is through the reading and interpreting of individual texts.

Index

Library of Congress Cataloging in Publication Data

Kahn, Victoria Ann.
  Rhetoric, prudence, and skepticism in the Renaissance.

  Bibliography: p.
  Includes index.
  1. Rhetoric—1400-1700. 2. Prudence. I. Title.
PN173.K34   1985   808'.009   84-21362
ISBN   0-8014-1736-8